Discipleship and Dialogue

New Frontiers in Interfaith Engagement

Essays in Honour of Dr. Israel Selvanayagam

Discipleship and Dialogue
New Frontiers in Interfaith Engagement

Essays in Honour of Dr. Israel Selvanayagam

EDITED BY

Eric J. Lott,
M. Thomas Thangaraj
and
Andrew Wingate

2013

Discipleship and Dialogue: New Frontiers in Interfaith Engagement - *Essays in Honour of Dr. Israel Selvanayagam* – published by the Rev. Dr. Ashish Amos of the Indian Society for Promoting Christian Knowledge (ISPCK), Post Box 1585, 1654, Madarsa Road, Kashmere Gate, Delhi-110006.

© Editors, 2013

ISBN: 978-81-8465-275-8

Cover painting: 'Journey to Emmaus', by Jyoti Sahi

© Jyoti Sahi

Laser typeset by

ISPCK, Post Box 1585, 1654, Madarsa Road, Kashmere Gate, Delhi-110006 • *Tel:* 23866323

e-mail: ashish@ispck.org.in • ella@ispck.org.in
website: www.ispck.org.in

Contents

Preface

It was at the time of our friend Israel Selvanayagam's 60th birthday that we first thought of publishing a *Festschrift* of this kind. Presenting specially prepared essays that relate in various ways to the polar concerns of Israel's life and ministry - typified in our title as 'Discipleship and Dialogue' - seemed to be the most fitting way to honour a man whose outstanding ministry of preaching, teaching, and inspiring leadership has been distinguished especially by his prolific and prophetic writing (both in Tamil and English). The extent of that writing can only be grasped by a look at the bibliography listed at the end.

The wide range of contributors to this volume witnesses to the range of Israel's impact. Many more friends could have been part of the project, but the size of the volume obviously had to be carefully restricted. We apologise to those who feel they should have been invited.

Our engagement with the faith of others in the name of Christ takes many forms and these diverse ways of 'dialogical discipleship' are clearly reflected here:

-       from reflection on the tensions between dialogue and witness, to the recognition of inner compulsions to dialogue lying within an evangelical heart such as Israel's;

-       from rigorous study of religious experience and theologies found in other faiths, to analysis of the pastoral issues raised within Christian communities by interfaith engagement;

- from identifying often overlooked biblical compulsions to engagement with people of other faith, to acceptance of the inspiration to interfaith seen in someone like Gandhi;

- from analysis of the need for interfaith engagement in socio-political situations globally, to reflection on the inner struggle and even suffering involved in interfaith engagement.

All these and more are the themes explored in these essays. With whatever questions readers may come to this crucial issue of interfaith discipleship, few will not find many passages that reflect their questioning.

We are sincerely thankful to all who contributed to this volume with their essays and/or their financial support; and to Jyoti Sahi for kindly allowing his picture 'Journey to Emmaus' to be used on the cover. We are deeply grateful to Rev. Dr. Ashish Amos and team ISPCK, Delhi for taking on the publication of this book.

Eric Lott
Thomas Thangaraj
Andrew Wingate

October 2012

Israel Selvanayagam:
Editors' Tribute

This Festschrift in honour of the Revd. Dr. Israel Selvanayagam is intended primarily in recognition of his excellence in theological reflection, scholarly writing, and ministerial practice. Through this volume we also wish to acknowledge the invaluable and lasting friendship each of the editors has had with Israel over many years. Along with the essays, therefore, we offer our personal tributes to him.

M. Thomas Thangaraj writes:

I met Israel in 1973 when he was enrolled as a student in the Bachelor of Theology programme of Tamilnadu Theological Seminary (TTS). I had joined the faculty only two years earlier. Israel came as a young student from Kanyakumari Diocese of the Church of South India. His parents were economically very disadvantaged and hence did not have access to either good education or decent healthcare. His father's work was climbing palmyrah trees to tap juice from them and make brown sugar from it. Israel's mother was a home maker. Even though they had eleven children, only six of them survived, others dying due to malnutrition and illnesses. Israel was the only one among them able to finish high school, and soon became a bread winner for his family. The family was very committed to the life of the church and Israel was deeply involved in its life, especially in the Youth Fellowship.

Within a year or so after high school, Israel was invited to work in the church as a Pastoral Assistant. Given the congregational polity of the churches in that area, Israel was functioning as a full time Pastor to the local congregation. He would spend several hours every day visiting the homes of the people in his congregation, reading the Bible with them, and praying with them. He would lead the worship in the church every evening and on Sundays led several services. He had no theological or ministerial training to assist him in these tasks; rather it was his sincere and firm vocational commitment that sustained him in his work. One should not fail to note that pastoral assistants like him received extremely low pay for their work.

Yet, his pastoral work was greatly appreciated and there were clear signs of revival in the congregations where he served. This was also the period in which he began to compose devotional songs for congregational use. As a pastoral leader he was able to bring unity within his congregations. The Bishop of Kanyakumari at that time, Bishop A. R. H. Gnanadason, sought Israel's help in settling quarrels and disputes in some other churches. Israel loved the Bible and read it and studied it with great devotion and care, which sustained him in his evangelical piety.

As a student at TTS, Israel was exposed to students and faculty who seemed to subscribe to cultural values and theological views very different from his own. At times he felt a sense of inferiority and inadequacy in the company of students who came from city churches, who spoke fluently in English, and had a different style of life. But Israel was not discouraged by any of these and he was determined to work harder than others and to do well academically. He found the seminary to be a place that offered him an opportunity to realize his full potential. When he graduated as a Bachelor of Theology, he had won the All India Highest Proficiency Award given by the Senate of Serampore College. Since he showed clear signs of scholarship and leadership, the Seminary invited him to take up the newly formed Interfaith Dialogue Program and to serve as the Organizer of Religious Friends Circle which consisted of Hindus, Muslims, and Christians who met once every month for dialogue, discussion, and prayer. Israel proved himself to be an able leader with great organizational skills.

TTS became the venue for Israel to improve his command of English and to develop nuances in his musical skill. Margaret Harris on the TTS faculty took up the challenge of helping Israel to improve his English fluency. Thanks to her and Israel's own determination, he developed an impressive mastery of the English language. I still remember him telling me that he would choose a new English word for each day and build up his vocabulary by using that word several times during the day. He also improved his poetic and musical skills by his association with Dr. V. P. K. Sundaram, Tamil professor at TTS. I had played only a minor role in helping him to play the harmonium with a keen sense for the formation of chords. Every time Israel found an opportunity to learn more and improve his skills he would immediately seize it and work with that new skill in a determined manner.

Israel was married to Leela in 1977 and continued to work in TTS. One of the vocational traits in Israel is this: he would never ask the question: What do *I* want to do? Rather, he would ask: What is needed in this situation? He took upon himself several duties and activities within and outside the seminary not because he *liked* to do them, but because they needed to be done. Such was his commitment to the needs of the context. A good example of this trait is the way he chose the area of study for his Master of Theology program at United Theological College in Bangalore. While his New Testament teacher thought that Israel would do well in New Testament studies, the Principal wanted him to consider Old Testament, and his own mentor Sam Amirtham suggested theology, Israel chose to study Religions because he firmly believed that seminaries in India needed teachers of religions. This decision had put on him additional demands in terms of learning new languages and upgrading himself to study Hinduism in depth. He moved to United Theological College with Leela and their two children Ani and Arul to pursue his studies.

The other two editors have much to say about Israel's contribution to TTS and UTC, and also to the study of religions. Therefore let me end with highlighting two things that I admire in Israel. The first is that Israel was a persistent writer. He had and still has a great ability to sit for hours and write and rewrite. The huge number of publications he has done over the last thirty years bears ample witness to this. He has published widely in Tamil and in English. He was able to do all these while taking on several administrative and pastoral responsibilities. He was always able to find time to write. Many academicians tend to see administration and pastoral ministry as major distractions to their writing and publishing. This was not the case with Israel. He viewed those as boosters rather than blockers, and consequently all his writings had practical and pastoral concerns interwoven with academic rigor. That he was able to retain a lively mind, with strikingly fresh ideas in so many of his writings, is another thing of wonder.

Secondly, Israel kept the dialectic between commitment and openness alive at all times. His earlier rootedness in evangelical piety served him well never to lose sight of his deep commitment to Christian faith. Therefore easy and quick theological solutions to religious pluralism were never attractive to him. All his writings exhibit the tensions involved in combining commitment and openness. Moreover, his openness to other religions was never a matter of either expediency or fashion; it sprang out of his deep love for Christ and his profound concern for the Christian church.

Eric Lott writes:

It was in 1981 that Selvanayagam Israel came to United Theological College, Bangalore, for post-graduate studies. Having up to that point worked and studied almost entirely in Tamil, first there was the need for an intense and sustained *linguistic* struggle. Along with this, the transition to more advanced theoretical work called for a grappling with the difficult concepts relating to Religious Studies. Rather than a clearly marked-out 'field', with a well-defined 'discipline', there are those who see Religious Studies as a dense and darkly tangled 'forest'. Some of the theories about the nature of religion that the student is expected to grapple with actually distort religious realities, making the initial task that much more difficult for the earnest student. But our friend Israel has never been one to back off merely because a task is daunting.

There were other 'struggles' too. We rightly denounce the earlier assumption that all we need to know about Hindu religious history is found in classical Sanskrit texts. Yet, reading key texts from that tradition was inescapable. The anti-Brahmin, anti-Sanskrit stance in modern Tamil political history, as well as the thoroughly non-elitist and non-Brahmanic, socially and economically underprivileged rural background that is Israel's, made even more intense the 'struggle' to enter and become at home in this religious 'forest'. (Being able to empathise at least with the early experience of a remote rural background, thoroughly non-intellectual, perhaps helped me as Israel's initial guide).

Even in rural Tamil Nadu pride in their region's richly cultural heritage is considerable. For Tamil students entering Religious Studies, therefore, there are also some outstanding advantages. The pro-Dravidian bias may be all too clear, but awareness of a rich cultural diversity is not lost. Especially in Israel's case, there was already awareness of the pluralist character of Indian cultural life, even appreciation of its plethora of religious traditions. He was already well-experienced in forms of inter-religious dialogue. His earlier teachers at Tamilnadu Theological Seminary had done a fine job.

Speaking in this cursory way about a positive 'inter-religious' attitude could well hide what was probably the greatest 'struggle' for someone from Israel's background. Given the new Christ-based identity to be expected of the devout Christian in Tamil Nadu, the attraction of building clear, even exclusive, faith- and community-boundaries is very great. It is not only my 19th century missionary fathers who preached the need for radical difference from idolatrous Hindus, with their 'superstitious myths and obscene immorality.' Similarly today, the religious 'other' is demonised by great numbers of fundamentalist preachers in Tamilnadu. Well before coming to UTC, Israel struggled against this tendency.

And yet, an unresolved tension remains between commitment to Christian faith and openness to the experience of others. Perhaps we have to confess that some degree of 'tension' is in the end unresolvable, that it is innate to being a faithful Christian theologian in Religious Studies, perhaps even a necessary characteristic of the most fruitful interfaith engagement. The words 'Discipleship' and 'Dialogue' in the title of this felicitating volume, give some idea of this inner tension, pointing to both commitment and openness, faithfulness and responsiveness to others. Even at that early stage Israel rejected not only any idea of being 'objective' about the faith of the other (when one's own subjectivity is crucially shaped by an all-embracing faith in Christ, certainly by Christian tradition); aiming to be 'dispassionate', 'neutral', and certainly 'methodologically agnostic' in describing the faith of others is equally impossible in Israel's view. And here, from time to time, he and I have found ourselves holding a slightly different approach. That 'empathy' in relation to another's faith is essential we both agree. At times I have felt that empathy somewhat compromised in Israel's approach. Perhaps this merely reflects our different personae, and Israel's greater natural assertiveness results in a more forcefully expressed account of the issues.

Interestingly, a fellow-student in his MTh class, Professor P.Pratap Kumar (University of KwaZulu, Natal) moved on to a very different position from that of Israel's. His article in this volume makes clear his rejection of any positive role for a 'theological' stance within Religious Studies. His well-argued critique of my own (originally written 1981) account of the inter-penetrating relationship of 'Theology' and 'Religion' makes it clear that in responding to my view, Pratap and Israel moved in opposite methodological directions.

Having said this, I immediately need to stress how wonderfully *empathetic* was Israel's account of the inner life and poetic outpouring of the Tamil *Bhakta* in the Saiva tradition, Manikkavachakar (Note the Sanskritic form of my transliteration here: I have long mourned my lack of Tamil – knowing only Telugu and, to a less extent, Kannada of the South Indian languages). As editor of the *Bangalore Theological Forum,* I invited Israel to submit a shortened version of this fine account of the Hindu saint's faith (his first weighty publication in English?), and still regard this as one of the most important articles the Forum published. His appreciative description of the Saiva saint's heart being melted by the divine love shows very clearly Israel's empathy and perceptiveness.

In 1986 it was a joy to welcome Israel back to UTC, Bangalore, as a doctoral student. First there was the need to work his way through our quite rigorous pre-dissertation programme, the first six months of this involving interdisciplinary engagement with other doctoral students and faculty supervisors. Suffice it to say that Israel's work output during this period was so prolific, as his supervisor I had great difficulties in keeping up! An assignment given one morning would result in a lengthy and heavily documented essay the following morning, often I suspect with little sleep for him during the intervening night. Israel's single-minded focus and the intensity of his commitment were unparallelled in my experience. Even then, early in the morning he would be circling the college lawn, vigorously exercising every limb as he jogged, and then seemingly fresh for college morning prayers.

The fact remains, though, that his will to work and his dedication to the desk took its toll. For example, the neck-pains that distressed him later in life began even then. Other health problems may well relate to his intense and total commitment to any task in hand.

Yet, a sense of fun and a typical Tamilian sense of humour were never far away. I had the privilege of taking the Religions' post-graduate students for a tour of Karnataka's places of special religious significance: pilgrimage centres such as Jaina's Sravana Belagola, the Tibetan Buddhist monastery and refugee centre south of Mysore, the first Sankara Matha at Sringeri, the Sri Vaishnava centre at Melkote, and an important Vira Saiva monastery. In meeting numerous Swamijis and Pontiffs, Israel's contribution to discussion was always positive and to the point. Then, as we motored from place to place, he was often the leading joker in the group!

Well before the end of that first year, his DTh Proposal was prepared, refined and even partially developed. By the end of the second year, it is almost unprecedented that he had completed the main body of his outstandingly well-argued, well-documented Thesis on a very difficult topic, involving issues that are crucial to the changes that took place within Hindu tradition. The title given to the book in which the thesis was published by a 'Hindu' publishing house in 1996 is perhaps rather limiting: *Vedic Sacrifice: Challenge and Response.* In reality the issues that are analysed and discussed in this remarkable book take us to the heart of key elements in the wider Hindu tradition, and does so very perceptively.

As it happened I left UTC at the end of Israel's first year of thesis writing, and I had no hesitation in recommending Israel (I recall using the phrase, 'still a rough diamond but great potential') to be a student with Professor Julius Lipner at Cambridge University. Later (1993), invited to give the prestigious Teape lectures at Cambridge, Israel drew on this research material very effectively. This in itself bears testimony to the high regard in which Julius Lipner holds Israel, as a student, and very soon as a friend.

At least briefly I should refer to three further aspects of Israel's two periods of study at UTC, Bangalore. (a) There was his intense interest in indigenous music, lyrics and liturgy. We appreciated his talent as a frequent composer of some topical Tamil lyric. Thus he often contributed to our attempts (with myself as Co-ordinator) to develop forms of 'Intercultural Worship', attempting to weave together styles of liturgical expression from a wide range of sources – classical, local-indigenous and even modern.

(b) There was his mature influence on the student body throughout these periods at UTC. His wish to identify himself with the whole student body once led him into a spot of bother! Happening to meet a group of students protesting about a perceived injustice, he was urgently asking about their noisy grievance. Just at that moment the Principal came around the corner and saw what looked like an Israel-led protest procession! Allaying the Principal's suspicions after this took a long time!

(c) More than once Israel has expressed (e.g.in his biographical essay mentioned above) disappointment at the lack of Interfaith Dialogue programmes at UTC while he was there as a student. He does value the opportunity he had for numerous discussions with Stanley Samartha, who had returned from his WCC position in Geneva to live in Bangalore and teach part-time at UTC. I cannot here go into the complex reasons for the paucity of systematic interfaith engagement by UTC as a community from 1981-87. On those occasions when I managed to arrange ad hoc group or public meetings with people of other faith (several Satsangs and suchlike at the Indian Institute for World Culture for example) Israel was a key person, especially in leading vernacular Bhajans. Then, I recall a very fruitful time at the ancient Sri Vaishnava centre in Melkote, where Israel, M.Lakshmi Thathachar and myself had a long indepth discussion together.

As my final comment concerning Israel's postgraduate study years at UTC, Bangalore, I refer again to the astonishing level of concentrated focus he was able to sustain in his study and essay-writing. This called for almost superhuman effort on the part of a young man from a somewhat remote Kanyakumari village. In Israel, though, we have a person never afraid to strive to the uttermost and even beyond that in order to achieve a desirable goal. In this story we can even see something of the stuff of classical heroes and their struggles.

Andrew Wingate writes:

In 1995, I was approached by John Taylor, then responsible for ministerial education in the British Methodist Church. He asked me to recommend an Indian theological educator to take up a post at Wesley College, Bristol. I was delighted to be asked this question. It had always disturbed me that I was invited to teach at TTS for an indefinite period, straight after my curacy. I had limited experience, and no more than an M.Phil. But TTS trusted the missionary society to make a selection. I had been deeply disturbed at Queen's, when I had received a request for an outstanding teacher from TTS with a Doctorate in New Testament, to spend one sabbatical year in the college as a Visiting Fellow and Teacher. The Principal of the time brought the proposal to the staff meeting. He came back to me with great sadness, to say that they would not agree to his coming. He might disturb the biblical teaching, and his radicalness might upset the students. The Principal, to his credit, said it was not Queen's greatest hour! I replied that it was one of my saddest, knowing how much I had received from my cross-cultural opportunity, not least my meeting Israel in TTS. Hence my excitement a few years later, when I received the Methodist request.

I had no hesitation in recommending Israel. I felt his scholarship would be much respected in the Methodist academic tradition, but also that his ability to be alongside students to bring challenge, was a very transferable skill. So also the way he did not remain within narrow subject limits, but could integrate biblical teaching, both Old and New Testament, with theological and missiological questions, and within the multi religious world that Britain was increasingly conscious that it had become. I knew how much I myself had learnt from Israel, about theological education, and the importance of lay training, as witnessed by his introducing me to Theological Education for Commitment and Action (TECCA), involving Israel in long weekends away in distance places challenging lay people on new attitudes to theology, mission, religions, liturgy and music. Fellow editors have written about his gospel centred approach to Hinduism from which I had also learned so much, and is referred to in my article on Hindu-Christian Forums UK and in Leicester.

Israel was involved in various wider organisations in these Bristol years and beyond. He was a member of the influential Mission Theology Advisory Group of the Church of England. He was Education Secretary of the Friends of the Church in India. He was a member of the Network for Inter Faith Concerns of the Anglican Communion. And he was on the World Council of Churches Inter Faith Advisory Group, in Geneva. At Bristol, he initiated the exchange programme with TTS, following on that already established in Queen's College. These were rich years for most valuable interaction between these three colleges.

Israel made an impact in Bristol, not just on students, but on staff, and within the Methodist Church and beyond. Israel was never an academic who delinked himself from the local church, as happens with some South Asians who make the journey from East to West. For Israel, his preaching and teaching ministry are always part of the life of church as well as of classroom.

His contract in Bristol was coming to an end when he was asked by the Methodist Church to be their candidate for the post of Principal of the United College of the Ascension at Selly Oak. The college had been high church Anglican since its foundation in the 1920's, until it became the United College in 1996, upon the demise of Kingsmead. These were big challenges for USPG, as well as Israel, who was quite clear that he came from a United Church, and there was no ounce of Anglican tradition within him. He wrote an article on the Anglicanisation of the CSI, something he felt strongly negative about, with its effect on architecture (the building of towers and chancels) music with the introduction of organs, church governing structures, and above all on the way the episcopacy in the CSI, which was supposed to be locally conditioned to South India, had in fact become more hierarchical than anything seen in the Church of England.

When I became Principal of the C of A, in 1990, the then President of the Federation, Martin Conway, said 'Welcome to the best job in the Church of England.' In some ways he was right, with the immense variety of challenge from around the world church and especially the Anglican Communion, the daily variety of worship and music in its chapel, the theological challenges from all six continents, the privilege of being a leading member of staff of the oldest missionary society, and the travels that came with this. But at the same time, it was a very difficult post, with a new cross-cultural community to create three times a year, and to work within a complex Federation of Selly Oak Colleges with a major university growing more powerful every year.

Israel came to Selly Oak at a difficult time in its history. The great times of its mission were in the past. By 2001, the flow of mission candidates had become little more than a trickle, a trend I had already experienced when I became Principal. Bursars, coming to study at Birmingham University, or within the Colleges, filled the gap for a decade or so, but these also began to reduce quickly, with the increase in fees in Birmingham, and the establishment of alternative much cheaper institutions in Africa and Asia. Both USPG and the Methodist Church had their respective financial crises, and keeping their own college took over much of their slender budgets. Working with the British churches was no real substitute, where the energy was in Diocesan and church to church links, which rarely looked to the college.

In addition, CMS made their own decisions, without consulting USPG. They decided to close Crowther Hall, without looking at the alternative of considering the establishment of one strong mission college. The Principal of Crowther had little sympathy, it seems, for the kind of approach to mission found at UCA. The decision to close the Centre for Anglican Communion Studies (CEFACS) was also taken unilaterally. This had been a significant joint project of the two colleges and CMS and USPG since 1994. Israel had been a loyal joint Principal of the programme, even though he was not an Anglican, which is typical of his commitment to service.

Overall, Israel led the college well through these difficult years, where the clouds were on the horizon.

The entrepreneurial minded Principal of Queen's College offered to take world mission training under his umbrella, and this led to the formation of the oddly named SOCEMS, the Selly Oak Centre for Mission Studies. This all happened quite rapidly, and was a decision which Israel backed, but he found it very hard, seeing it as a personal failure. He could be faulted perhaps in one respect, for being determined to claim his agreed sabbatical in India during the time when decisions were taken. Some may have seen this as not fighting for the college. But it is doubtful if this would have made much difference. In general, he had found the administrative role which dominated his time at UCA difficult, as it held him back from focusing on teaching, and, above all, on research and writing. His last months in Selly Oak were blighted by illness, and uncertainty about his future, and this was a deep shock to Israel's confidence.

But to Israel's credit, he offered to the Birmingham District of the Methodist Church, to assign him to a suitable posting. He became District Inter Faith Training Officer, and oversight of two Methodist churches in a majority Muslim area of East Birmingham. This was not an easy time family wise, but Israel rose to the challenge of the local church work, as well as by developing a much valued course in new reading of the Bible in a Multi Faith Context, for ministers and interested lay people. He was free to be used more widely in the Methodist Connexion, and he was also able to fulfil his wish to write in the area of mission.

Four much valued books have come out of these years: *A Second Call: Ministry and Mission in a Multifaith Milieu* (CLS, 2000), *Relating to People of Other Faiths: Insights from the Bible* (Thiruvalla CSS, 2004), *Samuel Amirtham's Living Theology* (Bangalore BTESSC/SATHRI 2007 – 900pp), and *Being Evangelical and Dialogical* (ISPCK, 2012). They all deserve to be better known, both in India and in Britain. Israel has always felt sad that he has not found it easy to find a British or Western publisher for such works. This is probably related to the general decline in western publishing of religious books in these years.

Israel had a longing to return to South India, to offer something back to the church that had nurtured him. He was encouraged in this by all of us friends. He was someone deeply earthed in his background, and never a kind of transglobal Indian Christian who had lost touch with his roots. When the Principalship of UTC fell vacant, in 2008, he eventually decided to apply. The power realities were against his chances of being appointed, but he felt he should offer himself, in the year before its centenary was to be celebrated in 2010.

To his surprise, he was appointed to the post, as clearly the best qualified candidate. He returned with high hopes that this would be the crowning experience of his ministerial, teaching and academic career. He had visions of strengthening the faculty by giving them adequate remuneration in the very expensive context of Bangalore, of reviving a very run down Religions department, and celebrating a grand centenary year. He had hopes too of making UTC a centre for cross-cultural placements, in the way that Selly Oak had been. Symbolic of this was for UTC to host in 2009 an international conference on *Gospel in a Pluralist Society*. This was one of the preparatory conferences for the Edinburgh 2010 centenary conference.

Sadly, before this conference could happen, Israel fell ill again. It was clear that his illness was connected with the very difficult and complex context in which he was trying to bring about his vision for UTC. He had little alternative but to resign and return to the UK, for a period of recovery with his family and friends. He carries with him the pain of this period, and it was more than a year before he felt ready to return to India, to a teaching post at the Lutheran Seminary of Gurukul, in Chennai. He does not find Chennai congenial, but he has fulfilled his obligations at Gurukul, and has begun to write again, and has edited the Gurukul Theological Journal.

The post comes to an end within the next year, and he is looking to various possibilities for his future. These include returning to his beloved south Tamilnadu, and discussing whether there are ways of realising a dream of establishing some kind of Truth and Reconciliation teaching centre, for lay people as well as clergy in South India. There are other possibilities, including the proposal to set up a Post-graduate Department in Religions at Gurukul.

I end with two personal reflections. One is to pay immense tribute to Leela, and the way she has been the deeply steadying influence in these difficult years; so also have Ani and Arul, and their spouses. It has been the journey of a family together, an inspiration to many whose families find it hard to stay together in the stresses of today's world. The other is to appreciate deeply his encouragement to others, the most important gift of a colleague in the ministry. Even in dark times, Israel has been able to show the kind of interest and support that has enabled my years since we first met. My hope, and I am sure the hope of all three of the editors of this volume, and all the writers whose lives Israel has touched, is that still 'the best is yet come', and Israel's creativity will flourish in the coming years. He has so much to offer, in both English and Tamil, to a world thirsting for original thinking on inter faith theology and mission. This includes a return to a preaching and music ministry, the like of which I have rarely seen in combination.

Editors' final afterword

This has been, we hope, an honest account of our friend and colleague's life and ministry. The words of the old hymn come to mind, 'Through all the changing scenes of life, in trouble and in joy, the praises of my God shall still my heart and tongue employ.' And it is fitting that we end with some words of Israel in his latest book 'Being evangelical and dialogical' (p.225), about Sadhu Sunder Singh, the great north Indian Sikh convert, who also suffered much, and rejoiced much: 'Sunder Singh demonstrated by his life and teaching that it was not his calling to make judgments about other religions, but to advocate life in Christ with a focus on the cross. He presented the cross as a challenge to immersion in materialism. He refused to accept fabricated portrayals of heaven as fulfilling all worldly desires. For him the cross is heaven.'

Interfaith Dialogue: Compulsions and Tensions

S. Wesley Ariarajah

It gives me pleasure to join Israel's friends and colleagues to felicitate him on his special birthday and to congratulate him on the contributions he has made to the cause of Interfaith Dialogue and Theological Education. His writings on interfaith dialogue weave together his life experiences, his thorough knowledge of the Bible, the learning experiences he has had from actual engagement in dialogue, and his academic scholarship. In so doing, he has also been open about the tensions and issues that one confronts in interfaith relations both from the perspective of one's own faith commitments and the realities of living in religiously plural societies. I am, therefore, glad that the editors of this volume asked me to reflect on some of the "compulsions and tensions" in interfaith relations and dialogue. What I hope to do is not to write an academic article on interfaith dialogue but share some of the compulsions and tensions that had been part of my own experience of participating in and facilitating interfaith relations during the past few decades, especially during the time I served the interfaith ministry of the World Council of Churches. In the first part of this brief paper I shall highlight just three of the compulsions for dialogue, and in the second part deal with the tensions and problems that are associated with it.

COMPULSIONS

Confronted by the tide of history

In the year 2010 there were a number of events in many parts of the world to mark the first World Missionary Conference of 1910 in Edinburgh, Scotland. In all these events the most remembered words from the 1910 meeting were John R. Mott's rallying call for the evangelization of the whole world in that generation. There was indeed a bold conviction that if the missionary movement could mobilize its human and financial resources and develop a clear strategy, it would make Asia and Africa into Christian continents even as Europe and Latin America had become by that time. Enormous effort was put into India and China as the main targets of the missionary endeavour in Asia. This was easily done because, at that time, most of Asia was under colonial rule. The Christian colonizing powers were confident that their religion and culture were superior to those of the "natives" and that the "natives" would readily respond to the missionary message - if only it was taken to them.

The missionary movement totally underestimated the deep religiosity of the Asian peoples based on a variety of religious systems that have withstood the test of time, and the intricate and entrenched social structures that have been built on them. It was simply assumed that people could be easily moved from what it assumed were "pagan" beliefs to the "truth" of the missionary message. Because of this conviction the missionary movement was also theologically intolerant to religious plurality and was unwilling to allow Christianity to be inculturated by Asian religions and cultures as it had, in fact, done in the Greco-Roman world. This approach made it impossible for the Gospel to impregnate the Asian cultures and to transform them from within.

These observations are some broad generalizations, for one is aware that Christianity had been brought with a very different spirit to Asia well before the missionary era, and that even during the missionary era there were many individual missionaries and movements that ran contrary to the main thrust of the missionary movement. However, when the colonial period was over, not even 2% of India and China had embraced Christianity. With the exception of the Philippines (which was colonized by Spain) most of Asia remained "unevangelized" by the standards set by the 1910 missionary conference. With the end of colonialism the tide of history had changed: now Hinduism, Buddhism and other religions and ideologies not only revived and withstood Christianity, but were presenting themselves as credible alternatives to it.

Perhaps the missionary movement had forgotten or had not taken into full account the way Europe and Latin America had become "Christian" continents. The Roman Empire imposed Christianity on the European population, and as Latin America was conquered by Portugal and Spain it became automatically Roman Catholic because of the strict convention that all the areas that came under the political control of the emperors of Spain and Portugal as a matter of course came under the spiritual control of the Pope in Rome; the people had no choice in the matter. The British Empire, not being Roman Catholic, never followed this convention, except to facilitate missionary work. In Asia people had a choice to embrace or reject the Christian faith.

Enthused by the Great Awakening in the United States and under the influence of Pietism and spiritual revivals in Europe, the missionary movement had no plan "B" for Asia. What happens if people hear the Gospel but do not respond to it by becoming part of the Christian community? How do we respond if having heard the missionary message people react by saying that they have been able to find answers to their ultimate questions within their own religious traditions? What is the place and role of a tiny minority Christian community within a predominantly Hindu, Buddhist or Confucian community? The missionary movement never anticipated or answered these questions. Even today the mainline missionary movement refuses to face these questions; it has no alternative to making Christians of the population of the world.

In post-colonial Asia, however, many Christians and Christian groups were searching for answers. The need to face and deal with these questions with honesty has been one of the significant compulsions of interfaith dialogue.

Does God listen to prayers of my Hindu neighbour?

As Christians began to live in closer proximity with neighbours of other religious traditions, deeper questions began to emerge. Would the God of love, whom we have come to know in Jesus Christ, refuse to listen to the prayer of my devout Hindu neighbour, simply because he or she calls God by a different name or has notions about God that had been developed in their own cultural context? The question, simple as it sounds, has enormous theological implications. It is indeed true that religions have different understandings of God and those differences matter, because what we think about God affects the way we look at and relate to our neighbours and the world. It also would dictate the values one holds. In this sense not all religions are the same. But if one were to look at the issue from God's side (so to speak, for who can see things from God's side!) would God who created all, cares for all, and loves all refuse to listen to the sincere cry of the heart of a Hindu or Muslim because they have not had the opportunity to hear the Gospel or had not responded to it in the way the church stipulates?

Even though Christians living with people of other faiths do not articulate the issue as a theological problem, deep down they have had difficulties in denying the spiritual life of their neighbours, their ethical and moral convictions, and their self-less actions even when they saw them. Nor could they dismiss the spiritual sages and saints that their neighbours' religious traditions have produced. In Africa the question was put in this way: "Was God absent in Africa until the coming of the missionaries?" No doubt, Christians were aware that they have understandings of who God is, how God relates to us, and what God requires of us through their discipleship to Jesus Christ, which they consider to be precious and unique. However, in actual practice they increasingly realized that this conviction did not necessarily warrant the dismissal of other ways of believing and being.

I recount in my book, *Not without my Neighbour – Issues in Interfaith Relations*, my personal experience of living next to a devout Hindu family. Already in my student days I could not believe that God would favour us, the Christian family, over the Hindu family next door, simply because their piety and values of life, exemplary as they were, were not drawn out of devotion to Christ. Eventually I was driven to the conviction that if there were a 'heaven' I wouldn't want to be in it if my neighbours could not get in simply because they were Hindus. Hence the title of the book: "Not without My Neighbour." Asian Christians may not articulate this experience in these words, but deep down there is disquiet about dismissing other religious traditions even in their best expressions. This theological struggle would eventually become the compulsion to engage in dialogue.

Am I my brother's keeper? The Challenge of Interdependence

The post-colonial realities in all Asian countries brought in the third compulsion I seek to highlight. This has to do with the question of Christian participation with neighbours of other religious traditions in rebuilding the nations that were newly independent of colonial rule. During the colonial period Christians were a privileged minority with power and influence disproportionate to their numbers. The post-colonial situation cut the Christians down to size. Any meaningful place for them in the society can only come from meaningful participation with their neighbours in nation building. And yet, they had not developed the habits nor established institutions that shared power and helped them work with others as equal partners. The situation was so desperate that M. M. Thomas, for instance, developed the concept of a "secular fellowship in Christ", which meant that while being committed to Christ, Christians could forge alliances with others based on the secular principle of humanization of life.

The concept gave some basis for Christians to engage in nation building, but soon it became clear that one cannot find a secular basis for all areas of life. The reality was that the human community was deeply interrelated and interdependent and no one community could accomplish by its own efforts what the larger community or the nation needed. There were no Christian questions awaiting Christian answers but human questions that needed to be tackled in community. The search for a "community of communities" or a "community of heart and mind" that cut across the religious and ideological barriers became indispensible. Christians, even as all other religious communities, had to readjust to living in the context of irreducible and persistent pluralism, exemplified in most situations as religious plurality. This compulsion moved the Christians, albeit unwillingly, to enter into a new relationship and dialogue with neighbours of other religious traditions.

Even though many Christians and a considerable section of the church have come to recognize interfaith dialogue as an essential part of their existence and ministry, many doubts, tensions and uncertainties continue to plague large sections of the Christian community and the churches. By this I do not mean the more conservative evangelical sections of the Christian community, both inside the mainline churches and outside, that stay with the conviction that still our calling is to evangelize the whole world and to bring it to Christ in its totality. This kind of internal plurality with regards to the mission of the church would always be there and we need to respect one another's convictions. However, I wish to highlight here some of the tensions that continue to trouble that part of the church that has already accepted interfaith dialogue. Among many such tensions, four stand out.

TENSIONS

Does the Bible support interfaith dialogue?

From early days when I began to advocate interfaith dialogue to this day in my class room at Drew, the question that surfaces most concerning Christian relationship to peoples of other faiths has to do with the Bible. Despite all the developments in Biblical Studies for more than a century and the critical study that the students do in the seminaries, most Christians have an understanding and approach to the Bible that puts them at odds with interfaith dialogue. It would appear that one could never have a conversation with a believing and practicing Christian on interfaith dialogue without him or her raising the problem presented to them by Matt. 28, commissioning us to go out and preach the Gospel to all nations, and the conviction about Christ in John 14.6 that he is "the way, the truth and the life" and that no one can come to the Father except through him. Many of us, including Israel, have written books and articles attempting to interpret these and other exclusive verses and lifting up other verses, passages, stories, and streams of thinking within the Bible that can be helpful for interfaith dialogue. My own impression is that the problem over the Bible is endemic and Christians cannot be helped on this issue without a much more concerted effort, not so much to explain these exclusive verses, but to help Christians at the congregational level to own the Bible in a whole new way.

Most Christians do not know that there had been no Christian Scriptures for nearly the first two centuries of the Church's life, that none of the writers of the New Testament wrote them in the hope that they would become 'scriptures', that none of them (perhaps with the exception of the Book of Revelation) claim that what they were writing was 'revealed' to them or that the Holy Spirit was inspiring them to write them. They have no idea that the books of the New Testament Canon were selected out of a larger group of writings, not so much because they were inspired but because they were a collection believed to preserve the best memories of the life and teachings of Christ and of the faith of the early church. No one dares to tell them that such ideas as 'infallibility' and 'inerrancy' of the Bible came much later and are idolatrous.

It is important to demystify the Bible and to tell the truth about it. The congregation should know that the Bible is not the "words" of God in the sense that the Muslims believe the Qur'an to be, but that it is the "Word of God" only because it witnesses to the "Word" that "became flesh and dwelt among us." There is little realization that in Christianity it is Christ and not the Bible that is the revelation of God.

The church in general is very reluctant to tell the congregations the truth about the Bible and help them own the Bible in a more mature, informed, and intelligent way. It is hesitant to help them speak of and relate to the Bible as the "word of God" for the right reasons. But until we can do this the tension in relating to interfaith dialogue based on the Bible will continue.

Mission or dialogue? The unresolved tension

The second tension relates to the first. If the Bible asks us to go out and convert all the nations to Christ and to baptize them in the name of the Father, Son and the Holy Spirit, is it legitimate to engage in interfaith dialogue except for the purpose of evangelism? In the light of what I have said above about the reading of the Bible there is no need here to deal with the biblical aspect of the question. There are more important issues about the understanding of mission itself that need to be resolved if we are to engage in meaningful interfaith dialogue.

Because of the limitation of space this cannot be dealt with in the detail it deserves. There are *four* important questions about mission that Christians need to deal with in order to overcome the tension between mission and dialogue. The first is whether Christian mission is about converting the whole world to embrace the Christian faith. The Jewish understanding of mission was that they were a "witness" to the nations, but that God was the God of all nations and that God would eventually bring them unto Godself. The concept of the "Mission of God" was developed within the missionary movement in the 1960s which helped us to move away from the anxiety to convert the whole world. Over a period of time this concept of mission was set aside and has been replaced with an aggressive understanding of mission. We should recover the concept of *the mission of God* as a way to overcome the tension between mission and dialogue.

An even more important issue concerns the purpose of mission. In Jesus' understanding mission was about bringing healing and wholeness into the life of individuals, communities and the world. It was about discipleship to the Reign of God and its values rather than in believing in any propositions of truth; it was about solidarity with the poor, oppressed and the marginalized. The attempt to replace other religions with Christianity was a misguided understanding of mission that was developed during the colonial era when the colonial powers thought their own religion and culture to be superior to those of others. Until we remove religions as the target of Christian missions we can never resolve the tension between dialogue and mission.

Is religious plurality within God's providence?

The question of mission is tied to an even deeper issue on which Christians are still perplexed, namely, whether it is within God's providence that peoples of the world have numerous ways of understanding and relating to the mystery of life. Whether there is 'one truth' to which we must bear witness and call all others also to come to it, or whether we should learn to be at home with many ways of expressing and celebrating the Truth, is a matter of tension for Christians. Quite unfortunately, the Christian tradition, already in its early development, moved into a philosophical environment that saw 'one' to be better than 'many' and in which the one 'truth' is arrived at by a process of exclusion. The condemnation and expelling of heretics had to do with a genuine attempt at arriving at the 'one truth' that had to be preserved, guarded and handed down by a recognized teaching authority. At the heart of this issue is one's approach to plurality.

Christians are ill at ease with the Asian philosophical environment where 'manyness' is not seen as a problem. Many ways to express the reality of God, many ways to attempt to reach God, and many religious streams living side by side etc. are easily accepted in Asia but is not part of the Christian ethos. In fact, the Christian understanding of God, its understanding of salvation, its interpretation of Christ, and especially its understanding of mission are all exclusivistic because of the tradition's inability to deal theologically with plurality. The tensions in relating to peoples of other religious traditions cannot be resolved until Christian theology is rethought in the context of plurality.

Is dialogue viable in the context of religious extremism and militancy?

In addition to these built-in theological tensions, today we are faced with the reality of religious fundamentalism and militancy that raises the tensions between religions and casts doubts on the viability of dialogue as a way of relating to one another. Much can be said on this, but it would be sufficient to highlight three aspects of the issue. The first is to acknowledge the reality of religious extremism and violence and to take whatever steps necessary to safeguard the interests of those that are affected by it; there is no place for romanticism in interfaith dialogue. However, many fail to deal with the issue intelligently by imputing to a whole religious community the evils perpetrated by a small group within it. It is important to recognize the prevalence of internal religious plurality within all religious traditions. The majority of peoples in all religious traditions seek to live in peace and harmony with others.

The second need is to realize that most religious traditions have lived for centuries as rival or alternate religious traditions and in some cases have been in conflict and war with each other. Others have grievances about the way their traditions were treated during the colonial era. Therefore it is important to engage with one another and to build intentional bridges of mutual understanding so that we would have a new experience of each other as partners and fellow pilgrims. Forging new relationships is the best way to keep extremism at bay.

Third, we need to build interreligious institutions at all levels of societal life so that interfaith dialogue becomes a way of life and not an exotic activity undertaken by a few within the community.

Understanding the Religious 'Other' in a Violent World

Elizabeth Harris

I first met Israel when he was World Church Tutor at Wesley College, Bristol. I was then Inter Faith Officer for the Methodist Church in Britain, having lived for a number of years in Sri Lanka. During the years I have known Israel, I have consistently admired his dedication to helping Christians grapple with the challenge of interfaith encounter in a world shot through with injustice, within which religion is not innocent. In this work, Israel has been prophetic and insightful. For instance, well before the term 'scriptural reasoning' entered the western academy and western interfaith encounter, Israel was calling for a diligent reading of scriptures between people of different faiths.[1] In Israel's honour, therefore, I would like to offer some reflections on one of the most important issues in understanding the religious 'other': how to deal with difference.

When I was working for the Methodist Church in Britain, I often encouraged Methodists to embrace two interfaith tasks. The first was the 'internal' task of making theological space for interfaith encounter through reading the Bible with new eyes.[2] The second was the 'external'

---

[1] See for example Israel Selvanayagam, *A Second Call: Ministry and Mission in a Multifaith Milieu* (Madras: The Christian Literature Society, 2000) pp 172-188.

[2] See, for instance, Elizabeth J Harris, 'Being Christian and Living in a Multifaith Society: A Perspective from Britain' in *Dialogue* (Colombo), New Series XXXVII & XXXVIII, 2010 – 2011, pp. 102-121; Elizabeth J Harris, 'Telling the

task of understanding what is important within the lives of our neighbours of other faiths by empathetically entering or learning about their world views. The topic of this chapter is the second task, central to which is dealing with difference. For when we encounter the world views of other faiths, differences as well as similarities leap out. The religions of the world touch at many points but they are not the same. The indic world view, for instance, diverges dramatically from the abrahamic and, within each of these, there is internal diversity.

My argument will first tackle the accusation that understanding other world views is impossible anyway. I will then examine similarity between faiths, before passing to how difference can be approached. To do this, I draw on my experience of interfaith encounter in South Asia, work with the Methodist Church in Britain and teaching religious studies at Liverpool Hope University. I also build on a short talk I gave at Burngreave Ashram, Sheffield, in 2011.[3] My main argument is that difference need not be a source of threat or fear but can be one of the most challenging and enriching elements of interfaith encounter, although it can, where there is trust, involve what could be called, 'hard talk'.

Is understanding the 'other' impossible?

Some western thinkers believe that truly understanding the 'other' of another faith is impossible because religious world-views are simply so different that comparison is impossible. Paul Hedges has named this approach, 'particularism'. He links it with Michel Foucault, Karl Barth, Gavin d'Costa and George Lindbeck, describing it as a post-liberal philosophy rooted in the conviction that religions are incommensurable and therefore cannot be compared without an illegitimate exercise of power.[4] Hedges rejects this view through appealing to the history of religions, as I do.

Christian Story in a Multi-Faith Context' in Prabo Mihindukulasuriya, Ivor Poobalan & Ravin Caldera (eds), *A Cultured Faith: Essays in Honour or Prof. G.P.V. Somaratna on his seventieth Birthday,*(Colombo: CTS Publishing, 2011) pp. 182-196.

[3] 'Understanding the Precepts and Practices of the Other's Faith' at 'Interfaith Praxis 2010', organized by the Multifaith Chapel and Library Burngreave Ashram, Sheffield, 21 November 2010.

[4] Paul Hedges, *Controversies in Interreligious Dialogue and The Theology of Religions* (London: SCM, 2010) pp. 146-196.

The religious systems of the world have never operated in separate spheres and certainly do not do so now. Throughout history, their devotees have interacted with each other. Christians interacted with the religions of Greece and Rome in the countries surrounding the Mediterranean in the first centuries of the Common Era. Buddhists interacted with Muslims in Afghanistan in the 8th and 9th Centuries. Hindus interacted with Christianity in nineteenth century India. Sikhs created their own identity within the cultures of both Hinduism and Islam. Change and adaptation resulted in all cases. This suggests that human beings, although usually nurtured by one culture and religion,[5] have the potential to move outside this heritage to interact with the 'other'. What the particularists might say, however, is that, in all these cases, power relationships skewed the resulting adaptations. It is a warning that must be heeded but not, I would suggest, to the extent that any inter-religious learning or inter-religious understanding is invalidated. Just as we, as human beings, have the potential to learn another language and thus enter another linguistic world, so we have the capacity to enter empathetically other religious worlds.

Similarity Stressed

When interfaith encounter was young in the cities of Britain, in the middle of the last century, Christians involved in it tended to stress the commonalities between faiths in order to soften the ground for those who were rather frightened of Britain's growing religious plurality or who saw faiths other than Christianity and Judaism as so different as to be utterly false, even demonic. They, therefore, asserted, 'All religions affirm the Golden Rule: do to others what you would like them to do to you', or 'All want to work for the good of society', or 'But we all worship the same God'.

Particularists might dismiss this as an illegitimate exercise of power. These Christians, they might argue, had no right to make these judgements, as part of a powerful religious majority. I disagree. They were right to stress commonality at this time. It was a necessary counterbalance to the negative representations of other faiths that many

---

[5] The term, 'usually' is important. Inter faith and inter-cultural marriages and partnerships mean that a growing number of children are growing up with a dual cultural and/or religious heritage.

Christians had inherited from the era of British imperialism.[6] It was just such a stress on commonality that enabled the first interfaith groups to form in places such as Leeds and Wolverhampton. And it also pointed to something that is the core to interfaith encounter and inter-religious learning. When we meet as people of different faiths, commonalities emerge continuously. The existence of commonalities enabled a wonderful interfaith event, held in the Palace of Westminster in London, at the beginning of the year 2000 to mark the Millennium. Its culmination was an Act of Commitment, when people of nine faiths[7] affirmed that they held seven key values in common: Building community; personal integrity; a sense of right and wrong; learning, wisdom and love of truth; care and compassion; justice and peace; respect for one another, for the earth and its creatures.

This Act of Commitment is still being used in Britain and I am deeply grateful for it. Today, we must continue to affirm the commonalities that bind people of different faiths together, whether these are in the fields of values, spiritual practice, social engagement, insight into truth or devotion to God. These can be discovered in joy when we talk together. And there must be joy in interfaith relations.

The Dignity of Difference

Empathetically entering the world-views of others, however, involves more than the affirmation of commonalities, and those early interfaith pioneers knew this too. It had been their conscious choice to stress commonality over difference at a particular point within the history of inter faith relations in the West. In 2002, however, Sir Jonathan Sacks, the Chief Rabbi in Britain, head of the Orthodox Jewish community, wrote, *The Dignity of Difference: How to avoid the clash of civilizations*.[8]

---

[6] See for instance, Geoffrey A. Oddie, *Imagined Hinduism: British Protestant Missionary Constructions of Hinduism, 1793-1900* (New Delhi &London: Sage, 2006); Sharada Sugirtharajah, *Imagining Hinduism: A Postcolonial Perspective* (London & New York: Routledge, 2003), particularly pp.74-89; Elizabeth J Harris, *Theravâda Buddhism and the British Encounter: Religious, missionary and colonial experience in nineteenth century Sri Lanka* (London & New York: Routledge, 2006) particularly pp. 53-75; 101-109.

[7] The Baha'i tradition, Buddhism, Christianity, Hinduism, Islam, Jainism, Judaism, Sikhism and Zoroastrianism.

[8] Jonathan Sacks, *The Dignity of Difference: How to Avoid the Clash of Civilizations* (London & New York: Continuum, 2002)

By that time, the public imagination, in response to events such as 9/ 11, was stressing difference between religions in the context of religion's potential for violence. That religion could be the cause of violence had long been a fact of history but now it was being voiced at a popular level, with Islam as the unfortunate illustration. At an academic level, it had become acceptable to speak of a clash of religious civilizations in preference to a clash of ideologies.[9] Sacks, however, did not respond, 'Oh but you've got it wrong – there are no differences between religions and therefore no potential for violence'. He affirmed that religions were different from one another and sought to assert the dignity and worth of this difference rather than its potential for conflict. Drawing on his own theistic religious heritage, he affirmed:

> The God of Abraham teaches humanity a more complex truth than simple oppositions – particular/universal, individual/state, tribe/humanity – would allow. We are particular *and* universal, the same *and* different, human beings as such, *but also* members of this family, that community, this history, that heritage. Our particularity is our window on universality, just as our language is the only way we have of understanding the world we share with speakers of other languages. God no more wants all faiths and cultures to be the same than a loving parent wants his or her children to be the same.[10]

If we enter inter faith encounter, seeking to understand the world-view of the 'other', in the belief that we will find only a clone of our own faith, we will be the losers. For it will lead to a projection onto other faiths of our own preconceptions and our own categories. And these very preconceptions may indeed lead to an illegitimate use of power over the 'other'. If we are truly to understand the world-views of faiths that are not our own, we must first of all listen to how people within those faiths define themselves and expect that these self-definitions will be different from those from within our own faith. We must resist the temptation to compare everything that is said with what we believe, as far as possible letting go of our own religious lenses so that what is different can arise with its own inner integrity.

---

[9] See Samuel P. Huntingdon, *The Clash of Civilizatons: And the Remaking of World Order* (Simon & Schuster, 1997).

[10] Jonathan Sacks, *The Dignity of Difference: How to Avoid the Clash of Civilizations* (London & New York, Continuum, 2002) p. 56.

Two Examples of Encounter

Let me give two examples of this kind of encounter from my own life: first, studying and empathetically 'entering' Buddhism over a period of twenty five years; second, what resulted after I was asked to teach Judaism at Liverpool Hope University, albeit only at a preliminary stage. Both involved in-depth encounter with the 'other'. The study of Buddhism took me to Sri Lanka, where I spent nearly eight years immersing myself in the religion and studying it academically. The teaching of Judaism sent me to the prayer books of Judaism, to friends who were Jewish and to the dialogue groups I had been involved with for several decades.

In both these journeys, the commonalities between faiths leapt out at me. Buddhism's view of the world as radically scarred with greed, hatred and delusion resonated with me and seemed to touch the Christian doctrine that humans, when alienated from God, are entrapped by Mammon or greed.[11] The call of the Hebrew prophets that righteousness and justice should flow through society touched, for me, what engaged Buddhists are calling for: action that addresses institutional greed and the violence and injustice that flows from it. In both Buddhism and Christianity, compassion is also important, particularly to one's enemies. Jesus, in the Sermon on the Mount, exhorts his listeners to, 'Love your enemies and pray for those who persecute you,' (Matthew 5: 44). In the *Mettâ Sutta*, the Buddha encourages a similar quality of mind and heart:

> Just as a mother would protect her only child at the risk of her own life, even so, cultivate a boundless heart towards all beings.

> Let thoughts of boundless love pervade the whole world; above, below and across without any obstruction, without any hatred, without any enmity.[12]

In one traditional meditation on loving kindness that many Buddhists practise daily, meditators at first visualize a revered teacher, then a family member or a dear friend, then a person towards whom they feel neutral and then someone they do not like or actually feel hatred

---

[11] See Matthew 6: 24; Luke 16: 13.

[12] *Mettâ Sutta, Sutta Nipâta* v. 149-150 (adapted from a translation by H Saddhatissa).

towards. Loving kindness has to be enwrapped around all. Both Christianity and Buddhism, I discovered, encourage letting go of resentment and revenge, and impulses towards violence, as an essential part of the spiritual life.[13]

When I was preparing to teach Judaism, the knowledge I already had of the Hebrew Bible was deepened and, again, commonalities leapt out. Both Jews and Christians stress the inseparability of love of God and love of neighbour, expressed in the creating of a just society where the vulnerable are cared for. The first verses of the Shema (Heb. 'hear') are revered by both, beginning, 'Hear. O Israel: The Lord our God, The Lord is One. And thou shalt love the Lord thy God with all thy soul, and with all thy might'.[14] Both are challenged by the words of Amos, 'But let justice roll down like waters, and righteousness like an ever-flowing stream' (Amos: 5: 24). Both speak of a God of love, a God who can be called 'father' but who, at the same time, is beyond description.

However, in my encounter with both Buddhism and Judaism, differences also emerged. Buddhism is a non-theistic faith. More accurately, it does not recognise the existence of a creating, all powerful God. Those who include Buddhism in the phrase, 'Oh but we all believe in the same God' are misled – or are projecting onto Buddhism something that most Buddhists would not own. There are gods in Theravâda Buddhism and, in Mahâyâna Buddhism, a myriad of celestial beings. The former, however, lie below the Buddhas in cosmic hierarchy. They can be petitioned for mundane blessings but are still in need of the Buddha's teaching if they are to reach *nibbâna* (Pâli; Skt. *nirvâṇa*) Some of the celestial beings in Mahâyâna Buddhism have reached enlightenment and can help beings on the path to *nirvâṇa* but they have no cosmos-creating function.

---

[13] I have attempted to communicate what I believe Buddhism can offer the world, using my own experience, in Elizabeth J Harris, *Buddhism for a Violent World: A Christian Reflection* (London: Epworth, 2010).

[14] The Shema consists of three passages: Deuteronomy 6: 4-9; Deuteronomy 11: 13-21; Numbers 15: 37-41. Translation taken from, A Cohen (ed.), *The Soncino Chumash: the Five Books of Moses with Haphtaroth* (London, Jerusalem & New York: Soncino Press, 1985).

The belief of most Buddhists that we are reborn within the cosmos, within its heavens and hells as well as the human plane, again and again, over aeons of time, also differs radically from the Christian worldview. In one commentarial narrative within Theravâda Buddhism, the Buddha has a conversation, in a cemetery, with a woman who is mourning the death of child. The conversation goes something like this:

> The Buddha: 'Why are you crying?'
>
> The Woman: 'I cry because of the death of my daughter, Exalted One'
>
> The Buddha: 'Which one are you weeping for? Cremated in this cemetery are 84,000 of your daughters.[15]

The story, therefore, implies that the woman had had at least 84,000 previous births, all in the same geographical location. Ten rebirths can perhaps be understood by someone coming from a Christian worldview but tens of thousands of rebirths, each governed by the Law of Karma, the Law of Action, is a different matter. The cosmology of Buddhism and the path of living beings within it, for someone nurtured by a non-indic viewpoint, can be difficult to understand, let alone empathize with.

As for Judaism, it is all too easy for Christians to assume that Judaism is familiar territory. It is not! The hearts of Christians may leap in recognition when they say the first verses of the Shema. The other verses, however, lead into a world that Christians do not share. Deuteronomy 11: 20 enjoins Jews to write God's words on the doorposts and gates of their houses. Jews today tie small receptacles containing the Shema on their front door and on most doors in their house. Numbers 15: 37, also part of the Shema, enjoins Jews to attach fringes to their garments as a reminder of God's commandments, a practice that has led to the tassels (*zitzit*) on the Jewish prayer shawl (*tallit katan*).[16] There are realms of practice and law within Judaism that Christians are usually unaware of. Practice, what is done, in fact, can

---

[15] The commentarial story connected with the verses of the nun Ubbiri in the *Therîgâthâ* (Verses of the Sisters) vv. 51-3. Also quoted in Elizabeth J Harris, *Buddhism for a Violent World: A Christian Reflection* (London: Epworth, 2010) p.56.

[16] Some Orthodox Jews will wear a prayer shawl all day under their garments; others will wear it only for the morning service and all day on the Day of Atonement.

be more important within Judaism than belief or faith. As Clive Lawton, a prominent Jewish educationalist, said at a lecture on, 'What in my faith could I not live without?':

> I don't think Jews do faith. Culture is more important. It's an odd fact that we live in this corner of the globe and think that faith is synonymous with religion. But I'm not sure how much faith I do. When I was Head of King David's School, a Roman Catholic girl who was taking part in a sixth form programme said to me, 'I can't get a handle on what Jews believe. What do you believe?' And I found myself immediately switching to what Jews do. Jews switch straight into practice.[17]

Both contemporary Judaism and Christianity grew from a shared baseline: the Judaism of the Second Temple Period in the 1st century CE when Judea was under Roman occupation. Both developed in different ways, diverging from this baseline and from each other. After the destruction of the temple in Jerusalem in 70 CE by the Romans and the further defeat of a Jewish uprising in 132-35 CE, the Jews largely became a diaspora community, forced to develop ways of being Jewish that were not dependent on having a centralized temple system. Rabbinic Judaism thus grew up. The Hebrew Bible (*Tanakh*)[18] remained central to Jewish law and practice but a vast corpus of texts grew up that Christians usually have little knowledge of, most notably the Talmud, a commentary on the Oral Law or Mishnah. To enter this is to enter a religious world of hermeneutical struggle that, for me, was different and challenging. It certainly destroyed any vestige of the view that Christians can learn all they need to know about Judaism from the New Testament or that Jews relate to the *Tanakh* in much the same way as Christians relate to the Bible. Nothing could be further from the truth.

Dealing with Difference

In both of these encounters, the differences led to enrichment. It is my conviction and indeed my experience that tremendous creativity may arise when we encounter both difference and similarity with humility

---

[17] Part of a series of lectures sponsored by Liverpool Hope University and the Merseyside Council of Faiths in 2010-11 entitled, 'What in my faith could I not live without?' It is hoped that the series will be published.

[18] An acronym for the three sections of the Hebrew Bible: Torah (Pentateuch); Nevi'im (Prophets); Ketuvim (Writings).

and the wish to learn. I do not say this glibly. The way we deal with difference is one of the most important issues within interfaith encounter. Some differences simply invite respectful acceptance. Some need to be struggled with. Some may turn out not to be differences as much as practices that can complement our own or help us to uncover something we have overlooked. And some need to be contested.

The non-theism of Buddhism was one source of struggle for me. I did not condemn it but sought to respect and understand it. This, in turn, eventually led me to costly interrogation of the Christianity I had brought to interfaith encounter. As I wrote in 2002, 'I found myself reversing the gaze'.[19] I still believe that there is a personal force, characterised by love, wisdom and justice, at the heart of the universe, which Christians call God. However, Buddhism has helped me to see more clearly that the religious path involves much more than belief in such a force and that reliance on a saviour, if this is unthinking and simplistic, can actually hinder walking the walk of the spiritual life.[20]

Walking the walk of the spiritual life, Buddhism has taught me, involves work on the mind and heart, namely meditation, and it was within this realm that I found what has complemented and deepened my own spiritual practice. Buddhist meditation is different from prayer. When I first encountered Buddhism, I was already interested in Christian contemplation, particularly Ignatian forms. When I first attended Buddhist meditation sessions and centres, my heart at first yearned to seek God in the silence. Eventually, I resisted this. After all, my aim had been to enter the world of Buddhism empathetically. As I wrote in the biographical article already cited, it was only then that, 'I began to glimpse what meditation could be in Buddhism – not a search for spiritual experience, not a movement towards God, but a hard, rewarding path of coming to know the mind and the heart'.[21] Practising Buddhist forms of meditation led me into a use of silence that was different from Christian prayer but it was a complementary difference.

---

[19] Elizabeth J Harris, 'The Beginning of Something Being Broken: The Cost of Crossing Spiritual Boundaries' in *Spirituality Across Borders, The Way Supplement,* 2002/104, pp.6-17, here p. 15.

[20] The article mentioned in footnote 19 explores this in much more detail.

[21] Harris, 'The Beginning of Something Being Broken'. P. 13.

A form of *vipassanâ* or insight meditation is the one I practised most when in Sri Lanka. I still practise it. It involves sitting in quietness, and watching in a non-judgemental and non-clinging way all that arises and passes in the mind and heart. Such watching can be hard work. It can be accompanied by feelings of calm but, more often, effort is needed to keep focussed and alert. But the effort is worth it. As one of my teachers, Godwin Samararatne, used to say, such meditation is a way of making our demons our friends. We face what is violent, angry, egotistic or troubled within ourselves non-judgementally and therefore can transform it. Buddhism's emphasis on mental culture, on meditation, as a way of coming to know how our mind and heart work, has indeed given me more than I can say and I have held it alongside the practice of prayer.[22] It has also led me to a source of riches within the Christian faith that can be overlooked by western Christians - *hesychasm*, the tradition of contemplative prayer linked with the Eastern Church.

Judaism, on the other hand, has taught me that religious texts can be wrestled with in the most robust of ways. Respect for the texts does not mean unquestioning acceptance of what seems to be the literal interpretation, but the struggle for meaning. Holy texts combine myth, metaphor, mysticism, narrative, history, ethics and philosophy. Each has a different mode of expression and mode of interpretation. The ancient rabbis within Judaism knew this and have much to teach Christians.

Moving lastly to differences that have to be contested, I am in difficult territory. Nineteenth century Christian missionaries contested the differences between Christianity and religions such as Buddhism and Hinduism by demonizing them. Devotion shown in front of Buddha images was idolatry. Exorcist rituals were, 'devil dancing', a worship of the devil. Such demonization was informed by a culturally-influenced inability to understand the 'other'. I am not referring to this type of contestation. I am referring to the challenging questions we may feel impelled to ask devotees of other religions if we witness practices that seem to flout values that we hold dear. The discrimination

---

[22] See Elizabeth J Harris, *Buddhism for a Violent World: A Christian Reflection* (London: Epworth, 2010) chapter 4 for an in-depth appraisal of what I believe Buddhist meditation can offer to the wider world.

that can arise from the Hindu caste system might be one such area of practice or the severe penalties imposed for apostasy in Islam. For me, in Sri Lanka, one aspect of Buddhism that I found difficult was popular interpretations of *Kamma*, the Law of Action, for instance when a friend told me that she felt she had to believe that all those who suffered from the release of poisonous waste at Chernobyl must have been involved in some collective misdoing in the past.

Sometimes, our wish to contest is because we have not understood deeply enough the world-view of the other, or because we have not fully realised that practice often diverges from ideal values. Respectful conversation can help to resolve this.[23] Sometimes, the practices that worry us are popular expressions of a religion that differ from the texts or the teaching of scholars. I discovered I could discuss the Law of Kamma with my friend by citing Buddhist texts that affirm that not everything that happens to a person is due to past action. The teaching of the Buddha as recorded in the Theravâda texts is much more nuanced than she had feared. Sometimes, however, our questions may be rooted in a challenge that some people within other religions need to hear. It may also touch on internal dialogue within that religion. Where trust has been built up, we should not be afraid to ask questions about the Hindu caste system, Muslim penalties for apostasy or a mechanistic view of the Law of Kamma. As a result, we may find that not all Muslims believe that apostasy should be punished and not all Buddhists interpret the Law of Kamma in a mechanistic way. If we do become involved in conversations of this kind, however, we should not forget that people of other faiths may have some very challenging questions to ask of Christians, particularly about the violence with which Christian history is permeated.

Concluding Thoughts

In this paper I have attempted to explore what understanding the religious 'other' involves. I have argued that it involves more than the affirming of commonalities, although this is important. If we are truly to understand the religious world views of our neighbours of other faiths, we must be prepared to encounter and struggle with difference.

---

[23] I am indebted to Inderjit Bhogal who has always stressed respectful 'conversation' as a more compassionate and user-friendly term than dialogue.

If we do this, the riches are immense and we will avoid projecting onto others what they may not own, which is no less than an illegitimate use of power.

So let me commend in this paper the in-depth face-to-face encounter or conversation that leads towards an understanding of how our friends and colleagues within other faiths see the world. The journey is, at one and the same time, joyous and challenging.

Commitment and Openness:
The Vision of the Faith Guiding Course

Ruth Tetlow

I was privileged to serve as a Tutor at the United College of the Ascension in Selly Oak Birmingham from 1999 – 2006, when, for most of that time, Israel Selvanayagam was Principal of the College. It was a formative time for my own development as a Christian engaging in inter faith relationships, and one in which Israel Selvanayagam's influence played a significant part. He enabled me to use my previous interfaith experience in running and contributing to numerous short courses and events. He also encouraged me to study for a postgraduate degree in Interreligious Relations at the University of Birmingham (M Phil completed 2004), which has provided a vital foundation for the work I have been able to do since. **In this essay I shall describe and reflect on that work and attempt to show how it has been rooted in Israel Selvanayagam's theological thinking and Christian practice.** Since 2007 I have been the Co-ordinator for the Faith Encounter Programme, a small inter faith educational project based in the West Midlands, which has mainly become known for developing the Faith Guiding course, accredited by the Institute of Tourist Guiding.[1]

---

[1] *www.itg.org.uk*

The nature and context of the Faith Guiding course

The Faith Encounter Programme was set up in 2007 with the objective of developing mutual respect and understanding between people of all faiths and none in the West Midlands. It has been steered by a small group of people with considerable inter faith experience and coming from 6 different faiths. With myself as self employed Co-ordinator we have developed a pioneering 'Faith Guiding' course as a means of achieving this objective. We began training people of all faiths from local places of worship to lead guided tours for groups of visitors of all ages and faith backgrounds at their own place of worship. The need for this work had become apparent in the multi faith city of Birmingham during the preceding 20 years, as more and more school, college and adult groups had undertaken such visits either as part of their religious or theological education, or motivated by a wish to build positive relationships. Many places of worship were not equipped to receive this attention and although they offered warm hospitality and did their best to provide informed guides, these people often had little appreciation of the religious or cultural standpoint of their visitors or their purpose for visiting. The result was that real communication was limited and sometimes the encounter was open to misunderstanding or even gave offence. The training offered on the course enables such visits to be more educationally productive, spiritually enriching and sensitively tailored to the backgrounds of the visitors.

The name of the project, Faith Encounter Programme, reflects my conviction based on experience, that 'encounter' is sometimes a more appropriate word than dialogue to describe meetings between a number of people of different faiths. It arose out of the study I undertook for my M Phil dissertation on 'The Missing Dimension: Women and Interfaith Encounter in Birmingham,'[2] in which I carried out participant observation of a group of eleven women of six different faiths. The word 'encounter' is likely to

I refer to several people or positions, including groups of people. The participants encounter one another with body and spirit as well as mind, and often with several senses, such as smell, touch and sight. Examples include the beauty of flowers, candles and incense frequently experienced on visits to places of worship. The communication is

---

[2] University of Birmingham M Phil dissertation 2004.

holistic and may be non-verbal. The word dialogue, on the other hand, should mean 'talking through', in contemporary English, but it tends to evoke the picture of a verbal intellectual exercise where two sides are engaged in a discussion of theological issues. Where it is 'interfaith dialogue' it implies people of two different faiths trying to understand one another but on opposite sides of a debate. Israel Selvanayagam favours the definition of dialogue offered by Stanley Samartha, who said,

> 'It is not a gathering of porcupines, nor is it a get-together of jelly fish ....(rather) communities of concerned people (must be) ready to take the risk, to move beyond safe boundaries..'

Israel Selvanayagam adds that dialogue

> '...involves serious commitment to one's convictions and openness to the extent of being vulnerable.'[3]

I use both words, encounter and dialogue, depending on the context.

The context of the city of Birmingham, well known to Israel Selvanayagam and with some similarities to the South India he came from, is significantly more multi-ethnic and multi-religious than the national average for the UK. According to the last census figures available (2001), 29.6 per cent of people described themselves as other than 'white', amongst whom the largest groups were Pakistani, Indian and Caribbean. The same census identified significantly higher numbers of Hindu, Muslim and Sikh residents than the national average, significantly lower numbers of Christians and those professing no religion, while numbers of other faith communities (chiefly Buddhist and Jewish) were roughly in line with the national average. The city is the scene of long standing inter faith work, some of which Israel Selvanayagam took part in when he was at the United College of the Ascension. After the attack on the World Trade Centre in 2001, the need for greater understanding was particularly urgent, and this realisation was only increased by the tragic London bombings of 2007. In 2005, a Department for Communities and Local Government report on 'Race and Faith' found that half the population perceived an increase in racial and religious tension in Britain. Government policy began to prioritise 'community cohesion'.

---

[3] I.Selvanayagam 'A Second Call' CLS 2000 p203.

In this context, the Faith Guiding Certificate was developed, with the accreditation of the Institute of Tourist Guiding (Level 2 as it is site specific) and the support of staff of University College, Birmingham with expertise in leisure and tourism. The course has now been completed by about 90 people, mostly in the West Midlands, together with a small group in Leicester. They have been drawn from the following faiths: Buddhist, Christian, Hindu, Jain, Jewish, Muslim, Sikh, Unitarian and Zoroastrian.

The course comprises three elements: faith knowledge, guiding skills and understanding of other faiths. Besides 36 hours in class (usually 3 hours per week over 12 weeks), extensive private study (or evidence of prior learning) totalling over 100 hours, is required by the Institute of Tourist Guiding. Participants keep a weekly journal of their responses to the course. The assessment is through a one hour written examination and a short assessed guided tour conducted at the participant's own place of worship. Each participating faith has a university calibre Faith Tutor, so for example the Muslim participants will spend 10 hours at the beginning of the course with a senior Muslim scholar, learning how to put across their faith accurately and concisely to complete outsiders. They should be able to speak about the faith as a whole, not just their own particular tradition, and should have a sense of how it is seen by outsiders. This makes up the first and foundation element of the course, known as **'Faith Knowledge'**. The second, **'Guiding Skills'** (18 hours) is taught by a Blue Badge Guide (Institute of Tourist Guiding) and the third **'Understanding other faiths'** (8 hours) is taught by a qualified and experienced inter faith practitioner (often the Co-ordinator herself). Even those experienced in guiding at their own place of worship find they have much to learn from the professionalism of the Blue Badge Guide, for example about repeating any question that they are asked, before answering it, in order to make sure the whole group has heard. The course includes four visits to different places of worship to experience good practice and learn about the different faiths. Much learning also takes place incidentally during the course, as participants get to know one another as friends and practise presenting their faiths.

The influence of Israel Selvanayagam's work

Israel Selvanayagam is known for being both **'evangelical and 'dialogical'**. He frequently teaches and demonstrates that mission and dialogue are not incompatible, but are two sides of the same coin. He set this out in a seminar in 1993, which was later published and became known as his position paper. He expounded the same position in his Teape lectures and in his book, 'The Second Call: Ministry and Mission in a multifaith milieu.'(*CLS Chennai 2000*). In this book he talks about 'actual encounters undertaken with mutual respect and courtesy' (p 388). This is what happens to participants in the Faith Guiding course. The Faith Knowledge aspect of the course trains people to witness to their own faith with clarity and confidence (being evangelical), but without preaching or attempting to convert. The conversion, if any, is left in the hands of God. They learn to interpret specialised language, which makes them think deeply about the real meaning of words and phrases that may have been familiar all their lives, such as, 'God is known as Father, Son and Holy Spirit', to give a Christian example. Those participants belonging to faiths which are rooted in other cultures and commonly use words that cannot be accurately translated into English, learn to explain them. Sikhs, for example, have to explain '*langar*' and '*Guru Granth Sahibji*, while Muslims have to translate '*hajj*' and '*halal*'. Christians too learn that their faith has cultural expression, and that, for example, Arabic speaking Christians may call God '*Allah*', while Christian women in India often remove their shoes and cover their heads for worship. In England Christians put up Christmas trees in church and celebrate harvest festival in the autumn – which is not biblical and would be thought strange in other Christian churches around the world. Faith guides learn to distinguish between religion and culture, to respect the integrity of each other's faith and to recognise and understand differences while building on areas of common ground. This means starting sentences with the words, 'As Hindus/ Christians/Jains etc. we believe.....' rather than making general statements that imply a particular belief is universal. This enables them to engage in dialogue as well as witness.

The Faith Guiding course embodies many of the principles that Israel Selvanayagam lives, and continues to write about and teach. One of his central principles for interfaith dialogue is that of 'Commitment and Openness,'[4] which lies at the heart of the Faith Guiding course. By this he counters some of the suspicions sometimes

---

[4] I.Selvanayagam 'A Second Call' CLS 2000 p189.

held against interfaith practitioners, that they are compromising their own faith positions. Selvanayagam has shown that compromise is not only unnecessary but may even be unhelpful. Mutual respect develops between people of different faiths who are clearly committed and able to express that commitment. They find they are speaking the same language and each recognises a deep spirituality in the other that forms a genuine bond. On the other hand, there must be openness to the other position, a serious attempt to understand intellectually and enter into the experience of the other spiritually. The result is usually a growth in faith on the part of both participants in the dialogue, as new light is shed on their own faith. For instance when Muslims speak to Christians of their reverence for Isa/Jesus and the way in which they see him as a prophet, the Christians see their Lord in new ways.

Other themes frequently examined in Selvanayagam's work are those of community and of concern for the oppressed. He is quick to point out injustice wherever it occurs and to see the point of view of those who are discriminated against. Although these themes are less explicit in the Faith Guiding course, they are there in the way it has been conducted. No-one is excluded from taking part. This is done by keeping fees low and waiving them for those on benefits or very low incomes. Hindu priests, for example are often paid only a subsistence wage by their congregations but several have taken part in the course. People of widely varying age and status often take part in the course and find they are all treated as equals. In a recent course a friendship developed between a Buddhist man in his 70's and a Muslim woman in her twenties. During the course a strong sense of community is fostered through participative exercises, especially in the Understanding other Faiths section. One of the most memorable is when participants are paired with someone of another faith and are asked to speak without interruption for 2 minutes on topics such as 'how does your faith help you cope when times are hard?' The partner listens and then shares, again without interruption, on the same topic. Mutual friendships are also fostered among the group through the experience of overcoming nervousness when speaking in front of the group. Some find this a very daunting prospect but grow in confidence bit by bit, until they are able to take the practical examination in front of two examiners and the whole group in their place of worship. The sense of community on that day is powerful, as each wills the others to succeed. As Gareth Jones has said,

'People (of different faiths on the course) gain from each other's enthusiasm, and there's also a sense of shared vulnerability...... arising out of this I've noticed a real mutual encouragement – people want each other to do well, they want each other to fulfil their potential.'[5]

Benefits of the course

The Faith Guiding course is of benefit in a number of ways, but first and foremost to the faith guides themselves. Some of those who start the course have experience in hosting visitors and are not sure that they have much to learn, while others are very nervous and don't believe they will ever be able to lead a tour with a group. Those with experience find they value the multi faith context of the course and the opportunity to stand in the shoes of visitors at other places of worship. They often gain additional professional skills such as maintaining eye contact with everyone in the group. Those who lack self confidence gain it through the mutual encouragement of the group, the non-judgemental atmosphere and the opportunity to practise among friends. A sense of the benefits to participants, who become faith guides, can be conveyed from their own responses:

'...it was an excellent opportunity to ask all those questions to each other about our faiths that you would otherwise never have the courage to ask.' (Sikh faith guide)

'I am inspired by the camaraderie and I now have the ability to receive groups confidently and professionally.'(Zoroastrian faith guide)

'I learnt how to explain concepts for my own faith while being sensitive to others.' (Christian faith guide)

'Since finishing the course I have been getting regular visits from schools... to our Mandir, and I have also been asked to do presentations at schools.' (Hindu faith guide)

As this quotation indicates, faith guides have the opportunity to gain other forms of speaking experience. Requests come into the Faith Encounter Programme for speakers to visit schools, colleges and adult groups in the West Midlands and beyond. A good example was the invitation to take people of six faiths to Pershore High School in Worcestershire, when they engaged with several hundred pupils aged 15-18. They are also invited to take part in interfaith events and can thus develop their dialogue skills.

---

[5] Gareth Jones (Christian and Inter Faith Tutor) at Walsall Faith Guides' Awards Evening 06.06.11.

Secondly, there are significant benefits to the places of worship and faith communities involved. As Gopinder Kaur Sagoo has said (personal communication 28.20.11) many different types of encounter take place during a visit. The visitors encounter a sacred building, with all its sounds, symbols, practices and atmosphere. The faith guide encounters the visitors, who may themselves be of different faiths. There is an encounter of different cultures and the faith community is challenged to see itself as outsiders see it. While recognising differences of doctrine, tradition and practice, profound areas of common ground are also usually discovered, which can form the basis for future relationships. These include a seeking after the eternal perspective on life, care for humanity and all of creation, and a commitment to work for peace and reconciliation. Faith guides become more aware of intra-faith diversity, as they seek to respond to the perceptions and questions of the visitors. For example a Sunni Muslim may find s/he is asked a question about Shia practice that a visitor has seen on television. All these experiences can be shared with others in their own faith community. The host community is challenged to engage more fully with the locality and wider area, and to find new ways of sharing its insights without proselytising. The new faith guide may encourage his/her place of worship to improve the quality of its presentation, its system of booking visits and its backup literature, so as to improve the warmth and efficiency of the welcome that can be offered. This reminds me again of Israel Selvanayagam's emphasis on community. He was inspired by the thinking of S. J. Samartha, who writes about 'dialogue in community,'[6]

> 'There must be dialogues within particular communities of faith and also between different communities , so that new communities might emerge – communities of concerned people ready to take risks, to move beyond safe boundaries, to replace old particularities with new profiles.'

The Faith Encounter Programme moves communities in this direction.

The third group of people to benefit from the Faith Guiding training, is naturally, the visitors. The Faith Encounter Programme has enjoyed the support of the Birmingham Standing Conference on Religious Education (SACRE) for the last five years, not least because

---

[6] S.J.Samartha 'Courage for Dialogue – ecumenical issues in inter-religious relationships' WCC 1981 p100.

the Faith Guiding approach has fitted in with their development of a new approach to the RE syllabus.[7] This involves learning *from* religion, as well as learning *about* religion, and its promotion with Birmingham schools has been the responsibility of the RE Adviser, Simone Whitehouse. She has written:

> 'The value of having someone trained as a faith guide should not be underestimated....This is at the heart of community engagement, of interfaith dialogue, where pupils can openly ask 'Why does that happen?' 'What is this?' and 'Why are they doing that ?' and be given the chance to reflect on what those answers might mean for them. This is the crux of meaningful ...religious education.'[8]

She also says how important it is that the visit meets the needs of the class in terms of linking with the curriculum. Even faith guide training does not fully equip guides to manage this, so the Faith Encounter Programme holds follow up workshops to introduce the dispositions that are the focus of the Birmingham syllabus.[9] Pupils on a faith guided tour are enabled to see the place of worship as the heart of a religious community on their own doorstep. They may be offered a rare spiritual experience in a beautiful building (or a building containing beautiful artefacts), that a classroom based talk, even by a visiting speaker, could never replicate. The faith guide is able to serve their community by bringing their own commitment to life in the context of the building, for the visitors, reminding us again of Israel Selvanayagam's principle of 'committed openness'.

The future

The course has already been extended throughout the West Midlands and to Leicester, and there are hopes of extending it elsewhere in the country. What lessons have been learnt that will have to be borne in mind if this process is to be successful ? The delivery of the course, with its three elements, is a complex process and needs an experienced hands-on Programme Director to coordinate all the parts. It is a new development for the Institute of Tourist Guiding, so compromises have to be made in order to retain its essential ethos while complying with their requirements for accreditation. These require a firm grasp of the

---

[7] *www.faithmakesadifference.org.uk*

[8] Personal submission.

[9] *www.faithmakesadifference.org.uk*

aims and purpose of the pioneering concept of Faith Guiding. The Institute's requirements give a very useful framework, assuring quality and recognition. However, it is essential that the course is tailored to the local situation, not just in terms of the number of different faiths that can take part, but also the needs of local school groups and the context of local faith communities. This may mean forgoing the Institute's accreditation and running a shorter, simpler training programme. In some places there may be an inter faith centre that can take responsibility, in others a local Steering Group will have to be established. In some cases a university or college may be involved, while in others all the practicalities will have to be set up for the first time. In some places, a local multi faith forum, offered the course, has felt it had other priorities, while in others a similar body has welcomed the course as a valuable part of its on-going programme. In a large monocultural area the variety and needs of places of worship will be different from those in a very diverse city, but the course will still be useful even if only two or three faiths take part and some of the diversity comes from different Christian denominations.

Conclusion

In terms of models of interfaith activity, the phrase coined by Sir Jonathan Sacks, the chief Rabbi, 'face to face and side by side', is relevant and has become widely used, particularly by the Department of Communities and Local Government.[10] 'Face-to-face' is where people of different faiths get to know each other and each other's faiths by talking face to face; 'side by side' is where people of different faiths cooperate with each other on common activities, usually to benefit their local community. Gareth Jones, in his address to the Faith Guides' Awards evening in Walsall in 2010, made the point that the Faith Guiding course enables faith guides to do both. They work alongside each other to benefit their local communities and in the process, they meet face to face and get to know what faith means to each other. They learn not just about the outward expressions of faith, what people do or wear, but they appreciate their inner commitment, ethical behaviour and deep spirituality.

---

[10] '"Face-to-face and side-by-side":a framework for inter faith dialogue and social action' Consultation document from DCLG 2007

Some quotes from faith guides bear this out :

'I learned how people live their lives by their religion, the group members are real people not just 'Christians' or 'Hindus'. (a Sikh)

'I am grateful for the insights into other people's religions – there was a feeling of warmth and love.' (Christian)

A visit to a place of worship should be a rich experience, intellectually, emotionally and spiritually. When the visit is interpreted through the eyes of a follower of the faith, who is enthusiastic, warm hearted, knowledgeable and also appreciative of the background of the visitors, it becomes a unique opportunity. Faith guides themselves

'discover the emotional connection that each of us has to our own faith and how for each of us faith is a source of inspiration, joy and comfort.'[11]

A tour will make a lasting impression if the visitor,

'has journeyed within themselves and been stimulated to think how we can better learn to live together and enhance the world around us.'[12]

This deep understanding is the foundation of the informed and committed openness that Israel Selvanayagam continues to live and teach, both in India and Britain.

---

[11] Gareth Jones in Walsall 2011.

[12] Gopinder Kaur Sagoo (Sikh Tutor) in a personal reflection 2011.

Some Exegetical and Hermeneutical Options in Reading the Gospel According to John to Promote an Inclusive Understanding of God

Dhyanchand Carr

A Preamble

It is a matter of great delight and privilege to make this small contribution to the Festschrift in honour of Dr. Israel Selvanayagam, a one time student, long time colleague and a person who bonds with unwavering consistency. This little piece is written partly in response to frequent off the cuff discussions we both have had on the issues relating to interfaith dialogue as well as to a comprehensive and lucid essay on the theme of interfaith relations jointly written in Tamil by him and my former teacher and theological godfather The Rt Rev Dr. Samuel Amirtham (E.Note 1). It is hoped that this little piece will help strengthen a concern we both share namely that somehow the people who belong to the Church in India should be brought out of their exclusivist attitudes abetted by a fundamentalist treatment of texts taken out of context. Because the oft used text to warrant this attitude is John 14:6, I thought it may help at least those who are keen to understand the words of Jesus and make them a guide for their life, if they are enabled to see the meaning of the self designation of Jesus as "I Am" as understood by the author of the Gospel.

1.   Some Important Reminders

In John's Gospel belief in God implies responsive love which implies an unfailing commitment to follow God's ways as revealed by Jesus, God's Son. One cannot be seen in isolation from the other. Such a combination alone leads to truth and consequent liberation from slavery to sin. Sin is not predominantly moral violation but blind slavery to tradition, which makes it impossible to recognize who Jesus is and therefore to understand who God is! (cf Jn 8: 24-32 & 44-56). Truth is not doctrinal truth but the ability to recognize God at work among those who suffer and among those who are alienated (see Jn 4:7-32 & 5:1-17 and the follow up discussion in 7:19-24). This inability is highlighted through the story of the Cross. For it is on the Cross that Jesus the Son of Man is recognized as none other than the "I AM" of Median. John uses the lifting up of the Son of Man on the Cross in an anachronistic manner because for him that it is an ongoing reality and not a onetime event.

It is also necessary to keep in mind the metaphor of eating the Bread of Life (Jesus' flesh) and drinking, drinking of the water that never makes one thirst again and the drinking of the blood of Jesus. For the self designation "I Am" is linked with I am the Bread of Life and Bread is linked with the flesh of the Son of Man which means sustenance of life provided by exploited human labour (cf 6:52-55). We shall see how these references help us to understand our Lord's words:

> "...And you know the way to the place where I am going. Thomas said to him, 'Lord we do not know where you are going. How can we know the way?' Jesus said to him, "I am the way, and the truth and the life. No one comes to the Father except through me. If you know me you will know my Father also...the Father dwells in me does his works...the one who believes in me will also do the works that I do..."

The works that Jesus does are the works that the Father does in him. These works are linked to the words that Jesus speaks from the Father. Therefore it is plain that the way to know the Father is through understanding the works of Jesus.With these basic reminders let us enter into a detailed exegesis of the self designation "I AM" of Jesus in the Gospel according to John.

A List of "I Am" Occurrences

First, the well recognized ones with explanatory notes:

i. "I am the bread of life" (6:35); - Bread gives life; Jesus gives his flesh as bread and gives us his life - But to understand the metaphor of eating the heavenly bread to live in unison with Christ, we need to understand how Jesus lived by life given to him by the Father - "Just as he living Father sent me and I live because of the Father, so whoever eats me will live because of me" Most certainly Jesus could not have eaten the flesh of the Father. Neither did he have access to the Heavenly Bread from the Father through participation in any sacrament. Then how did he live because of the Father? Let us read Jn 4:31f "Rabbi, eat something" But he said to them "I have food to eat that you do not know about....My food is to do the will of him who sent me and to complete his work". It is abundantly clear, therefore, when Jesus asked his disciples to eat his flesh and drink his blood he was asking them to be wholeheartedly involved in doing God's work and in turn be sustained by the very life God had given to Jesus himself. No wonder then in John the work of God (cf 6:29) is explained as belief, for true faith and living in unison with God doing the work of God are inseparable from one another. So we shall have to reach an understanding of faith also via doing the work of God. To know what that is we shall have to wait a little longer.

ii. "I am the light of the world, whoever follows me will never will never walk in darkness but will have the light of life" (8:12) - The chosen path of Jesus distinctly differs from the path set for themselves and the people by the religious leaders of his day. Following this path is following the "light of life". How does the way of the light of life differ from that of the path shown by religion and "this world". The saying "I am the light of the world"(8:12f) follows the story of the way Jesus dealt with the woman caught in adultery (8:1-11). Religion and this world condemn the women who are pushed into adultery by the male world. According to Jesus, as explained in the Syn Gospels, the one who causes the weaker to stumble is the more guilty. We do not know what our Lord wrote on the ground which scared away all the men who wanted to stone the hapless woman to death. When Jesus said let the one without sin cast the first stone, it was the elders who began the retreat first! All the men left, except Jesus. He sent her home without condemning her with a word of counsel to beware of the world of men (a bold rereading of the "sin no more" in resonance with Jesus' response to the men who brought the woman).

iii. I am the Good Shepherd: The Good shepherd gives his life for the sheep. He knows them intimately and they also know and recognize his voice without paying heed to the voice of the thieves and robbers - the false shepherds. In addition to these well known sayings it is good to remember that the shepherd image is drawn from the nomadic life of Abel the first victim of human jealousy and Abraham who relinquished settled urban life and became a nomad/shepherd. The letter to the Hebrews commends Abraham for remaining in the Promised Land without any take over bid. Isaac and Jacob also followed suit. It is also good to remember the metaphor of the shepherd aptly described the kings of Israel and Judah, though many of them never lived up to that designation (see Ezek.ch 34). Finally the Good Shepherd is keen to gather in sheep which do not belong to his pen.

iv "I am the Resurrection and the Life" - These are the famous words of Jesus spoken to Martha. Lazarus is raised to life after having been in the grave for four days. We should take this incident along with Jesus voluntarily bringing back to life the son of the widow of Nain and the incident of giving life to the 12yr old daughter of Jairus. Jesus did not go about raising many from the dead. His interventions were against untimely deaths. Therefore as we see in the raising of Lazarus a definite sign of the end time of hope of resurrection for all we should also take note that it is the bringing back to life of an unfortunate victim of the forces of death prematurely. Thus, this saying "I am the Resurrection... yet once again connotes God's involvement in the unfortunate victims of the forces of death and destruction playing havoc in the lives of many.

The Not So Well Recognized Occurrences

We now move on to see some othertexts which have gone unnoticed by people who cannot read the Greek New Testament because of some arbitrary decision taken by most translators to introduce a "he" thereby distorting the intended meaning of the author.

i. Speaking to the Samaritan woman Jesus declares that he is the Messiah saying, "I am". The "he" in the translation is not present in the Greek text. This is recognized by modern translators. For some odd reason, however, they choose to introduce a "he", thereby distorting the intended meaning of the author. The author of the Gospel clearly wants us to understand that the Messiah is "I am" recalling the Median episode in which God made it known that God was right there in the midst of the burning bush of Israel suffering persecution, guarding it from getting totally scorched. Here in this episode Jesus offers the Distraught Samaritan Woman life giving water. His reference to her present living with a man who was not her legal husband should not be understood as an indictment. She must have been repeatedly thrown out of marriage perhaps because she could bear no children. In any closely knit society single women always ran the risk of being preyed upon by pleasure seeking men,quietly winked over by all. Of necessity women are forced to live under the protection of a man. It is because the woman understood the sympathy of this strange man from a community which despised them and spurned their religion she was pleasantly surprised and later came to understand who he really was. Later in the same episode this meaning is alluded to when Jesus going against custom stayed in the Samaritan village helping them to understand the true nature of the Messiah. So when Jesus simply says "I am" the author wants us to understand that God who spoke to Moses is at work again. God through his Messiah who would not judge according to what his eyes were made to see and what he was forced to hear was hear taking the side of a despised woman. Thereby he gained over a despised and estranged Samaritan community. This memory has been preserved for us which means that there must have been a Samaritan Christian community who cherished it and passed it on.

ii. The next two occurrences of "I am"(he) appear in John ch 8. Jesus is talking to the Jews in the Temple precincts in Jerusalem. "...I told you that you would die in your sins unless you believe that I am"(8:24). Again translators introduce a "he" in the translation. For them the phrase "unless you believe that I am **he**" seems to connote a recognition of Jesus as the Messiah, the "he" stands for that. While John wants to convey the meaning that they ought to believe in Jesus as the Messiah who is none other than the "I am" of Median revelation of God's presence in the midst of people who suffer. This inference is clearly warranted by 8:28 "When you have lifted up the Son of Man, then you will realize that I am **he.** In this verse also what John wants to convey is that the crucified Jesus is the Son of Man of Daniel 7 who represents the People of the Most High who in fact symbolize all those who suffer as a result of their struggle against injustice. The author of the fourth Gospel strains his literary skills to bring about a fusion of the Son of Man, the Messiah and the "I am" in 12:31-36.

The sin from which God wants to save the world is the sin of not being able to understand that God is always involved and implicated in the lives of the oppressed. God is involved in the lives of all Abels of the world. Thereby God achieves a twofold purpose. God redeems the Abel community from their quest for vengeance. They are converted to make their plea along with Jesus, "Father forgive them..." Though this word of the Cross is taken over from Luke it is not contrary to the declared purpose in John. Remaining on the Cross, the Lifted Up Son of Man - I am will draw all people to himself. This drawing together will come about only through the Abel Community being constant in the struggle against injustice. For the struggle of the Abel Community will expose the world and lead to its judgement. Its ruler then loses his grip over the world. the Mega Exorcism will take place. The Cain Community will undergo a thorough repentance. All people will be drawn to the lifted up Son of Man saying a "NO" to the devil once for all. When repentance does come about the victim sector will extend forgiveness completing the task of Christ's suffering. This is clearly implied in the central passage of the 4th Gospel ch 12:27-36.

iii. Two more occurrences of "I am" which clinch the argument. In John ch 8 the contention of Jesus is that the people of the Jewish community, the chosen people of God stubbornly remain in their orthodoxy. Jesus shares in their convictions about God being One. He joins in their worship of the One True God in their synagogues. He happily accepts invitations to preach. Yet, Jesus is deeply perturbed that they are unable to understand God. They had become proud of their exclusive Abrahamic lineage. But they do not realize Abraham their ancestor had seen God's purposes that would one day be made known to the whole world through Jesus the Messiah, the I am. It was because he had understood this he was prepared to give up the urban elite life he enjoyed and become a nomad making no claim for even a small piece of burial ground even in the very Promised Land to which God had led him. So Jesus asserts, "...before Abraham was I am, your father Abraham wanted to see my day and I say he saw it."

It is in fact the utterance "I am" when the hired men of the high priests coming along with Judas saying that they had come in search of Jesus of Nazareth is most significant. No sooner the people hear Jesus saying "I am" they draw back and fall to the ground because they had heard the unutterable Name of God revealed to Moses in the Median desert. This story is full of irony as it is a key text to understand all "I am" utterances in the rest of the Gospel. The irony is that even the thugs and the rowdies have a religious deference to the Name of God. Thus those who sent them are shown for what they really were.

What Then Are the Implications of the Exegesis Thus Far?

Hope the reader would have been able to see the subtle connection between the well known 'I am' sayings in the Fourth Gospel and the not so well recognized ones. It is the latter which really enshrine the intended meaning of the author. Belief in Jesus is not confessional. Rather it arises out of a sense of who God is. God is everywhere where people suffer unjustly. God's presence enables them to struggle against the injustice which causes the suffering without losing their humanity. They are not to reek vengeance. Rather, they are expected to join with Jesus and pray "Father forgive them for they know not what they do". Although the above cited word is borrowed from Luke's Gospel, the Mission mandate in John authenticates our understanding. Breathing on the disciples on Easter evening Jesus sent them out into the world asking them to declare forgiveness and assured them that their plea for forgiveness would be heeded. Rather, it may even be that there may be many without any belief in God are led to express their solidarity with the suffering sections of humanity. They should be considered to have seen Christ as Abraham was able to see Christ. Abraham chose to become a nomad and remain although he had arrived in the Promised Land. How sad, however, that his descendants today have taken the path of the Zionists intent on driving out the Palestinians from their home land.

The letter to the Hebrews echoes the same sentiment.It declares that in the act of Moses walking out of the palace choosing to take the side of his enslaved and oppressed people he saw Christ who was yet to come. When Moses did that he did not know that he was serving the God of Abraham the Father of the Future Christ. But to the author of the letter to the Hebrews what Moses did was nothing but an offering of his service to the Christ who was yet to come. There are also people like Rahab, who are alien in the reckoning of people like Joshua. Rahab, nevertheless was added to the community of the saved simply because she empathized with the unfortunate history of the Hebrews.

All this means that among many who claim to be believers there is a vast majority who worship the Father of our Lord Jesus without knowing who he is and what he is up to. In fact they are opposed to all that God is doing constantly without rest. And, there are those, who quite unknowingly are serving the Parent God of our Lord Jesus. The task of interfaith dialogue would be first to challenge our own people who refuse to understand the True God and be liberated from all the deeply ingrained falsehood. Only those who are so liberated can share together the love of God made known in Christ with all those who are already without knowing are in tune with the purposes of the God who is Truth and life.Such a dialogue, however, can happen only in so far as join hands and are involved in the work of God "I am".

End Note

The above essay could be considered by all Tamil knowing readers as a supplement to the extensive article, *People of Other Faiths*, in Samuel Amirtham and Israel Selvanayagam, *Let Us Return to the Bible*, pp 323-387, Madurai, 2011.

Would Paul Have Approved of 'Christians'?*

Neil Richardson

The word 'Christian' occurs only three times in the entire New Testament (Acts 11.26,26.28, 1 Peter 4.16), and not at all in the writings of St Paul. It seems to have been a nickname given to the church by 'outsiders' – Roman or Jewish authorities. It is likely that Paul knew of it since, according to Luke, the term was first coined at Antioch. But even if it was not yet an 'in-house' term, there may be deeper reasons why the apostle would have preferred not to use it. This paper explores what some of those reasons might have been.

1.   St Paul's Critique of Religion

I begin with a suggestion by the American New Testament scholar, Paul Meyer:

> 'A more adequate penetration of Paul's diagnosis of the condition under which all human religion suffers may lead to a more profound understanding of his gospel'.[1]

At first sight, Paul's criticisms of religion seem to be directed almost entirely towards the faith of the Jewish people. This has rightly become a sensitive area, as New Testament scholars have sought to free their discipline of caricatures of Judaism.[2] Yet, on closer inspection of his writings, Paul's critique of religion can be seen to have a universal application - the Christian Church not excepted. Paul's letters, after all, came to be regarded as Scripture because the Church had come to see that the significance of these writings transcended the original context to which they were first addressed.

Romans 1.18-32 provides a good example. These verses were originally directed at contemporary Gentile idolatry and the immorality which, in the eyes of a devout Jew such as Paul, that idolatry engendered. But today, despite interpretative difficulties with particular verses, the downward spiral which Paul traces in Romans 1.18-32 has a particular challenge in an age when market forces predominate : when human beings worship what is less than God, their idolatries make them less than human; such dehumanization fractures human relationships and human communities.[3]

With this wider, contemporary significance in mind, we turn shortly to some of Paul's strictures against the religion of Israel. But first we look at one word which, more than any other in Paul's writings, encapsulates his critique of human religion. It is the word *sarx*, translated misleadingly in older English versions as '(the) flesh', in more recent versions by a variety of interpretative phrases. Like the word 'world' (*kosmos*) in John's Gospel, *sarx* in Paul has a neutral[4] and a negative[5] meaning. It is the latter with which we are concerned, and here I combine the insights of two scholars. First, Leander Keck defines *sarx* in its negative sense as 'the physical or phenomenal when it inappropriately exercises power'.[6] Second, Ernst Kasemann notes that the word is used in the Old Testament and in Judaism to denote the difference between the creating God and the creature, referring both to the creature's weakness and sinfulness.[7] *Sarx*, therefore, in this negative sense in Paul, comes to characterize not only defective or inadequate human living, but also defective or inadequate religion.

Paul's use of this key word shows that his strictures are not limited to Judaism. His criticisms of both Jewish and Gentile religion are criticisms of what might be called their outcomes. But he has positive things to say about the best exemplars of Jewish faith, (and even of Gentile religion).[8] Meyer suggests that

> 'nowhere in Romans does Paul draw a distinction between an authentic Jew (2.28-9) and an authentic Christian (4.18-25; 9.24, 15.7-13)'.

Meyer goes on to add:

> 'nowhere does Paul draw a line through himself, to distinguish the authentic Jew from the non-Jewish Christian in his own person, or

> through God, to distinguish a God of the one from the God of the other (11.1-5).' Rather, 'a person is a Jew who is one inwardly, and real circumcision is a matter of the heart – it is spiritual and not literal' (Rom. 2.29a).[9]

However, the universal extent of Paul's critique of human religion when it belongs to the domain of the *sarx* becomes clear when the apostle accuses two of his churches of sliding back into that same domain. Of the Galatians, prompted by 'Judaizers' to adopt Jewish rites to complement their Christian faith, he asks: 'Are you so foolish? Having started with the Spirit, are you now ending with the flesh (*nun en sarki epiteleisthe*)?' (Gal.3.3b; compare a similar accusation levelled at the church in Corinth – 1 Cor. 3.1, 2c, 3a).[10]

Thus the contrasting terms 'flesh' (to retain the old, more literal translation) and 'Spirit' cannot be simply identified with Jewish and Gentile religion on the one hand and Christian faith on the other. The real antithesis is not between 'Jewish' and 'Christian' at all – a distinction which would be questionable in any century, but which, applied to the first century, is both questionable and anachronistic. In other words, Paul's use of *sarx* points up the universality of human failure and weakness in all religion, Christianity not excepted.

There are passages, however, where Paul is explicitly critical of his fellow-Jews. One such passage is Romans 2.17ff, especially verses 21-24, where Paul, in effect declares that the Jew who does not practise what he preaches forfeits his place as a member of God's people, and becomes, to all intents and purposes, a Gentile:

> '... If you break the law, your circumcision has become uncircumcision' (v.25).

Yet, as Karl Barth saw, the Church must hear these words as words spoken against itself:

> 'Where law is, the world expects a doing of the law; where the impress of revelation is, it expects actual revelation. It is not unsusceptible to reality, but it harbours no illusions.... The children of God present nothing peculiar, nothing new, nothing that exercises compelling power.[11]

There is, in Paul's view, one critical element of authentic religion: knowing and 'submitting to' the righteousness of God, (Rom.10.4). Not to know and submit to that righteousness results in two divisive, destructive consequences which are particularly pertinent to our exploration. We shall examine each in turn.

The verb *kauchaomai*, translated in older English versions by the word 'boast', is a key word in Pauline theology.[12] It serves to differentiate between true and false religion.[13] Boasting, according to Kasemann, 'is an expression of human dignity and freedom'. What is crucial is a person's 'lord'; by his boasting a person 'tells to whom he belongs.'[14] So human religion, (*not* Jewish religion *per se*), becomes the sphere for inappropriate boasting – although I note that Paul, addressing 'the Jew', says 'you boast in God' (Rom. 2.17) and 'you boast in the law' (Rom. 2.23). This brings us to the second of the two divisive, destructive results of not knowing and submitting to the righteousness of God.

The words 'zeal' and 'zealot' in Paul's writings illustrate how boasting can be disfigured or distorted by the power of sin and the weakness of the *sarx*. Paul thus describes himself:

> 'as to zeal, a persecutor of the church; as to righteousness under the law, blameless' (Philippians 3.6; cf Gal. 1.14 and Rom. 10.2).

Once more: we cannot possibly say that such 'boasting' and 'zeal' were or are distinctively Jewish. Kenneth Grayston comments as follows on Romans 7.1-6:

> 'God's bond with Israel has become too closely confined by the flesh – the habits and impulses of Jewish society: Paul wishes to free it to receive the energy of the Spirit'.

But he goes on to say:

> 'Devout Christian groups may recognize themselves…. in particularism that denies faith and sincerity to groups that revere God differently'.[15]

To summarize: we need to set on one side an older, long-established way of interpreting Paul which focussed on perceived antitheses between 'Jewish' and 'Christian' faith in ways which did less than justice to Jewish faith.[16] That misinterpretation has been widely acknowledged and corrected during the last few decades. We must now re-appropriate his critique of human religion, recognizing its universal application – the Christian Church included.

2.   Is there an 'Us' and a 'Them' in Paul?

Let Paul Meyer be our starting-point once more. Commenting on Paul's use of the words *pneumatikos* ('spiritual') and *sarkinos* ('fleshly') in Romans 7.14, Meyer observes that, under Augustine's influence, the two adjectives have been used to differentiate between 'two classes of humans: the religious person who is righteous, wise, re-born... and the irreligious, the ungodly and the sinner'. This, says Meyer, is 'the language of binary opposites, used by triumphalist religion to separate humankind into two groups of people, the saved and the damned'.

Meyer's comments represent a striking, if not revolutionary departure from a very widespread understanding of Paul. Does Paul not deal in 'binary opposites' after all? It will be instructive to summarize briefly the evidence. First, we note Meyer's later development of the main argument:

> 'the depth to which any reading of Paul that clings to such a division between the "godly" and the "ungodly" has misunderstood the apostle is sounded accurately only when one realizes that the whole of Paul's epistle (i.e. Romans) is but a single massive argument against the conventional uses of this distinction'.[17]

Is Meyer correct? I bracket out of the ensuing search for binary opposites in Paul the words *ecclesia* (church) and *hoi hagioi* (lit. 'the holy ones'), not because they are not important – they clearly are – but because they do not function as one half of binary opposites. Even when Paul uses the expression 'holy ones' – normally in his opening salutations,[18] there is no contrast. (We note shortly the few exceptions). So is there any basis in Paul for Christians, 'believers', 'the faithful', (or whatever self-referential terms Christians may use), distinguishing themselves from the rest of humankind? And if we do, have we reverted to the very binary language which Paul, according to Meyer, sought to exclude from religion?

When we turn to other Pauline words, we might well have expected his letters to be dominated by a contrast between *dikaios* ('just', 'righteous') and its opposite, *adikos*. In fact, this is not so. In this respect, Paul is quite different from some contemporary Jewish writings such as the Dead Sea Scrolls and the Psalms of Solomon.[19] There are only two instances in Paul to note, (apart from isolated occurrences of *dikaios* and *adikos* without their opposite): first, an implicit contrast in Paul's extended critique of Jewish (and, *ipso facto* as I have argued, human) religion:

> 'For it is not the hearers of the law who are righteous in God's sight, but the doers of the law who are justified' Romans 2.13);

secondly, there is an *ad hoc* contrast between 'the unjust' and 'the saints' in 1 Corinthians, where Paul is addressing the possibility of Christians taking fellow-Christians before pagan courts notorious for their corruption and injustice:

> 'When any of you has a grievance against another, do you dare to take it to court before the unrighteous (*adikon*) instead of before the saints (*ton hagion*)?' (1 Cor.6.1)

We turn to another pair of binary opposites which we might have expected to be prominent in Paul: *pistos* ('believer or 'faithful') and *apistos* ('unbeliever' or 'unfaithful'). There is a clear example of these words functioning as binary opposites in 2 Corinthians:

> 'What agreement does Christ have with Beliar? Or what does a believer (*pisto*) share with an unbeliever (*apistou*)?' (2 Cor.6.15).d

In fact, this is not typical Pauline language at all. Some scholars have questioned its authenticity, particularly as it sits somewhat awkwardly with the preceding and following passages.[20] If we allow that it is Pauline, the sharp language here may be due to the situation at Corinth, where some over-confident Christians were inter-acting with paganism to the detriment of others' faith, if not their own.[21]

Paul uses the word *apistos* several times in 1 Corinthians, but always when addressing specific problems. This word and its opposite *pistos* never occur together in the more generalizing, systematic way which would indicate that Paul does indeed divide humankind into the godly and the godless, the saved and the damned. Instead, we have much more nuanced discussions of sensitive, complex situations. We look briefly at the two most important examples.

In 1 Corinthians 7.12-15 Paul discusses what Christians married to *apistoi* should do. He concludes that they should not seek a separation unless their partner wants one, in the hope that through the marriage the *apistos* might be 'saved' (v.16). (Paul, interestingly, has acknowledged that the 'unbelieving partner' has already been 'sanctified ' (*hegiastai*) (v.14). This teaching is a striking reflection of Jesus' teaching - and actions - that purity can overcome impurity, whereas the Qumran literature (for example) reflected a concern about the reverse process.[22] Two other verses in this letter – 5.10 and 10.27 – suggest that the Christians at Corinth inter-acted quite freely with their non-Christian contemporaries.

When Paul envisages, later in the same letter, the possibility of 'an outsider' or 'unbeliever' (*idiotai e apistoi*, 1 Cor. 14.23-4, cf. v.22) entering a Christian meeting, he is again using this language in an *ad hoc* way, and not in the more thorough-going way which Meyer – rightly, I believe – is challenging. But we must test this by looking at further evidence.

The present participle 'perishing' is contrasted twice with 'being saved' at 1 Corinthians 1.18 and 2 Corinthians 2.15. It is significant that Paul uses present participles for both verbs: no-one is yet saved – i.e. 'home and dry'; compare Rom.8.24 and 1 Cor.15.2 – nor yet wholly lost. There *is* a contrast, brought about by the preaching of the cross,[23] but it is not a fixed or final one. As for 2 Corinthians 2.15, the contrast is due to the image of a victory procession in war which Paul is using here.

So Paul's use of opposites is largely *ad hoc*, when he needs to make a contrast in order to formulate some ethical teaching. Otherwise, he very rarely contrasts 'the holy', 'the righteous', 'the believers' etc. with their opposites. This does not mean that the response of a person to the gospel was a matter of indifference to Paul. Paul's language of 'salvation', of 'being saved' and 'perishing' shows otherwise. So it is all the more remarkable that his language is largely devoid of the binary opposites which divide humankind into 'sheep' and 'goats'.[24]

Paul's main 'binary opposites' are 'flesh' and 'spirit', and 'letter' and 'Spirit'. These make a contrast, as we have seen, not so much between two groups of people, as between authentic and inauthentic religion.[25] Instead of binary opposites, the emphasis in Paul's writings is different. For example, the word *pisteuo* ('believe in' or 'have faith') occurs over 40 times in the undisputed letters. It is frequently used in conjunction with the words *pas/pantes* ('every', 'all'), whilst in Romans 4 and Galatians 3 Abraham is represented as the prototype of all believers. Following the suggestion of Meyer with which I began this paper, I believe that Paul's critique of religion will indeed help us to understand more fully his gospel. So, in the final section of this paper, I explore the nature of that gospel in the light of the foregoing discussions.

3. Paul's Gospel in the Light of his Critique of Human Religion

According to Paul, all religion, including Christian faith, is easily distorted. Adherents of distorted religion tend to boast of their god, to direct their zeal against their opponents, imaginary or real, and to perceive humankind as divided into two camps, those who 'belong', and those who do not. This Pauline critique of human religion has far-reaching implications for the Church. Most churchgoers, if asked whether the Church has any rivals, would respond, 'But of course it has!' If asked whether the distinction between 'Christian' and 'non-Christian' was theologically sound, would insist that it was. It is precisely here that Paul's perspective acquires its cutting edge.

Identifying the heart of Paul's message – his gospel – is not a straightforward task, since all his surviving letters were occasional writings, directed to specific contexts. In Paul there is no such thing as a gospel in general, only the gospel for Galatian Christians challenged by the 'Judaizers', for the Corinthian Christians, seduced by contemporary culture, and so on. But we can get close, by paying careful attention to Paul's language, and some of the patterns or paradigms which might be said to carry most of the theological weight in his letters. Two features, in particular, deserve our attention.

First, the words 'one' and 'all', as we briefly noted above, appear with remarkable frequency. One of the most important occurrences of the word 'one' occurs at 1 Corinthians 8.6:

> 'Yet for us there is one God, the Father, from whom are all things and for whom we exist, and one Lord, Jesus Christ, through whom are all things and through whom we exist'.

We might call this Paul's 'meta-narrative'; it frames his entire thought and theology. It is inclusive, as the repeated 'all things' indicates. It is also exclusive, since 'one God' precludes all idolatries. But how inclusive or exclusive is 'one Lord'? This is where Paul can easily be misread, and when that happens, we are back to a religious world of binary opposites. So we turn to a second fundamental pattern in Paul's language.

At the heart of Paul's theology lies the divine 'interchange', later expressed in patristic writings: 'God in Christ became what we are, that we through Christ might become what he is'. In Paul, this 'interchange' is expressed in language contextualized for the situation he is addressing. So in urging the Corinthians to contribute generously to his 'collection' for famine-stricken Christians in Judaea, he says this:

> 'For you know the generous act of our Lord Jesus Christ, that though he was rich, yet for your sakes he became poor, so that by his poverty you might become rich' (2 Cor.8.9).

There are several other expressions of this divine exchange in Paul's letters.[26] But its creative heart - not always explicitly stated - is the cross and resurrection of Christ:

> 'For our sake he (sc. God) made him (sc. Christ) to be sin who knew no sin so that in him we might become the righteousness of God' (2 Cor.5.21).

It is the cross and resurrection which have changed the old frames of reference, including the old opposites of 'righteous' and 'sinners', 'Jew' and 'Gentile'. For example, in Galatians the letter's prescript includes a reference both to the resurrection (1.1), and to the sacrifice of Christ 'for our sins', the purpose of which is to 'rescue us from this present wicked age' (1.3-4). Paul, however, does not proceed to divide humankind into those who have been rescued and those who haven't, but in a quite different direction. He proceeds to demolish a familiar binary opposite, one half of which was 'Gentile/sinner' (The two words are treated as synonyms at 2.15).

The *conclusion* of Galatians expresses the outcome of the divine exchange (expressed at 4.4-6): a 'new creation' (6.15). Such a concept, both eschatological and universal, cannot be defined over against any other human grouping. It might be differentiated from *all* human groupings, though the New Testament itself seems to discourage that. Even if it were, it would still remain true: God has abolished the old world of binary opposites: 'believer' and 'unbeliever', 'righteous' and 'unrighteous' etc. This is the 'scandal' of Paul's gospel.[27] The 'new creation' is all-embracing, as other verses in the Pauline corpus clearly show:

> At Romans 5.19 Paul writes,

> 'For just as by the one man's disobedience the many were made sinners, so by the one man's obedience the many will be made righteous' (cf. 1 Cor.15.22).[28]

Hultgren, in his recent commentary, quotes Karl Barth here:

> 'In the light of this act of obedience (i.e. of Jesus) – there is no man who is not in Christ. All are renewed and clothed with righteousness'.[29]

This does not make Paul a universalist. The lordship of Christ is universal (Rom.10.12, Phil.2.9-11), though not yet universally acknowledged. But we risk over-looking the strongly universalist tone in Paul's writings because we tend to read into them the binary opposites which, we have argued, are simply not there. 2 Corinthians 5.14 provides another example:

> 'For the love of Christ urges us on, because we are convinced that one has died for all; therefore all have died'.

It is not easy to say what Paul meant by 'all have died', but the 'all' here cannot be narrower than the 'all' in the preceding clause: 'one has died for all'.

4.   Paul's Language in a World of Many Faiths

What are we to make of Paul's language in a world of many faiths? In our day the words 'one' and 'all' may suggest aggressive proselytizing and triumphalism. It will be instructive to return to the words 'boast' and 'zeal' which we looked at in the first section. First, it is noteworthy that Paul's intolerance and zeal are now re-directed towards fellow-Christians – just as the strongest words of Jesus seem to have been reserved for religious people who divided their world into 'us' and 'them'.[30] But this is very different from the universalizing of humankind into two opposed groups of believers and unbelievers.

Second, what Paul now 'boasts' in is the key to understanding his theology. The grounds for religious boasting, and, therefore, the basis of human dignity and freedom[31] have shifted. Boasting which differentiates from another group - as, implicitly, in Romans 2.17 and 23 - is misplaced. The only grounds for boasting is 'the Lord' (i.e. Christ):

> 'Let the one who boasts, boast in the Lord (1 Cor. 1.31b, 2 Cor. 10.17; cf. Rom.5.11).

It must be said at once that such boasting in Christ can be - and sometimes is - as divisive and destructive as any other. But two extraordinarily counter-cultural references by Paul to boasting show why it must not be so. To the Romans Paul writes of how 'we ... boast in our sufferings, (Rom.5.3a; cf. 2 Cor.12.9 and 11.18-30). Such a statement turned all contemporary boasting upside-down. The explanation for it lies in an even more counter-cultural reference to boasting:

> 'May I never boast of anything except the cross of our Lord Jesus Christ, by which the world has been crucified to me, and I to the world' (Gal.6.14).

What does this mean for our understanding of human religion? We do not do justice to Paul's message of the cross, unless we acknowledge its anti-religious implications. The cross undermines all grounds for divisively saying 'our god', as it undermines all forms of religion which divide humankind into opposite categories, whether 'believers' and 'unbelievers' or 'righteous' and 'sinners'. God in Christ has shifted the grounds for human 'boasting': now the only grounds for boasting is the crucified Christ who undercuts all boasting which exalts one group at the expense of another.

Christian faith, therefore, cannot be a reason for believers deliberately or self-consciously distinguishing themselves from others; a distinctiveness will emerge from faithful witness, but that is a different matter. The holiness of Jesus should be our guide here. Faith is expressed, not primarily in making distinctions, but in *agape* (Gal. 5.6). The key words are not 'us' and 'them' but 'one' (i.e. God in Christ) and 'all'.

Other references to boasting in Paul's letters support, rather than undermine the argument here. The apostle frequently speaks of his 'pride' (literally, his 'boasting') in his churches (1 Cor. 15.2, Cor. 1.14b, 1 Thess. 2.19, Phil.2.16). This 'boasting' is the outcome of the gospel of the crucified Christ. The divine interchange has prompted a corresponding interchange in human boasting: now a person boasts, not in themselves, but in their Christian brothers and sisters. Faith is characterized, not by marking itself from the world, but by the love which elicits and nurtures faith in others.

Conclusion

Paul's critique of human religion invites Christians to engage in serious self-examination. How appropriate is the word 'Christian'? It is a convenient term of self-reference, but it has become a label not only of differentiation, but also of division. The word hardly occurs in the New Testament, and when it does, it is as a nickname, a taunt or an accusation. Would Paul have approved of its contemporary use? We can only guess. Paul thinks of the Church and of 'Christians' eschatologically – as the firstfruits of God's 'new creation'. If they are thought of in this way, there can be no other grouping, or even religion, 'over against'.

Paul's critique, and our own self-examination (not least in dialogue with other faiths) may help us discover, or re-discover a truly universal religion which – if true to its cruciform centre – will not be triumphalist; nor will it aggressively proselytize. The apostle's rhetorical question in Romans, 'Is God the God of Jews only?' (Rom. 3.29a) invites a modern parallel: 'Is God the God of Christians only?' We cannot say, without the risk of grave misunderstanding on all sides, that 'in Christ there is neither Christian nor Hindu'. But, in faithfulness to Paul, it must be said that 'in Christ' there is no 'over against', no rival religious or human grouping. That is true also of 'the Body of Christ', Paul's use of which is 'catholic', rather than exclusive or divisive.[32] The only 'over against' is the 'weakness of the flesh', from which, as Paul's letters so clearly show, the Church is not exempt. Instead, we find in his writings the seeds of a universal *humanum*, the theological foundations for what G.K. Chesterton called a 'cosmic patriotism'.

Endnotes

[*] Part of this essay is in *The Conversation Continues* © 1990 Abingdon Press, kindly permitted.

[1] Paul W. Meyer, 'The Worm at the Core of the Apple', in *The Writings of St Paul*, eds Wayne A. Meeks and John T, Fitzgerald, (2nd edition, W.W. Norton & Co., New York 2007), p.524.

[2] See, especially, K. Stendahl, *Paul Among Jews and Gentiles*, (Fortress Press 1976, SCM 1978), and E.P. Sanders, *Paul and Palestinian Judaism* (SCM 1977).

[3] Although Paul no doubt envisaged the Gentile world here, it is worth noting that he writes, not *ethnon* at v.18, but *anthropon*, and subsequent pronouns and verbs continue this universal reference (vv.19-23).

[4] With this neutral sense, phrases such as *kata sarka* are translated by phrases such as 'on the human level' (REB, Romans 1.3), or 'by natural descent' (REB Rom.9.5), the translation being shaped by the context.

[5] This negative sense is reflected in English translations in phrases such 'our sinful nature' or 'our old nature', (thus the REB at Rom. 8. 3 and 12).

[6] L.E. Keck, *Romans*, (Abingdon New Testament Commentaries, Abingdon Press, Nashville 2005), p.186.

[7] E. Kasemann, *Commentary on Romans* (E.T. SCM Press, 1980) p.188.

[8] Romans 2.14-16.

[9] Meyer, *op. cit.*, p.517.

[10] A.C. Thistleton, *The First Epistle to the Corinthians* (Eerdmans 2000), p.292, translates *sarkinos* (v.1) as 'people moved by entirely human drives', and *sarkikos* (twice in v.3), as 'unspiritual' and 'centred on yourselves'.

[11] K. Barth, *The Epistle to the Romans*, (6th ed., O.U.P., 1933, E.T. by Edwyn C. Hoskyns), p.73.

[12] Whilst 'boast' is the older, more literal translation of *kauchaomai*; 'take pride in' sounds more contemporary, though it does not convey the full significance which this word had for Paul.

[13] Kasemann, *op. cit.*, p.69.

[14] Kasemann, *op. cit.*, p.133.

[15] K. G. Grayston, *The Epistle to the Romans*, (Epworth 1997), p.55.

[16] The discussion about Paul's theology of justification and related matters, such as the meaning of 'the works of the law', continues amongst Pauline scholars. Amongst the best of recent critiques is Stephen Westerholm's *Perspectives Old and New on Paul* (Eerdmans 2004).

[17] Meyer, *op. cit.*, pp.516-7.

[18] Romans 1.7, 1 Cor. 1.2, 2 Cor.1.1 and Phil.1.1.

[19] *The Psalms of Solomon* distinguishes sharply between 'the righteous' and 'sinners' (e.g. 2.34f, 4.8,23 and 13.6ff), whilst the Community Rule at Qumran makes a distinction between sons of light and darkness in, e.g. cc 1 and 2. The contrast with Paul is theologically significant, but not absolute in language.

[20] For a full discussion see, e.g. M. Thrall, *2 Corinthians 1-7* (I.C.C. T. & T. Clark, 2nd edit.2004), pp.25-36.

[21] A problem addressed by Paul in 1 Corinthians 8-10.

[22] M. Bockmuehl, *Jewish Law in Gentile Churches*, (T. & T. Clark 2000).

[23] H. Conzelmann, *1 Corinthians* (Fortress 1975), p.42.

[24] Matthew 25.31-46 – which is far from being a conventional or predictable use of binary opposites – note the surprise of both the righteous and the unrighteous.

[25] The implicit contrast between 'this age' (Rom. 12.2, 1 Cor.1.20 etc) and 'the age to come' – implicit because Paul never uses the expression 'the age to come'- is an eschatological one, and so, again, not a direct contrast between two groups of people.

[26] Other examples of the 'divine interchange' include Gal. 4.4-6 and Rom. 8.3-4.

[27] 1 Cor. 1.23, Rom.5.16 and 20 etc. For the (religious) offence and misunderstanding which Paul's gospel could generate, see, e.g. Rom.6.1.

[28] Here, as often in the New Testament, the expression 'the many' reflects the Semitic sense of 'all'.

[29] Arland J. Hultgren, *Paul's Letter to the Romans. A Commentary* (Eerdmans 2011), p.232.

[30] The precise reasons for Pharisaic opposition to Jesus are not easy to determine, but the heart of the matter seems to have been their sharply different attitude to 'sinners'. There is an important connection to be made here between Jesus and Paul's transformed and re-directed 'zeal'.

[31] See the earlier references to Kasemann.

[32] The probably deuteron-pauline Ephesians 1.15-23, perhaps editing the possibly deutero-pauline Colossians, (1.15-20), draws out the universal nature of the body of Christ, exemplified in the Church.

Who Needs "Conversion"?

Christy Femila Johnson

1. Introduction

In this paper the theme of religious conversion is examined in the context of conversions' being an impediment to interfaith dialogue between Hindus and Christians. The real basis for the controversy emerges from the fact that Christian conversions came along with Western colonial imperialism and the fact that most converts adopted a Christian way of life opposing the discriminatory hierarchical caste structures. The paper also envisages that there is possibility of a common project (through dialogue) to rediscover a new cosmology from what the East can offer to the West challenging Western technological approaches to Nature.

2. Hinduism

Hindu nationalists view 'conversion' of an Indian to any non-Hindu religion as a threat to the national integrity of the Indian nation state. In discussing why and how it is so, one must first ask, who is a Hindu, there being no single unified agreement on the term. It is an arduous task to define Hinduism in a sentence or two. Encompassed within the universal term 'Hinduism' is a wide variety of belief systems, practices, traditions and values. Despite the random and wide usage of the term 'Hindu' to represent the majority Indians, it carries geo-cultural, religious, legal, and political meanings solely depending on the perspectives of the observer. Geo-culturally, and in a broader sense, the term 'Hindu' or 'Indian' refers to all those who live east of the

Indus river having adopted India as their mother/father land. And the beauty of India is that its culture has never been monolithic; plurality being the quintessence and substance of Indian reality.

From a legal perspective, excepting Muslims, Christians, and Parsis all those who live in India are Hindus. Within this definition, even those belonging to Jainism, Buddhism, Sikhism, indigenous religions, and tribal religionsfall under the broad category of Hinduism. Hindus, Parsis, Christians, and Muslims have separate personal laws pertaining to marriage, divorce, adoption and inheritance. Before the passing of the Muslim Personal Law (*Shariat*) Application Act 1937, even Muslims were treated as Hindus within the same legal frame.

Religiously speaking, Brahminical Hinduism originated as Vedic religion which was like an umbrella under which a variety of religious phenomena were accommodated, making it difficult to define it as a religion that was either founded by a founder or based on a particular creed. One of the general definitions offered for "Hinduism" is: "*sanatana dharma*". The term *dharma* is difficult to translate and is generally rendered as "righteousness". Theoretically, Hindus are all those who follow the *sanatana dharma* (eternal law) as expressed in the timeless rituals, customs and scriptures of the community. The bottom line is in the construction of a rhetoric that Hinduism is the *only sanatana dharma*. Moreover, the main objective of the Hindu right-wing is to create a Ram-centered myth[1] that will unite Hindus against other religious minorities, especially Christians and Muslims. Thus, for example, when Sita Ram Goel uses the word Hinduism in his book it means:

> Hinduism in the sense in which Gandhiji used it, that is, to cover all schools of Sanatana Dharma – Buddhism, Jainism, Shaivism, Shaktism and Vaishnavism which includes the Santa-*mata* and Sikhism. Treating these segments of a single spiritual vision as separate religions is not only misleading but also mischievous.[2]

At the same time, Hinduism cannot be treated simply as pantheistic, or polytheistic. Diana Eck argues that within the classical Hindu tradition singularity and plurality is very much embedded:

> The Hindu tradition is both monotheistic and polytheistic. Oneness and manyness are not seen as true opposites. In the Hindu tradition, matters of importance are thought of quite naturally in the singular and in the plural. Singularity or uniqueness is not the sole mark of significance.

> Indeed, many of the most important aspects of the Hindu tradition are not unique, decisive, and final. If something is important, it is important enough to be repeated, duplicated, and seen from many angles. There are many gods (*devas*), many divine descents of the gods (*Avatars*), many ways of salvation (*margas*) and many philosophical systems (*darshanas*) and many scriptures. The profusion of gods and scriptures is matched by a polycentric religious life, social structure, and family structure. There is no one clear, unmistakable center. Manyness is valued; indeed, it is seen as essential.... Hinduism is, in one sense, a radically polytheistic tradition.[3]

This multifaceted nature of Hinduism creates confusion in legal jurisprudence. To clarify this, a comprehensive definition of Hinduism was attempted by Chief Justice P. B. Gajendragadkar quoted in the Indian Supreme Court ruling of *"Bramchari Sidheswar Shai and others Versus State of West Bengal"* on 2nd July 1995:

> When we think of the Hindu religion, unlike other religions in the world, the Hindu religion does not claim any one prophet; it does not worship any one god; it does not subscribe to any one dogma; it does not believe in any one philosophic concept; it does not follow any one set of religious rites or performances; in fact, it does not appear to satisfy any one set of religious rites or performances; in fact, it does not appear to satisfy the narrow traditional features of any religion or creed. It may broadly be described as a way of life and nothing more.[4]

In the backdrop of the West Bengal Government trying to put a control over Christian mission schools, a school run by the Ramakrishna Mission applied for minority status under the Indian Constitution. In this context the Court identified seven defining characteristics of Hinduism and by extension Hindus:

1. Acceptance of the Vedas with reverence as the highest authority in religious and philosophic matters and acceptance with reverence of Vedas by Hindu thinkers and philosophers as the sole foundation of Hindu philosophy.

2. Spirit of tolerance and willingness to understand and appreciate the opponent's point of view based on the realization that truth is many-sided.

3. Acceptance of great world rhythm, vast period of creation, maintenance and dissolution follow each other in endless succession, by all six systems of Hindu philosophy.

4. Acceptance by all systems of Hindu philosophy the belief in rebirth and pre-existence.

5. Recognition of the fact that the means or ways to salvation are many.

6. Realization of the truth that Gods to be worshipped may be large, yet there being Hindus who do not believe in the worshipping of idols.

7. Unlike other religions or religious creeds Hindu religion not being tied-down to any definite set of philosophic concepts, as such.[5]

The Court refused to bestow minority status to the school. Political definition of who Hindus are varies according to different viewpoints of political groups and national leaders. Dr. Ambedkar didn't want to die a Hindu, while Gandhi was proud of his identity as a Hindu. According to a political point of view, Hindus are all those who are *not* Buddhists, Jains, Parsis, Christians, Muslims, or Sikhs. When social groups are identified on the basis of religion, a vast majority of Indians, who are classified as lower castes, exclude themselves from the broader category of Hindus. The reason is in the differences in their cultural and ritual practices from that of the classical Hindu system.[6] Kancha Ilaiah studied the differences between upper castes and Dalit bahujans in their worship of gods and goddesses, ritual practices, festivals, and lifestyles among others, and he concludes that the oppressed castes of Indian society cannot be called Hindus as the categories are different. According to Ilaiah, all the majority people who are exploited and suppressed constitute what he terms as Dalit bahujan and they are not Hindus. For Ilaiah:

> Hinduism has a socioeconomic and cultural design that manipulates the consciousness of the Dalit bahujans systematically. It has created several institutions to sustain the hegemony of the Brahminical forces. Through the ages it has done this by two methods: i) creating a consent system which it maintains through various images of Gods and Goddesses, some of whom have been co-opted from the social base that it wanted to exploit; and ii) when such a consent failed or lost its grip on the masses, it took recourse to violence. In fact, violence has been Hinduism's principal mechanism of control. That is the reason why many of the HINDU Gods were weapon-wielders in distinct contrast to the Gods of all other religions. No religion in the world has created such a variety of Gods who use both consent and violence to force the masses into submission. Thus, the relationship between the Hindu Gods and the Dalit bahujan has been that of the oppressor and oppressed, the manipulator and the manipulated. Of course, one of the 'merits' of Hinduism has been that it addressed both the mind and the body of the oppressed.[7]

Historically, the seclusion and isolation of the lower castes from opportunities, self-respect, equal participation in politics, equal power sharing, equality in worship, and so on have resulted in people of lower castes in harboring a deep sense of alienation from the upper castes and hence have defied identifying with Hinduism. The reactions have been in the form of mass conversions to Christianity in the last few centuries and to Buddhism or Islam in recent times.

It was in fact the British who popularized the term Hinduism to include the people of India belonging to various milieus under a single entity.[8] According to Wilfred Cantwell Smith, *religion* as a distinct concept and social category, evolved in the West.[9] The British used the word 'Hindus' to connote a group of people in India who were not Jews, Buddhists, Jains, Parsis, Christians or Muslim. Never did such unity exist, nor is it desirable. According to sociologists, India is "a summation of minorities".[10] Post-independence saw the immediate need to unify 350 and odd princely states into a country called India. Now the Hindutva ideologues would like to project India as a culturally, religiously and politically unified homogenous body, by promoting a false rhetoric that is Ram-centered, mono-cultural, mono-linguistic, mono-scriptural, and chiefly intended to maintain the hierarchical caste structure intact.

At the same time there is a general tendency to define Hinduism as a tolerant religion in the world. Francois Gautier, for example, views Hinduism juxtaposing Islam as "one of the most tolerant religions in the world and which on all evidence not only accepted coexistence with all the world religions but also accepted their divinity, pales in comparison with Islam, a creed which killed tens, if not hundreds, of millions, and for which all non-Muslims are "Kafirs", infidels"[11] This portrayal is specially aimed at a Western audience. However, this view is contested as there are many fundamentalist positions emerging within Hinduism today.

Academicians studying religions from a sociological and anthropological perspective have investigated the caste structure and its effect on people in the lower strata or outside the caste system. There is a strong religious mandate in the Vedas and other Hindu scriptures to strictly follow the caste system. *Karma* theory justifies the hierarchical structure, and the identification and sealing of caste by birth (and not by choice).

3.   Origins of Christianity in India

Church historians of earliest Christian community in India point to Christianity in India being as old as Christianity itself.[12] According to some traditions, the apostle Thomas and another disciple of Jesus, Bartholomew came and preached in India, particularly in North Konkan and Malabar areas. The apostle Thomas is believed to have travelled extensively in south India before he was murdered in Chennai (formerly Madras). Although the historicity of these events is ambiguous, the presence of some Christians who were known as St. Thomas Christians in South India before the arrival of Portuguese in the sixteenth century can be ascertained.[13] One of the reasons for the Portuguese expedition to India was to proselytize the local populace. Saint Francis Xavier was prominent among the Portuguese missionaries. The Portuguese exercised their influence over the coastal areas of India, though the territories under their control were small. They converted many indigenous people to Catholicism.[14] The approaches of other significant missionaries such as Jesuit Robert de Nobili, and the Lutherans Ziegenbalg and Pluetschau were different at the same time comparable. Their main aim was to convert individual converts by learning Tamil and engaging in conversations with Hindu priests.

The advent of the British in India saw the appearance of Protestant missionaries in the figures of Chaplains of the East India Trading Company in the years 1667-1700. The British resisted the coming of missionaries into India as their primary objective was not to proselytize, but to promote trade. The number of protestant missionaries in India increased after the Parliament in London nullified the restrictions on missionaries in 1813. During this period, there were considerable numbers of conversions to Christianity, both individual and mass conversions. John C. B. Webster traced the history of Dalit Christians from late nineteenth century to 1990 set within the context of modern Dalit movement. He mentions that primarily Dalits were not a uniform group in the nineteenth century regardless of how contemporary observers would like to place them. Webster observes that despite their dissimilarities there were several things in common that one could place them under an oppressed category. The common shared realities were: social discrimination, occupation, poverty, incorporation into *jatis*, complex and different life-styles, and little or no outside support.[15]

Conversion of Dalits, then, to Christianity or Islam was a representation of rejection of the caste system that suppressed them from social upward mobility.[16] Hence Webster traces the beginnings of the Dalit movement in the mass conversions[17] of Dalits to Christianity which were "initiated and led by Dalits".[18] This is the key to understanding why in the past and in contemporary times the Hindu-right wing is opposing conversions. If we conclude that mass conversions are a way of expressing protest against caste structures then the Hindu fundamentalists would not want that change to happen in society.

As for the contemporary Brahminical Hindu-right wing, the history of Christianity in India is concomitant to the European colonization of India. Sita Ram Goel surveys the history of Hindu-Christian encounters in five phases beginning with the coming of "Portuguese Pirates".[19] Another such view can be seen in the cover page of a book by Arun Shourie on Christian interpretation of Bible and Christian missionary activities in India mentions, "…for 500 years the Church has heaped calumny on our Gods – Krishna was thief, Rama lied, Shiva…"[20] While the Hindu right-wing criticism of Christianity may have its own merits, we also need to look at the connivance of Indian (primarily Hindu) elite in uncritically adopting Western technologies in almost all avenues of modern Indian civic life. This is contributing to the rape of nature furthering Western capitalism in the form of neo-colonialism and globalization. The essence of the "Hindu" (spiritual) way of a harmonious life with the Cosmos needs to be rediscovered to challenge Western hegemony (based on technical superiority). This can be attempted through a radical dialogue with the Hindu right-wing. The common project can be to 'convert' Western attitudes to humanize their technologies.

4.   Why is Conversion Politicized Today?

Defining the notion of conversion is as difficult as converting a person to another fold. Lewis R. Rambo, for example, mentions that a) conversion is a process over time, not a single event; (b) conversion is contextual and thereby influences and is influenced by a matrix of relationships, expectations, and situations; and (c) factors in the conversion process are multiple, interactive, and cumulative.[21] Religious conversions are diverse. It might start with a compelling meeting with the Divine in the form of a vision of God in some contexts as in the case of Saul becoming Paul. Or it might emanate from a very worldly that is non-spiritual conviction to change from one religion to the other. In ancient times the adaption of new notions of God, forms of worship and other associated rituals would have happened time and again as and when the need arose. But on the long run it is the rituals and praxis-based dimensions which sustain the new community's conversion.

Pushparajan studied conversion and it's inter-relationship between religions from a Gandhian perspective. He summarizes "the dangerous consequences of conversion visualized by the accusing party" [Hindu right-wing] as follows:

- It is an attempt to de-nationalize the converts

- That the converts will express allegiance to India should there arise a conflict between religion and state.

- Since the churches receive funds from churches in the west, it will be harmful to our national interests as the converts are likely to be loyal to the western countries.

- Indian states that are demanding separate statehood such as Jharkhand, Tripura, Nagaland and Mizoram are turning anti-national with the support and backing of foreign missionaries.

- Conversions have repercussions in the social front as well: converts are cut off from their previous family/community they were originally attached to and do not follow the caste obligations after conversion resulting in de-socializing; and converts go through a de-culturation of their customs, habits, traditions, and names as a result of Westernization.[22]

These are some of the reasons projected by the Hindu right-wing to create a false paranoia among Hindus against religious conversions. Christians defend against such allegations by referring to right to religious freedom enshrined in the Indian Constitution or in UN Human Rights documents and so on. Christian apologetics will swear upon the Bible to legitimize the Christian obligation to take the gospel to non-Christians or even to the so-called lukewarm Christians, who are not true Christians, according to them. K. P. Aleaz highlights the difference between proselytizing and conversion while discussing conversion of Hindus to Christianity in the context of Orissa, Madhya Pradesh and Arunachal Pradesh and the Freedom of Religion Bill. He views that "...conversion is always an individual's own wish, on his/

her own free will, whereas proselytizing of a person can be by another person. Hence, propagation and conversion are not opposed to each other; it is propagation and proselytizing which are opposed to each other."[23] Intentions being the same, what difference does it make to change words is another question. Hans Ucko sees no difference between the two terms namely conversion and proselytizing. He asserts that "I want to claim that seeking conversion of the other or targeting the other for conversion, is for me the same as proselytism."[24] Ucko adds that proselytism is a loaded word and that people these days use other terms such as seeking "invitation to join the Christian faith". On the other hand there is also the prevalent case of conversion by alluring in times of crisis known as "aid-evangelism". Ucko asserts that such "aid-evangelism is coercive proselytism."[25] Individual's right to follow the religion she/he is born into or to follow another depends entirely upon the individual. Conversion is becoming more controversial as the process of reification of religion is most complete in modern societies and nearing completion in pre-modern societies such as ours. We all know which religion we belong to and what are its basic tenets. Hinduism is a distinctly kinship-based society whereas Christianity and Islam are not. Within a kinship-based community there is a natural resistance to conversion which in most cases is manifested in the form of ostracizing the neophyte.

Religious conversions and its legal implications had been a subject of heated debate in the recent past. The connection between high level Christian missionary activities and spate of violence should to be studied carefully. For example the gruesome murders of Australian missionary Rev. Graham Staines and his two sons by Dara Singh will remain fresh in the memories of Indian Christians. Not only because of the sympathy it evokes because two innocent boys were killed in cold blood alongside their father, but also because Staines was a non-Indian missionary committed to social work in India especially among leprosy patients. Dara Singh was an active member of Bajrang Dal and that the assailants shouted *"Jai Bajrang Bali"* is recorded in the FIR filed by the pastor of Manoharpur Chruch. But, according to the Wadhwa Commission report what motivated Dara Singh to commit such a heinous crime was "misplaced fundamentalism".[26] In other words, his conviction that conversions of Hindus to Christianity by missionaries were threatening Hinduism led him to this act. The

Wadhwa Commission observed that the motive "appeared to be that non-Christian people were aggrieved on the ground that Christian fathers/missionaries are converting the people to Christianity in a deceitful manner by giving allurements."[27] The Commission's report gave a lot of emphasis to the anti-conversion laws of Orissa with a recommendation to enforce those provisions. Whatever be the motive behind Dara Singh' act, one can never legitimate the killing of innocents. That some individuals can be brainwashed into committing such crimes demands our attention in order to prevent such acts from happening in the future.

The spate of violence that erupted in Kandhamal district in Orissa and other places against Christians has a long history of Hindutva philosophy, power politics and strategies behind its beginning in the early twentieth century. From the writings of the Hindu right-wing it is evident that there is a fear of demoralization or even imminent annihilation of Hindu race, its culture and Hinduism first by the Muslims and then by the Europeans. The Sangh Parivar thus foment fear against Muslims and Christians by saying that these two major minority groups are anti-nationals as they cannot be loyal to India as it is neither their motherland nor their holy land. In other words, by limiting or eliminating the social work that specially emancipates Dalits and Adivasis, the Sangh Parivar would like to keep the status of the lower caste people of India discriminated economically, politically and socially so that they can retain the caste hegemony over them.

Analyzing the issue of conversions into Christianity in the context of the recent violence against Christians in Dangs in the state of Gujarat Joshi points out that while Christian missionaries have done a commendable work in impoverished Adivasi regions, the change in religion also leads to a shift in socio-political and tribal equilibrium:

The issue of conversion is thus a complex one. At a local level, Christian missionaries have often been appreciated for providing good educational opportunities for Adivasis in a situation in which government has failed to provide adequate facilities. Christianity is also providing many Adivasis with a set of cosmological beliefs which they believe are appropriate to their present situation. The bhakti variety of Hindu practice can equally fulfill such a role, and, in fact, it probably has in much larger number of cases, but as all forms of non-Christians and non-Islamic practice are recorded merely as 'Hindu' in the census report, we have no means for qualifying such a tendency. The desire of Christian

> converts to follow their own religious practices and disavow the
> community festivals and form of worship of the village community as
> a whole is deeply resented. This is because this represents a threat to
> one of the great strengths of the life of the people – their solidarity in the
> face of outsiders. But it also challenges the vested interests of the existing
> village elites, who resent this as a challenge to their social power and
> control. Initially, conversion gave rise to much bickering and bad feeling,
> but until two years ago there was no violence in this respect.[28]

For fundamentalist oriented Hindus, conversion can be and is a departure from one's own culture, language, tribal/caste affinities and shift of loyalties. Particularly, in the case of Christianity and Islam it is expected that the new converts will be steadfast in the new religion by completely shedding the elements associated with the old one. Such separation and cutting-off from Hindu religion also implicates that the new converts will enter into a supposedly casteless egalitarian system embodied within Christianity and Islam, at least in theory. Such changes in the social dynamics pertaining to disturbances in the caste hierarchy is perceived and projected as a threat to the integrity and unity of India. In the words of M. M. Thomas: "It is very clear that the strong opposition to Christian missions, conversions and evangelization arise out of a nationalism which is not prepared to grant the reality of any supranational Truth or recognize that man has a destiny beyond the Nation. It is the expression of a totalitarian nationalism, on which, the judgment of the jealous God must be proclaimed."[29]

It is no hidden fact that some of the Christian evangelistic groups engage in provocative proselytism and aggressive efforts at conversion. Such programs add fuel to fire of the already deteriorating Hindu-Christian relations. Hindutva promoters waste no time in intensifying their efforts to Hinduize and revert Christians back to Hinduism (*shuddi* movement). Portrayal of Hindu gods and goddesses in a bad light as opposed to the projection of sovereign God revealed in the Bible irks Hindus. So Hindus in turn try to show problems within the Bible. Arun Shourie studied the Bible in detail to point out that there are discrepancies in it. He challenges the notion that the Old Testament and the New Testament were authored by God as Christians claim.[30] In general the Hindu fundamentalists have constantly pointed out certain ideas in their writings. Some of them are as follows, not in the order of significance: opposition to conversion to Christianity or Islam, portrayal of Hinduism or Vedas in low light, Aryan invasion, post-dating the Vedic events, highlighting Muslim invasion as violent event and thus harming Hindus, associating Christianity as Western, and criticizing missionary activities.

5. Conversion as a Controversial Subject in Hindu-Christian Dialogue

Christian missionary work has passed through various phases since its early beginnings. Post political decolonization of the world has led us to the current phase of dialogue. Many attribute the beginnings of even a partial recognition of the need for Christians to associate with non-Christians to the period of the post International Missionary Conference held in Edinburgh in 1910.[31] Diana Eck would place the World Parliament of Religions held in Chicago in 1893 to be the first initiative of the modern interreligious movement. In a way it can also be seen as a modern Christian ecumenical movement as the event was planned and organized mostly by American Christians.[32] Swami Vivekananda has represented Hinduism to the Western world as a sophisticated religion compelling the West to revise the way it had gazed the East.

Historically one can study the evolution of interfaith theology from the point of view of the Vatican through their activities and statements as well as from the World Council of Churches. That is not our objective. It is our quest to grapple with the question of whether the agenda of conversion and interfaith dialogue possible at the same time. Orthodox Christian teaching is exclusive in character and its very essence is in underlining the notion that God wills everyone to be/become a Christian. Such a view depends on creating and sustaining a psychological feeling of superiority in being a Christian. Part of the reason for such extraordinary claims is because Christian theology was formulated and concretized when Christians were in power during and post-Constantine period. Moreover, Christian missionary activity reached a peak during the Western colonization. Christian missionaries reached out to regions where paganism was practiced with a clear vision of converting and hence civilizing the masses. In every sense, it is a venture of not selling but imposing an imperialist ideology whether the potential recipient required it or not. For example, the very core of being a Christian is described by Stanley Jones as thus:

"Conversion converts everything – from alcoholism to attitudes, and everything in between. There is no substitute for conversion. If the Church loses its power to convert it has lost its right to be called Christian."[33] But there were some differences in the approach of Western missionaries particularly Protestant missionaries within Indian context. Dalit and other lower caste people's conviction to embrace Christianity as a way of protesting the caste structure in effect challenged the Christian missionaries to alter their theological position, mission approach and join the cause of the socially deprived castes. Cobb clearly spells out our predicament:

> The encounter with Indian traditions challenges us to repentance in a quite different ways. There is the history of European imperialism in India and in some Buddhist nations. We must confess the role of Christianity in sanctioning this imperialism and in using imperial power to implement its proselytizing projects. But we must also reflect on the negative character of the dominant ways we have described God in all the Abrahamic traditions as this is perceived by Hindus and especially by Buddhists. Our rethinking of what we mean by God in light of the wisdom of India is a major task for the Christian community. It must be associated with rethinking of the nature of reality and of thought in general. Only a Christianity that has been transformed by the wisdom of India can make its full contribution to the salvation of the world.[34]

6. Conclusion

In today's context we have to re-examine our guilt-ridden theology that has come packaged with imperialist ideologies supporting colonization, neo-colonization and globalization. We need to critically engage the right wing Hindus, challenge their orthodox and fundamentalist positions. At the same time, we need to rediscover through dialogue the wisdom that Indian spirituality can offer to our understanding and practice of Christian faith. We need to question especially our approach to Nature, so that we can re-establish our relationship with the Cosmos, which is being threatened by an increasingly Western technological approach to our way of life. This can be the path to salvation.

Endnotes

[1] Ram or Rama is the name of one of the incarnations of God Vishnu and often seen as a unifying religious symbol among Hindus.

[2] Sita Ram Goel, *Catholic Ashrams: Sannyasins or Swindlers?* (New Delhi: Voice of India, 1994), vii. First published in 1988.

³ Diana L. Eck, *Encountering God: A Spiritual Journey from Bozeman to Banaras* (New Delhi: Penguin Books, 1993), 60.

⁴*"Bramchari Sidheswar Shai and others Versus State of West Bengal,"* *Hinduism Today* <http://www.hinduismtoday.com/modules/smartsection/item.php?itemid=5046> (19 January 2012). The complete text of the judgement is available online.

⁵ *Ibid.*

⁶ Cf. Kancha Ilaiah, *Why I am not a Hindu: A Sudra Critique of Hindutva Philosophy, Culture and Political Economy* (Calcutta: Samya Publications, 1996), 71-111.

⁷ Ilaiah, *Why I am not a Hindu*, 71-72.

⁸ Israel Selvanayagam, *A Dialogue on Dialogue: Reflections on Interfaith Encounters* (Madras: The Christian Literature Press, 1995), 31.

⁹ Wilfred Cantwell Smith, *The Meaning and End of Religion* (Minneapolis, MN: Fortress Press, 1991), 51.

¹⁰ Rajni Kothari. "From Religions to Religiosity," *Jeevadhara* (1990):74-75.

¹¹ Francois Gautier, *The Wonder that is India* (New Delhi: Voice of India, 1994), xii. Francois Gautier is one of the very few westerners actively defending *Hindutva*. This particular book is in effect an antithesis to A. L. Basham's classic, *The Wonder that was India*. Gautier particularly discredits Basham on the views that the European invasion spearheaded renaissance of India and his sanctification of the Christian missionary influence in India.

¹² For a detailed study see: A. M. Mundadan, *History of Christianity in India*, vol.I, Bangalore, 1984.

¹³ Thomas Chillikulam, "Rupturing Hindu-Christain Relations: A Christian Introspection," *Jeevadhara* vol.XXXIX (2009), 349-361.

¹⁴ J. Thekkedath, *History of Christianity in India*, vol.II, Bangalore, 1982.

¹⁵ John C. B. Webster, *The Dalit Christians: A History* (Delhi: ISPCK, 1992), 28-30.

¹⁶ Webster, *The Dalit Christians*, 31.

¹⁷ Mass conversion is a term used by Christian missionaries to indicate a group of people belonging to a caste converting mainly to Christianity. We can find similar conversions to Islam, Sikhism, tribal reform movement, Buddhism, and reverting back to Hinduism known as the *shuddi* movement initiated by Arya Samaj. Sociologist such as Rowena Robinson would like to term this phenomenon as group conversions. Rowena Robinson and Sathianathan Clarke, eds., *Religious Conversions in India: Modes, Motivations, and Meanings* (New Delhi: Oxford University Press, 2003), 17.

¹⁸ Webster, *The Dalit Christians*, 33.

¹⁹Sita Ram Goel, *History of Hindu-Christian Encounters: AD 304 to 1996* (New Delhi: Voice of India, 1996), ii. First published in 1986.

²⁰ Arun Shourie, *Harvesting our Souls: Missionaries, their Design, their Claims* (New Delhi: Rupa Publications India Pvt. Ltd., 2010). First published in 2000.

[21] Lewis R. Rambo, *Understanding Religious Conversion* (New Haven and London: Yale University Press, 5. In this book, Rambo analyses religious conversion from a psychological, sociological, anthropological and theological dimensions.

[22] A. Pushparajan, *From Conversion to Fellowship: The Hindu-Christian Encounter in the Gandhian Perspective* (Allahabad: St. Paul Publications, 1990), 79.

[23] K. P. Aleaz, *Theology of Religions: Birmingham Papers and other Essays* (Calcutta: Moumita Publishers & Distributors, 1998), 343.

[24] Hans Ucko, "Towards an Ethical Code of Conduct for Religious Conversions," *Current Dialogue* 50 (February 2008), 6-19.

[25] *Ibid.*, p. 12.

[26] Shourie, *Harvesting our Souls*, 15.

[27] *Ibid.* p. 20.

[28] Satyakam Joshi, "Tribals, Missionaries and Sadhus: Understanding Violence in the Dangs," *Economic and Political Weekly*, 11 September 1999, quoted in M.P.Raju, *Religious Conversion: Legal Implications* (Delhi:Media House, 1999), 94-95.

[29] M. M. Thomas, *Ideological Quest within Christian Commitment: 1939-1954* (Bangalore, Madras: Christian Institute for the Study of Religion and Society, & the Christian Literature Society, 1983), 148.

[30] Shourie, *Harvesting our Souls*, 81-109.

[31] Selvanayagam, *A Dialogue on Dialogue*, x.

[32] Eck, *Encountering God*, 25-30.

[33] E. Stanley Jones, *Conversion* (London: Hodder and Stoughton Ltd., 1960), 253.

[34] John B. Cobb Jr., "Multiple Religious Belonging and Reconciliation," in Catherine Cornille (ed.), *Many Mansions? Multiple Religious Belonging and Christian Identity* (Maryknoll, New York: Orbis Books, 2002), 20-28.

"I will make you fishers of human beings":
A Sermon by Krishna Mohan Banerjea

Julius Lipner

Introduction

In a spirit of dialogue with other faiths and Christian denominations, Israel Selvanayagam has rendered sustained, devoted and indeed fearless service over many years not only to the local communities in which he has found himself during his teaching and pastoral career, but also to the cause of the Christian Gospel in general. During the many years I have known him as a friend, it has been true to say, I think, that in witnessing to the Good News, Professor Selvanayagam has been unafraid to challenge entrenched complacencies in dialogic and other contexts, sometimes at considerable personal cost. It is therefore a pleasure and a privilege to contribute to this *Festschrift* in his honour.

Krishna Mohan Banerjea

In this contribution, a sermon delivered in Bengali by the well-known Bengali convert to the Christian faith, Krishna Mohan Banerjea (1813-1885), has been recovered and translated, I believe for the first time. We shall say more about the Sermon presently; first, let me make some introductory remarks about Krishna Mohan himself. Krishna Mohan was one of the most prominent Bengali Brahmin converts to non-

Catholic Christianity during the 19th century. From an early age he showed a precocious talent for study, entering the English-medium Hindu College in Calcutta at the age of eleven. There, he fell under the liberal intellectual influence of the Derozians and became a leading member of their iconoclastic faction, "Young Bengal". But unlike many Derozians, he did not dismiss *tout court* his ancestral Hindu faith. In order to understand it better, he simultaneously studied Sanskrit, the rich language in which the literary and philosophical achievements of Hinduism has been recorded for about four thousand years. This he did in Sanskrit College, which had been founded in Calcutta under the aegis of the British colonial authorities some years previously in order to further native learning. In time, Krishna Mohan's command of Hindu thought and practice by means of this elite linguistic medium as well as his own mother tongue was such that he was able both to record and to challenge for different purposes, Hindu tenets and customs through an impressive range of writings that showed his immense learning; these included various studies (e.g. on Hindu philosophy and the Vedas, the Kulin Brahmins of Bengal etc.), translations from Sanskrit works, the editing of Bengali journals, and editorship of the 13-volume *Encyclopaedia Bengalensis*.

After a number of dramatic personal upheavals, Krishna Mohan, now under the influence of the redoubtable Scottish educationist and missionary Alexander Duff, was baptised by Duff according to Presbyterian rites in 1832; Krishna Mohan was 19 years old. Within months, convinced that "Episcopacy was the form of Church Government established by the Apostles",[1] he joined the Anglican Church; in due course he studied theology at Bishop's College in Calcutta, was ordained in 1839, and became pastor of Christ Church in Cornwallis Square.

Though, like some of his leading Christian and non-Christian compatriots, Krishna Mohan considered British rule in India to be a providential dispensation (because in his estimation it could provide the legislative climate for purging native social abuses and foster the one religion that might regenerate his people), this is not the place to trace in detail his gradual move towards a moderate form of

---

[1] Cf. *A biographical sketch of the Rev. K.M. Banerjea* by Ramachandra Ghosha, Calcutta, Progressive Publishers, 1980, p.21.

nationalism. (Eventually, in 1875, he would join the Indian League, which sought Indian representation in Government, and in 1876 when the League gave way to the Indian Association, which had similar political goals, he would become the Association's President.) Here, we shall concentrate on his religious commitment.

Krishna Mohan's writing about Hinduism can be characterized in general as polemical. This does not mean that he was unsympathetic to certain features of his ancestral faith. However, his theological method relied on the so-called fulfillment approach, which maintained broadly that key themes and ideas of at least certain non-Christian faiths, judiciously considered, were "fulfilled" theologically by Christian doctrine. In the context of Hinduism, Krishna Mohan argued, like other Hindu converts to Christianity of his time,[2] that particular tenets of religious Hindu teaching prefigured or anticipated in some way pivotal aspects of the Christian message. Where Hinduism was concerned, this approach was developed more systematically several decades later by such thinkers as J.N. Farquhar (cf. his famous *The Crown of Hinduism*, published in 1913).

It is in the Vedas broadly considered that Krishna Mohan locates Hinduism's[3] true centre of gravity.

> The appeal to a glorious [Hindu] past, his Christian allegiance and his universalist predilections combined to produce his favourite Indian Christian themes....that the Vedic notions of 'saving sacrifice....of the double character of priest and victim....[and] of the Ark by which we escape the waves of this sinful world' bear witness to a primitive divine revelation vouchsafed to humankind's first parents but obscured by time and fulfilled in Christ's suffering and death.... 'On what grounds then', he asks,[4] 'can a Hindu advocate demand the ostracism of those who, by accepting Christianity, are only accepting a Vedic doctrine in its legitimately developed form.'[5]

---

[2] For examples, see the names discussed in J. Lipner, "A Modern Indian Christian Response": Ch.13 in Harold C. Coward (ed.), *Modern Indian Responses to Religious Pluralism*, State University of New York Press, Albany, 1987.

[3] In fact, Brahminical Hinduism's.

[4] In "The Relation between Christianity and Hinduism", (Calcutta 1881), reprinted in T.V. Philip, *Krishna Mohan Banerjea: Christian Apologist*, The Christian Literature Society, Madras, 1982, p.196.

[5] See J. Lipner, *op. cit.*, 1987, pp.305-6.

Some of these themes, e.g. that of Christ as the true Sacrifice for the salvation of the world, of the world as an arena of human sinfulness, and of the ostracism from Hindu society of (Hindu) converts to the Christian faith, appear in the Sermon we are about to consider. However, one would be hard pressed to regard Krishna Mohan's treatment of the Hindu dimension of these themes here as either eirenic or ecumenical. Indeed, in a contemporary dialogic context, this treatment may well come across as confrontational on the whole, even offensive in places. While on occasion, as we shall see, Krishna Mohan does give Hindu ideas a positive reception, overall they find meaning for him only in so far as they give way to or are subsumed under Christian teaching. But the underlying general point here is that such ideas are actually redeemable through their Christian transformation, that, in important respects, they prefigure Christian teaching, and that, therefore, they are not to be rejected out of hand. They provide the form for Christian content. In other words, the implication is that key Hindu ideas and beliefs were divinely implanted in Hindu soil in ancient times so as to rise to new life in a Christian form.

For all its defects, such an approach in its time, expounded withal in the vernacular, could be interpreted as a means of giving Bengali Hindu converts pride in their culture and mother tongue, and the confidence to reshape their faith with the passage of time in more dialogically equitable ways. By his life and example, Krishna Mohan gave to many Indian Christians the confidence to be truly Indian and truly Christian and to seek an effective synthesis between these two dimensions of their lives. A thorough study of Krishna Mohan's theology will give us a more nuanced grasp of the planting of Christianity in India, and is still awaited.

The Sermon

While working on another project, I came upon this Sermon by chance many years ago in the University Library at Cambridge University. The Sermon appeared in the form of a pamphlet tucked away among other booklets bound together as a small volume (class mark: 8833.d.30) whose label on the inside cover declared: "From the Library of Edward Byles Cowell....Professor of Sanskrit at Cambridge 1867-1903". Though I was aware that as a prominent Christian pastor in the capital city of the British Raj, Krishna Mohan would have preached regularly in both

English and Bengali, I had not previously come across a reference to this Sermon in any form, and it occurred to me at the time that I may well have made a salient discovery. For an expression of faith in homiletic form has a significance of its own. Sermons, by their very nature, are likely to reveal dimensions of religious commitment not easily found in more academic or "objective" pursuits. To an important extent they are "performative" acts, containing heartfelt recommendations for belief and courses of action that apply to both speaker and hearer. One bares one's soul, as it were, in a sermon; one "confesses" to who one really is, revealing what is important to one in context. In delivering a sermon, one cannot hide behind the so-called objectivity or neutrality of the academic exercise. Further, the Sermon was given in Bengali, at a time of political and linguistic sensitivity – political because, as we shall note presently, the nationalist movement was on the cusp of a new phase, and linguistic, because of the problematic nature of the Bengali language for Krishna Mohan's purposes (a point to which we shall return in due course). Surely, these considerations would add to the significance of the Sermon.

I made a draft translation of the Sermon soon after its discovery, but then abandoned it until such time as I thought suitable for polishing and publishing it. I am glad to present the finished product on this auspicious occasion.

In this Sermon, Krishna Mohan has laid bare the nature of his commitment to Christ and its priorities in the context of the ministerial vocation, at a crucial period of the development of (in particular) non-Catholic Christian faith in colonial Bengal. Through the lectures and activities of Surendranath Banerjea in the region, the "protonationalist" or incipient nationalist movement was about to take a more determinate turn.[6] And an important part of the rhetoric of nationalism in Bengal at the time was to adopt certain traditional Hindu religious *personae,* in particular Krishna Vâsudeva, as agents of the nationalist cause, either in the role of a religious counterpart to Christ or as a moral exemplar of selfless action (here the *Bhagavad Gîtâ* became an especially relevant text).

---

[6] See Julius Lipner, *Brahmabandhab Upadhyay: The Life and Thought of a Revolutionary,* Oxford India Paperbacks, 2001, pp.43-4.

In this atmosphere, it took courage, therefore, to convert to the religion of the foreign ruler, viz. Christianity, and to challenge the effectiveness of these ancestral saviour figures of Hinduism. Nevertheless, for a patriot, this challenge had to be made in a constructive fashion. In the Sermon, Krishna Mohan strives to do just this, walking a tightrope with his commitment to his Christian faith on one side and his regard for the culture of his ancestors on the other. If he veered to the former side while attempting to maintain his balance, we must take into account, on the one hand, the fact that key features of Brahminic Hinduism in the Bengal of his times were widely perceived in his circles as moribund and corrupt, and, on the other, the harsh criticism levelled by contemporary Hindu reformers against their own tradition. Krishna Mohan was by no means an exception in making such exacting scrutiny. Nevertheless, he saw certain salient features of Hindu belief and practice as susceptible of "redemption" in Christian terms, and this in itself intimated a positive appraisal of aspects of his ancestral faith.

Finally, as mentioned earlier, Krishna Mohan made the decision to deliver this Sermon in Bengali, his native tongue. In this respect, he was faced with a couple of major linguistic obstacles. As a language caught up in the travails of modernization, not least in the interface with the English education to which the Bengali elite were exposed, Bengali itself was undergoing among the intelligentsia a change towards an accepted uniformity of grammatical and literary style – in the process it lacked a certain kind of stability of literary form. This did not make its manipulation for the transmission of abstract thought in the context of an encroaching global modernity particularly easy. But it also lacked, equally understandably, a more or less established vocabulary by which it could reflect accurately those forms of Christian faith imported by foreign missionaries into the Bengal area, forms whose articulation had been constructed over many centuries by minds and tongues quite alien to Indian soil.

Let me give an example. Krishna Mohan's Sermon is profoundly scriptural in tone, and quotes often from the New Testament. But at the time, translation of the Bible into what could be called standard Bengali was still in the making. William Carey's valuable and pioneering effort, published from Serampore in 1801, though it did the inestimable service of starting the process and even providing the rudiments of an "established" Biblical vocabulary (for example, the word he uses for the Greek *haleeis*, "fishers" (of human beings) in the title of the sermon, resembles morphologically the very word used by Krishna Mohan three-quarters of a century later for the same Greek term), is nevertheless often stylistically and linguistically flawed. Subsequent attempts to translate the New Testament into Bengali built on this, but were either particularized in some way (e.g. "The Gospel of Matthew in Musalman Bengali", published in 1858), or still struggled to arrive at a form of non-dialectal Bengali.

So the question arises as to the source of Krishna Mohan's Bengali translations of the New Testament texts he quotes in his Sermon (which was delivered and published in 1870). A comparison of texts shows that he did not quote from Carey's translation, nor indeed from *The New Testament of Our Lord and Saviour Jesus Christ in Bengali Translated from the Original Greek, by the Calcutta Baptist Missionaries with Native Assistants* (published in 1854) – the texts, possibly the only relevant texts in existence at the time, with which viable comparisons can be made.[7] In this context, the New Testament Bengali text prepared by the Calcutta Baptist Missionaries in 1854 (mentioned above) is much closer to Krishna Mohan's quotations. The conclusion I can reach, therefore, is that Krishna Mohan made his own translations of the New Testament excerpts he quotes, *based on a close consultation of the text of 1854 (or a subsequent revision) produced by the Calcutta Baptists.* It is highly interesting to observe such important textual history in the making.[8]

The Sermon has two Introductory pages, the first in English and the second in Bengali. The English Foreward announces that the Sermon was "Preached by Command of The Right Revd. The Lord Bishop of Calcutta" by the Revd. K.M. Banerjea at Trinity Church, Amherst Street, and that it was published in 1870 at Chinsurah at D.E. Rodrigues' Printing and Lithographic Press. The Bengali Introduction provides more details. We are told that the Sermon was preached on

---

[7] I have also compared Krishna Mohan's Bengali texts with those from the New Testament in "Musalman Bengali". The two sides of the comparison diverge widely (see, e.g. footnote 11).

[8] Today, the fine Bengali translation of the New Testament, *Maṅgalbārtā* (*Nabasandhi*), made by Sajal Bandyopadhyay and Christian Mignon SJ, first published in 1984 and now in a new edition, is likely to supersede all previous versions.

the occasion of the Ordination (*niyogopalakṣe*) of two ministers (*duijan paricârak*), on 9ᵗʰ June, 1870; the name of the preacher (*pracârak*) is given in its Bengali form: Ũñkṛṣṇa Mohan Bandyopâdhyây.

Procedural Note: The reader will notice the inclusion of copious annotation in my translation of the Sermon. Since it is quite likely that there will be readers who are interested in the Bengali vocabulary Krishna Mohan uses to convey Christian terms and ideas during this period of the nineteenth century, I thought it appropriate to signal the Bengali words he uses. The more casual reader may wish to read the Sermon in the first instance for continuity without recourse to the footnotes, and then only later check the notes for more specific detail. Compulsive readers of footnotes, however, are invited to a footnote-*Fest* without more ado.

The Sermon translated

"And He said to them, 'Follow me, I will make you fishers of human beings'". Mt. 4.19.

The Lord said these words to two fishermen.[9] When He saw them casting a net into the sea to catch fish, He told them to follow Him;[10] He would make them "fishers of human beings".[11]

The expression "fishers of human beings" has the sense of winning others over through kind behaviour.[12] Just as the fisherman draws in fish by casting a net, so one can speak of "fishers of human beings" if one draws in humans by sound teaching and good behaviour.[13] When

---

[9] "The Lord": Krishna Mohan uses *prabhu* throughout this Sermon to refer to Jesus. The "two fishermen" refer to Simon Peter and his brother, Andrew (Mt. 4.18). We recall that the Bengali Introductory page mentions that this Sermon was preached on the occasion of the ordination of two ministers.

[10] I use pronouns with an initial capital when referring to Jesus, since Krishna Mohan invariably uses the honorific mode in the Bengali when speaking of Jesus.

[11] The expression used is *manuṣyadhârî*; *manuṣya* means "human being" (a generic term), and *dhârî* literally means "catcher" here, but to translate the sense meant one must bear the (Gospel) context of this Sermon in mind. The "Musalman Bengali" version here uses *âdmir mâchuyâ*.

[12] "kind behaviour": *saujanya byâbahâr*.

[13] "sound teaching and good behaviour": *sadupadeü o sadbyâbahâr*.

the word "fisher"[14] is applied to human beings in the language in which the Gospel was first set down, it can take on this meaning.[15] There are many examples of this in the works of the Greek savants.[16]

So the purport of the words the Lord spoke to the two fishermen is this: if they listened to Him and followed Him, they would become fishers of human beings; they would give up the business of catching fish and take on the role of catching humans. Instead of casting a net in the salty sea to catch mindless fish, they would draw in intelligent humans from the ocean of being[17] by spreading sound teaching and kindness.

The root cause of such drawing power is following the Lord. And following the Lord means listening to His teaching, accepting it, observing it, and proclaiming it. It is by doing these things that it becomes possible to catch human fish. In the same way that these words were uttered to those two fishermen, they can be spoken to all ministers even today. So I too repeat this great call[18] to those who, present here today, are desirous now of attaining the priestly state:[19] if you observe and proclaim the Lord's teaching, you will become fishers of human beings, and if you desire to become fishers of human beings your chief recourse is to follow the Lord.

One becomes a fisher of human beings if one listens to the Lord's teaching and proclaims it; the real reason for this is that the Lord's teaching is true. Upanishadic sayings about an imaginary Brahman, which is no more real than flowers in the sky,[20] such as "Brahman is

---

[14] Here Krishna Mohan uses the expression *matsadhârî*, literally, "fisher" or "catcher of fish", indicating what he had in mind by the use of the compound *manuṣyadhârî* (see footnote 11).

[15] The Greek word used in Mt. 4.19 is the plural of *halieus*.

[16] "savants": *paṇḍit*. These are the ancient Greeks.

[17] "the ocean of being": *bhabasâgar* – a familiar Hindu expression.

[18] "great call": *mahâbâkya*: reminiscent of the *mahâvâkyas* or pivotal statements (in the eyes of the Vedântins) of the Upanishads.

[19] "priestly state": *paricârak pad*.

[20] "imaginary Brahman": *kâlpanik brahma*, and "flowers in the sky": *gagan puṣpa* – a stock example in Sanskrit literature of imagined or contradictory being.

reality, consciousness, infinite",[21] are appropriate only with respect to the Lord Himself. For His part, the Lord Himself has declared, "*I am the way and the truth and the life*".[22] And He addressed the Father saying, "Sanctify them by your truth, for it is Your word that is truth".[23]

Now the glory[24] of truth is that it is free from doubt; people of all races have proclaimed truth's greatness. One can see many currents of falsehood[25] in the stream of life,[26] yet the force of truth continues to manifest within it. Falsehood, after all, asserts itself only by disguising itself as truth. Once this disguise is exposed, falsehood itself runs away, cowed like a snake under a spell. Like darkness when light appears, falsehood vanishes in the presence of truth. Unless falsehood disguises itself as truth, it cannot stand for even a moment! The behaviour of false and hypocritical prophets[27] provides examples of this!

In our country, people call the Vedic religion,[28] *sanâtana dharma* or "the eternal religion". Why is this? By the term "Veda" we understand "a collection of sounds or words" promulgated by God,[29] and, in truth, sounds or words promulgated by God are not fallacious! Nor is it untrue that from the beginning the Creator of the world[30] proclaimed many words for the instruction of human beings; this is certainly the

---

[21] A quotation taken from the *Taittirîya Upaniṣad* 2.1.1 – a well-known *mahâvâkya* for Vedântins (see footnote 18), regarded as defining the Supreme Reality or Brahman.

[22] See Jn. 14.6. For "truth" here and further on, Krishna Mohan uses the term *satya*.

[23] See Jn. 17.17.

[24] "glory": *mahimâ*.

[25] "falsehood": *mithyâ*.

[26] "the stream of life": the word used is *sangsâr*, for Hindus and Buddhists a term that also denotes the cycle of rebirth.

[27] "of false and hypocritical prophets": *kâlpanik o bhâkta prabâcakdiger*.

[28] "Vedic religion": *baidik dharmma*.

[29] "'a collection of sounds....God": *aiśwarik praṇîta "śabdarâśi"*: *śabda* can mean "sound" and/or "word". The Sanskritic sounds produced by ritually uttering Vedic words and sentences are regarded as having an inherent transformative power with respect to both the human psyche and natural forces, in traditional "orthodox" Hinduism. See J. Lipner, *Hindus: their religious beliefs and practices*, 2nd edition, Routledge, London and New York, 2010, esp. Chs. 2 & 3.

[30] "the Creator of the world": *jagatkarttâ*.

case! Our own Paul himself has said, "In the past God has spoken in various measures and ways to our ancestors through the prophets, but now at the end time he has spoken to us through his own Son".[31] Those diverse utterances can well be called "collections of sounds or words", and indeed it is only under this guise that the Ṛg, Yajur, Sâma and Atharva Vedas[32] have been accorded a popular welcome. So it is true enough that the Highest Lord has spoken, and it is not untrue that there is an eternal religion. But it is not the case that the four Vedas comprise that collection of utterances, or that the eternal religion is contained within them. That false collection of utterances has been revered under the guise of the true.

In the same way, the Vedic rituals and sacrifices[33] have been propagated under the guise of the true Sacrifice.[34] It is quite true that without the shedding of blood, sin is not cleansed, but it is not possible to destroy sin by such Vedic sacrifices as the Aúvamedha and so on.[35] Nor is sin taken away through the blood of bulls and goats.[36] It is the Lord who is the true Sacrifice. The Vedic rituals and sacrifices are no more than an imitation of this, and in fact lack substance.[37] Nevertheless, under the guise of truth they have gained strength in this land and have been given a welcome by passing themselves off as the truth.

Further, the currency of personal, chosen deities[38] like Ram and Krishna is based similarly on false pretences. The Lord alone is the true chosen deity, the longed-for one of every race. It is He who is the

---

[31] See The Letter to the Hebrews, 1.1. Modern scholarship does not attribute this Letter to the Apostle Paul.

[32] The four divisions of the Vedas or canonical texts of Brahminic orthodoxy.

[33] "rituals and sacrifices": *jâg jagña.*

[34] "true Sacrifice": *satya jagña.*

[35] "sin" (here and elsewhere): *pâp.* On the *aúvamedha* sacrifice, see Lipner, *Hindus,* esp. p.383, note 22.

[36] A reference probably to sacrifices practised by the Jews in Old Testament times, and to current sacrifices among Hindus to certain Goddesses such as Kâlî.

[37] "imitation" and "lack substance": *anukaraṇ* and *asâr.*

[38] "personal, chosen deities": *iṣṭadebatâ.*

true Remover of sin, the Rescuer of the fallen, the true Lord of sacrifice.[39] Only He is the Destroyer of sin, and the Creator, Protector and Saviour of the world. By offering up His own life, He has destroyed the sin of the human race and bestowed deliverance.[40] There is no work like this in the lives of Ram, Krishna and the others, yet these have been revered in so far as they have assumed the Lord's guise. Here too, we can see that under the pretence of truth, falsehood has taken a stand.

There is no need for rules, ritual ablutions, sacrifices, offerings and ascetic practices if one wishes to worship[41] the Lord; if one has loving devotion[42] then with regard to the possibility of salvation[43] this great saying of the Hindu scriptures is perfectly true: "Salvation comes from devotion, without the need for prescribed actions".[44] Nevertheless, the worship of Ram and Krishna is but vain effort, and it is only in so far as it mimics Christian loving devotion that devotion to Krishna has grown strong.

In the Vaishnava scriptures a voice from heaven[45] is recorded as saying in Sanskrit: "If you worship Hari, what's the point of ascetic practice? And if you don't worship Hari, still what's the point of ascetic practice?"[46] In other words, if you worship Hari, there's no need for ascetic practice, and if you do not worship Hari what benefit can accrue from ascetic practice? But Vâsudeva is not the true "Hari" or Deliverer;[47] the true "Hari" is our Lord who takes away sin, and it is only by pretending to be Him that Vâsudeva has become "Hari".

---

[39] "the true Remover of sin....true Lord of sacrifice": *tini-i jathârtha pâp hârak, tini-i patita pâban, tini-i jathârtha jajñeúvar.*

[40] The Bengali of this sentence runs as follows: *tini svakîya prânpane mânab mandalîr pâpaghna o moksada haiyâchen.*

[41] "worship" (here and elsewhere, unless indicated otherwise): *ârâdhanâ.*

[42] "loving devotion": *prem bhakti.*

[43] "salvation": *uddhâr.*

[44] "*niyam baddha kriyâ vyatireke bhakti dvârâ uddhâr hay*". I have not been able to trace this saying.

[45] "voice from heaven": *âkâúbânî.*

[46] "*ârâdhito yadi haris tapasâ tatah kim; nârâdhito yadi haris tapasâ tatah kim*". This quotation is taken from the *Nârada-pañcarâtra*, 2.6. I am grateful to the scholar Graham Schweig for helping me locate this quotation.

[47] There is a pun on the word *hari* here; *hari* is another name for Krishna Vâsudeva, but it also means "deliverer", "remover".

Since truth has such authority that under its guise even falsehood is taken seriously, surely then if we accept, follow and proclaim the Lord's true teaching, the desired goal will be achieved. Surely success can occur by authentically proclaiming that very thing through the guise of which even falsehood has acquired strength! How can the Ṛg, Yajur and other Vedas be a divinely inspired collection of sounds when all they contain is praise of Fire, Wind, Indra and so forth, without even a mention of a Highest Lord?[48] If people are acquainted with the facts, then the genuine divinely inspired scripture has a chance of coming into its own. And if the true scripture gets established, for how long can the counterfeit one stand?

If all that the Lord has done to take away sin – the sacrifice of His body on the cross, His death and resurrection[49] – were to be properly disseminated, then the standing of the fake deliverers from sin, such as Ram, Krishna and so on, would surely decline. And this too would be established – that it is our Lord who is the true Deliverer or Hari, and that Vâsudeva is but an impostor. In the face of true devotion, false devotion[50] cannot stand; it will melt away just as wax melts in the presence of fire. This is why the Lord said, "Follow Me, and I will make you fishers of human beings".

Now what the Lord has said in this regard must be understood in a spiritual manner, and not in some fleshly or bodily way.[51] The Greek savants too understood this expression in this sense. Moving someone physically from one place to another[52] is not what this expression means in its subtle sense. Both by word and deed, Paul was implicitly opposed to people moving physically from one place to another; he says: "Brethren, let anyone who has been called while staying in a certain

---

[48] This is not an uncontroversial statement; see Lipner, *Hindus*, Ch.2, esp. pp.33-41.

[49] "the sacrifice….resurrection": *kruǐer upar tâ(h)hâr úarîrotsarga, tâ(h)hâr maraṇo punarjîban.*

[50] "true devotion, false devotion": *satya bhaktir samakṣe kṛtrim bhakti thâkite pâribek nâ.*

[51] "in a spiritual manner….or bodily way": *âtmik bhâbe grahaṇîya mângsik arthât kâyik bhâbe nahe.*

[52] As in the case of real fishermen, who are taken from one place to another by the fish they seek.

place dwell in that very place with God".[53] And when sending back Philemon's slave Onesimus to his master, he taught that it was not right for someone who was the dependent of one individual to be appropriated bodily by someone else.[54] This is why we must accept the Lord's teaching in a spiritual manner, in its subtle sense, and not in a physical or gross sense.

One should always remember that the letter destroys, but that the spirit gives life. It is said that if someone lapses from the truth and that if someone else puts them right again, then the one who has put the errant person right saves that living individual[55] from death and covers a multitude of sins. This is what it means too to become a fisher of human beings. To give truth back to the person who has lapsed from it, to restore the path to someone who has strayed; to check erroneous and false notions by true teaching and sound counsel; to win the minds of the arrogant and foolish by charming them through good conduct and kindness – these are the marks of a fisher of human beings. If one has faith and devotion,[56] the Lord can be worshipped in every place; that it is necessary to worship in a particular place was but the empiricist and bodily preoccupation of the Jews.[57] Indeed, the Lord Himself has said:

> Such a time is coming and has now come when it will no longer be necessary to worship the Father either on this mountain or in Jerusalem. Such a time is coming and has now come when true worshippers will worship the Father in spirit and in truth, and it is a worshipper of this kind that the Father desires. God is spirit, and those who worship Him must worship in spirit and in truth.[58]

---

[53] Krishna Mohan seems to have I Corinthians 7.24 in mind (see also 7.17, and 7.20), but this is a strained interpretation of the text since Paul is speaking of life-situations rather than places. Perhaps this is why Krishna Mohan adds "implicitly" (*prakârântare*) to his explanation. I am grateful to my colleague, Dr. Simon Gathercole, who teaches New Testament in the Divinity Faculty at Cambridge University, for help in identifying Krishna Mohan's New Testament references.

[54] See St. Paul's Letter to Philemon, especially vrs.10-14. Paul feels compelled to return Onesimus to his rightful owner, Philemon, but with a request that he be treated kindly and even freed.

[55] The term used is *prânî*, the idea being that the life of the spirit is more important than the life of the body.

[56] "faith and devotion": *biŵâs o bhakti*.

[57] "empiricist...of the Jews": *kebal yihudidiger aindriyik o kâyik tâtparjya*.

[58] See St. John's Gospel, 4.21-24.

If one takes this utterance and a thousand other utterances of the Lord to heart then the meaning of "fisher of human beings" resolves itself. To make a Mount Sion of each and every person's heart by combining faith and devotion, to make of this the desired dwelling-place of the Holy Spirit - *this* is the subtle meaning of becoming a fisher of human beings. Stephen has said: "The most high God does not dwell in temples made by hands".[59] He is all-pervading and exists everywhere, and He dwells with delight wherever He finds a sincere and devout heart. That is His Mount Sion, that His longed-for abode!

So, if one applies this spiritual sense of being a fisher of human beings, one can appreciate how very responsible the work of a minister is. The Holy Apostle[60] has declared, "Our battle is not only with flesh and blood but with dominations and powers, with rulers of the darkness of this passing world, with the spiritual wickedness of high places".[61] In this battle, human strength and resources[62] are useless. For this reason he says, "Put on all the divine armour whence you will be able to resist the wiles of the evil spirits".[63] In this task, God Himself is our sole ally. The proper weapons in this battle are the shield of devotion and the scimitar of the spirit. Truth is the waist-belt, and righteousness the breastplate, and, for protective footwear, at every step the peaceable zeal of the Gospel.[64] Moreover, prepare yourselves through prayer, spiritual offerings, and perseverance. All these works are means for this great undertaking.

But note that it is in both practice and proclamation that the girdle of truth, the shield of devotion, the scimitar of the spirit, and vigilance and perseverance are essential. Though we must resist many deceits and deceptions, we are not allowed to resort to them, for we cannot

---

[59] A reference to the words of the deacon Stephen in the Acts of the Apostles; see 7.48.

[60] "Holy Apostle": *sâdhu prerita*.

[61] An exact translation of the Bengali. See St. Paul's Letter to the Ephesians, 6.12.

[62] "resources": *kalkauinl*, devices, artifices.

[63] See Paul's Letter to the Ephesians, 6. 13 (which is not quite the same thing).

[64] "the shield...zeal of the Gospel": *bhaktir phalak ebaṅg âtmâr khadga. satya, mekhalâ bandhan. Sâdhutâ urastrân. âr pade pade úântik susamâcârer udyog caran rakṣak pâdukâ.* See Paul's Letter to the Ephesians, 6.14-16.

accomplish our ends by this means. We shall have to destroy a great deal of falsehood yet it is not appropriate to overcome poison with poison in this case; we cannot destroy falsehood with the help of falsehood. It is for us to establish and safeguard the truth, but if we attempt to do this by deceit and guile we shall strike at truth itself; in our recourse to safeguarding the truth, we shall be striking an axe-blow at it.

In every matter we must remember that our work is really God's work, and that in God's work we are only His helpers. Ours is but to follow what He has commanded. If we see no immediate results in the process, we ought not, being anxious, to abandon the honest conduct that is prescribed and resort to the crooked path that is not prescribed. In our spiritual battle it is the Lord who leads us to deliverance, and we must conduct ourselves in the matter in the way He has commanded. So, whatever happens, we must never abandon the path prescribed by Him.

And the path prescribed by Him is this: that we make known His glory by both practice and proclamation everywhere and in every which way; that we try to convince everyone to the best of our ability that it is He who is the way and the truth; and that we make it plain everywhere, by deeply impressing it in our own hearts, that salvation consists in relying upon Him alone and that there is no other way to salvation.[65]

The people of our country do not deny that they look for a Saviour. They freely admit that we are naturally prone to sin, that we do commit sin, that we are sinful by nature, and that we are liable to sin.[66] But the difference is this, that by calling Devakî's son[67] Deliverer, the God of sacrifice, and the Remover of sin, they fail to revere Christ our Lord as the true God of sacrifice. Nevertheless, they never impute any fault to our Lord, and when they look at the life of their fictitious Hari as he frolicked in Vraja and so on, they also become occasionally beset

---

[65] "salvation": *nistâr.*

[66] This sentence runs as follows in the Bengali: *âmrâ je svabhâbataḥ pâpsvarûp, pâpkarmâ pâpâtmâ pâpsambhab ihâ tâ(h)hârâ spaṣṭa svîkâr karen.* The intention is to be emphatic by repetition.

[67] That is, Krishna Vâsudeva.

by doubt.[68] Here our proper stratagem should be to emphasise the doubt-free and blameless reputation of our Lord while opposing the reproachful character and false pride of their highly dubious son of Devakî. Indeed, I myself have never heard any intelligent Vedic or Vaishnava devotee either criticise Christ or impute any fault to his behaviour or teaching. On the contrary, I have heard many of them condemning the character of such chosen deities as Krishna Vâsudeva etc. In such situations we should win them over by kindly behaviour.

Further, intelligent Vedic and Tantrik devotees will certainly realise that the worship[69] of such chosen deities as Krishna Vâsudeva etc. was not current in ancient times; it has become so only in recent times. There's not even a trace of such chosen deities in the Veda;[70] in fact even the Vaishnava scriptures say that Krishna-worship has arisen after a long time, hundreds of years after the beginning of the Christian era, and that this was prescribed by some new revelation.[71] Careful consideration of the matter will show that Krishna-worship is but a distortion of the truth. It is necessary to explain this to people like the Vedists and Tantriks; once this is done, their old persuasions[72] can give way and new ones arise through the help of the Holy Spirit.

At present, two formidable obstacles to God's work in this country are apparent: first, the atheism[73] of a great many talented men proficient

---

[68] Vraja is the area in north India (not far from Delhi) through which the Yamuna river flows, and encompasses Vrndaban, the forest-village in which Krishna grew up, and Mathura, the city in which Krishna was born. For a more profound interpretation of Krishna's so-called frolics in this region, see G. Schweig, *Dance of Divine Love: The Râsa Lîlâ of Krishna from the Bhâgavata Purâna, India's Classic Sacred Love Story*, Princeton University Press, Princeton, 2005. Krishna Mohan's age had a shallow understanding of the nature of symbolic and mythic narrative.

[69] Here the term used is *upâsanâ*.

[70] This is a contestable statement. If the Upanishads are regarded as part of the Veda (as they generally are), then there is a clear reference to "Krishna Devakîputra" in the *Chândogya Upaniṣad*, 3.17.6. Krishna Mohan, however, is probably referring here to the Saṃhitâ or hymnic section of the Veda. Even here a Krishna is mentioned in Ṛg Veda 8.85.3-4 as the composer of the hymn.

[71] "some new revelation": *âkâśbânî*.

[72] *saṅskâr*.

[73] *nâstikatâ*.

in English and their antipathy towards scripture as such, and second, profound resentment towards and contempt for Christian followers associated with the offence of making sons and daughters abandon their homes by means of various tricks and artifices.

However powerful the usual opponents of the Vedic and Christian traditions, that is, the atheistic as well as the so-called Brahmo despisers of scripture, may be at present, their power will not last for long, for the human heart can never completely forsake the Creator of the world, and those who profess in their conceit to understand everything by natural cognition[74] and slight the divine teaching, will sooner or later come to realise the purport of this Upanishadic saying: "To the one for whom it is not known, it is in fact known, whereas for the one to whom it is known, he does not know it. It is not understood by those who understand it; it is understood by those who do not understand" (*Kena Upaniṣad* 2.3).[75] In other words, those who do not pride themselves on understanding it through natural means,[76] actually do understand it, whereas those who say that they understand it in their own right, in fact know nothing. It remains unknown to those who take pride in natural cognition,[77] and known to those who do not boast in this way. Those who boast that, without recourse to divine scriptural teaching, they have rendered religious truths[78] as obvious as a fruit on one's palm, in fact don't know the first thing about such truths. What we must do in this matter is preach against human arrogance by looking to God for assistance.

As for the second obstacle I mentioned, it must be considered most judiciously: if because of their worship of Christ someone is turned out by their parents, then that is to their credit; if, on the other hand, they are not turned out and if on their own accord and at a young age

---

[74] "through natural cognition": *sahaj jñâne*, that is, without recourse to supernatural knowledge or revelation.

[75] Krishna Mohan quotes the original Sanskrit: *yasyâmatam tasya matam matam yasya na veda saḥ, avijñâtam vijânatâm vijñâtam avijânatâm.*

[76] "those who do not pride themselves....natural means": *je svabhâvataḥ bujhibâr abhimân kare nâ.*

[77] "natural cognition": *sahaj jñân.*

[78] "religious truths": *dharmma tattva.*

they escape from their parents surreptitiously without saying anything, then that cannot be to their credit in the same way; rather, they place themselves in the position of transgressing the fifth commandment.[79]

If someone, like the first disciples and Apostles, gives up everything, and in the manner of a wandering mendicant[80] goes about from region to region in order to preach the Gospel, having received a special call from the Lord, then that too can be to their credit, as when Peter said, "See, we have given up everything and followed You; what then shall we receive?" and the Lord answered, "You who have followed me will, in the time of the new creation when the Son of Man is seated on the throne of his glory, also sit on twelve thrones and judge the twelve tribes of Israel. And the person who, for the sake of my name, gives up home or brother or sister or father or mother or wife or child or land will gain a hundredfold and will be eligible for eternal life" (Mt.19.27-29).

But the call to become a wandering mendicant in this way is not possible for a person who is young; it is possible only for an individual of more or less mature years. The Lord Himself remained subject to His mother and father till maturity, after which He wandered about to accomplish His own work. In the absence of a special sign of such a call, it is not right to arrogate it to oneself. To forsake elders deserving of respect[81] at a young age only on the pretext of religious devotion[82] is not necessary, and therefore should not be done.

For worship of Christ can occur everywhere. In the beginning, even though the Roman Emperor was a fierce adversary of such worship, how many worshipped in this manner even in his palace! Such deadly and formidable foes are not possible today, so what is the need to leave one's parents at a young age and live under the protection of another? One should keep in mind Prahlâda's conduct as mentioned in the Purânas.[83] Though Hiraṇyakaúipu was the deadly adversary of

---

[79] Which is: "Honour thy father and thy mother".

[80] *daṇḍî*, that is, a mendicant who wanders about with staff in hand.

[81] "elders deserving of respect": *gurujan*.

[82] The word used is *upâsanâ*.

[83] The story of the boy Prahlâda, holding firm to his faith in and devotion to Vishnu against all odds, even at the risk of his life, in the face of his father, the

Prahlâda's preferred form of worship,[84] the young prince neither forsook his father nor denied his own chosen deity. No one has a right to object to someone leaving their father's house when mature and independent in order to live on their own, but it would be to overstep one's priestly duty[85] to give refuge to some fugitive youth and set oneself up in the place of his natural and proper protector when at an early age he cannot live independently as a householder,[86] and a guardian or protector is absolutely necessary.

The public resentment and contempt that have arisen against us when shelter has been given to someone else's son or daughter after they've abandoned home is a cause of particular concern. In our opinion, this has become the main obstacle in this country to spreading the Lord's teaching, and it is through our fault that the Lord's name faces censure. Otherwise I see no particular opposition to Christ's teaching among the Hindus;[87] they have nothing to say against the Lord's character or teaching. They do not deny that they are sinners by nature, and they also admit that there's need for a personal God[88] who takes away sin. Further, they are having second thoughts about such fictitious deliverers from sin as Ram, Krishna and so on. Though they evince no special objection to the claim that it is our Lord who is the true deliverer from sin, their misgiving is that if one becomes a Christian one has to abandon one's home and live in abject dependence upon another.[89] And it is this misgiving that lies at the root of all blame.

Therefore, because Christian worship must occur in spirit and in truth, there is no need for a special place for it, since devotion and

---

demonic king Hiraṇyakaúipu's persecution of him, is famous among Hindus, especially Vaishnavas. See especially the *Viṣṇu Purâṇa*, Chs.17-20, and the *Bhâgavata Purâṇa*, 7th Canto (where Prahlâda's relationship with his father in connection with the former's devotion to Vishnu, is described in detail).

[84] "preferred form of worship": *abhîṣṭa upâsanâ*.

[85] "priestly duty": *paurahitya kârjya*.

[86] "as a householder": *saṅgsârâúrame*.

[87] "among the Hindus": *hindu sampradâyer madhye*.

[88] *iṣṭadeb*.

[89] "abject dependence upon another": *parer annadâs haiyâ thâkite hay* - literally, must wait on another for food.

faith[90] comprise its essence. Unless one's parents turn one out, there is no need to run away surreptitiously. Christ issued no prohibition or command concerning what one may or may not eat; you can remain the strictest of vegetarians, eating the simplest of foods,[91] and still worship Him. Nor is there any prohibition or injunction concerning popular customs, individual tastes, and forms of service.[92] Christ's chief injunction is to turn away from sin: "His will is to make you holy".[93] The more such words enter people's hearts, the more will the Lord's otherworldly spiritual kingdom flourish, and we too shall become progressively fishers of human beings.

Those who are present here today with the desire of becoming ministers will never, all life long, be able to fulfill the vow for whose undertaking they now stand ready. For the observance of this vow is a perpetual task, and the spiritual struggle that they must engage in by means of it has no rest in this transient world. For this struggle will have no respite so long as even one person remains unrepentant[94] and devoid of Christian faith. The enemy is Satan, the attendant evil dispositions of flesh and blood, and superstition.[95] There can be no truce, even for a moment, with any of these. When can one call a halt in the battle with these things? This is, therefore, a perpetual conflict: we should neither boast if we have a little success in it, nor, when success eludes us, should we run away, dispirited. It is necessary to remain engaged in untiring combat.

On the one hand, with respect to those who have been received into the community[96] and marked, through faith, with the name of

---

[90] "devotion and faith": *bhakti o śraddhâ*.

[91] "the strictest of vegetarians….simplest of foods": thus *habiṣyâśî haiyâ śâkânna bhojan kariyâ….*

[92] "popular customs….service": *laukik byâbahâr svaruci tantra,* though *tantra* can take on a number of meanings, including "cult", "doctrine", and "system of belief".

[93] See 1 Thessalonians, 4.3a.

[94] "unrepentant": *ananutâpî.*

[95] Reading *kusaṅgskâr* for *kusaṅgsâr* here (though, if the latter is accepted as the correct reading, it may be translated as "the wicked world"). The term used for "Satan" is *śaytân.*

[96] "community": *sabhâ.*

Christ, the task of the minister is to increase faith, to spread the joy of the Lord, to destroy doubt, and to inspire devotion;[97] however, for those still outside the community, unaware of or unbelieving in Christ's glory, the burden of the following tasks is placed upon the minister: to introduce Christ to them and familiarise them with His words, to make known the mystery of Christ's love, and to make them a part of Christ by drawing them into His community.[98]

Who is able to bear such a heavy burden by his own strength? It can be borne only through God's grace with the help of the Holy Spirit.[99] Hence the chief task of the minister is this: to strive continually to obtain that grace and help. And we should always keep this in mind that if we are to convince others, it is vital that we ourselves become knowledgeable; if we are to instruct, it is absolutely necessary to devote ourselves to study; if we are to spread virtue,[100] we must first spread it in our own lives, and that if we are to make known the greatness of love,[101] it is necessary to make it shine forth through our own conduct.

Every one of the Lord's devotees should behave in such a way that whenever outsiders observe their conduct they will come to know that "these have come close to God".[102] Just as iron manifests a distinctive trait in the presence of a magnet, so the human heart assumes a new state through devotion to the Lord,[103] and by seeing the fruit of this people are induced to give God a welcome.

If this is possible for devotees in general, then it is all the more fitting that it apply also to ministers consecrated to Christ.[104] For the sake of Christ's sovereignty,[105] we have turned over everything we

---

[97] "faith": *biśvâs*; "devotion": *bhakti*.

[98] "Christ's glory": *khrîṣṭa mahimâ*; "the mystery of Christ's love": *khrîṣṭa bhaktirahasya*.

[99] "through God's grace": *ûivar prâsâdât*; "the Holy Spirit": *pabitra âtmâ*.

[100] "virtue": *satkarmma*.

[101] "the greatness of love": *bhaktir mâhâtmya*.

[102] Perhaps Krishna Mohan has The Letter of James, 4.8 in mind.

[103] "through devotion to the Lord": *prabhur upâsanây*.

[104] "consecrated to Christ": *khrîṣṭbrata*.

[105] "For the sake of Christ's sovereignty": *khrîṣṭer adhikârâthe*.

possess to Christ in order to conquer human hearts. If we do not now devote ourselves with body, mind and speech to His service and to extending His reign, we shall have to stand accused of the crime of misappropriating what belongs to God.[106]

There was an ancient custom in our country that if one performed the Râjasûya Sacrifice one had to conquer all opponents – such conquest was the distinctive mark of that Sacrifice.[107] Our Lord too, having completed his self-sacrifice, is now engaged in accomplishing its remaining part of universal conquest, and in this matter we are his supporting army. In clear language John has described that which we too may experience with the eye of devotion[108] in joy and delight: that the Lord, mounted on a white steed, is even now conquering in every direction, and that before long all the realms of the world will become the kingdom of the Lord. Then that Sovereign Emperor, King of kings and Lord of lords, having conquered the world, will acquire a title by which the inhabitants of the three realms – heaven, earth and hell – will bend the knee, and every tongue cry out continuously, "Jesus Christ is the highest Lord! Glory be to God the Father!"[109]

---

[106] "misappropriating what belongs to God": *debatra apaharaṇ*.

[107] There is a possible confusion here with another well-known Vedic sacrifice, the *aśvamedha*. According to J.A.B. van Buitenen, "[O]n strictly Vedic terms the *râjasûya* does not really bestow universal sovereignty....this claim is reserved for another ritual [the *aśvamedha*]". In a personal note to me, the scholar John Brockington remarks in addition that the *râjasûya* tends to ratify the inauguration of a reign. "This would distinguish [the *râjasûya*] from the *aśvamedha*, which is typically performed by an established king, either to proclaim his overlordship....or to purify him/his kingdom from some fault". For both references, see J. Lipner, *Hindus, op. cit.*, p.396, note 4.

[108] "the eye of devotion": *bhakti cakṣu*; this expression recalls the *divyamcakṣuh* (the "divine eye") of the *Bhagavad Gîtâ*, 11.8, bestowed by Krishna to Arjuna to enable the latter to behold the all-conquering majesty of Krishna's *viśvarûpa* or Universal Form.

[109] For scriptural phrases and ideas consonant with this last segment of the Sermon, see The Revelation to John, 19.11, 19.16, and the Letter to the Philippians, 2.10-11.

Thinking Theologically in Tamil:
An Exercise in Comparative Theology?[1]

M. Thomas Thangaraj

I consider it a privilege to present this essay in honor of my colleague, Dr. Israel Selvanayagam. In addition to what I have written about Israel in the Editors' piece on him I want to highlight the fact that Israel and I have been involved in *Tamil* theological education for many years. As colleagues at Tamilnadu Theological Seminary (TTS), we were deeply committed to doing, articulating, and writing theology in and through Tamil language. As persons who grew up in the independent India and amongst the revival of Tamil language through the pure Tamil movement initiated by Maraimalai Adigal, and under the political aegis of Dravida Munnetra Kalagam (DMK), we were nurtured in a special love for and pride about Tamil. Prof. V. P. K. Sundaram of TTS provided a great inspiration for younger theologians like us to speak and write in good and poetic Tamil. Moreover, we both have been involved in inter-religious dialogue especially with the Saivites of Tamil Nadu who have a significant collection of religious and philosophical writings in Tamil. Is our thinking and articulating theology in Tamil an exercise in comparative theology? Before I attempt to answer this question, a prior question needs to be addressed: What is comparative theology?

To understand comparative theology we shall take the route Francis Clooney has suggested in his book on the subject. He writes, "Comparative theology is best understood by reflection on practice. If I am going to explain the field, explanation works well as reflection on my own practice."[2] I would like to extend such an approach to the story of Christianity itself because there is something peculiar about how Christian faith had to engage in the practice of comparative theology right from its beginnings. Let us first note that Christianity began as a religion of converts –disciples of Jesus who "converted" to a religious faith which was to be named as Christianity later. Of course the early Christians thought that they were simply extending their Jewish faith to include the recognition of the Messianic role of Jesus of Nazareth. So they called him Jesus the Christ. Not everyone around agreed with such an ascription. Yet they remained within the Jewish religious community. Soon the entry of Gentiles into the emerging Christian community and their own expulsion from the Synagogues forced the early disciples to forge a new identity for themselves as Christians. Such a process of identity- formation operated on a dynamics of difference – that is, highlighting the difference between Jewish faith and the new community of faith and also their faith's being different from the non-Jewish religious and philosophical traditions. In this dynamics of difference lay the beginnings of comparative theology.

The early converts to Christian faith had no other option than comparing and contrasting their newly found faith with their previous religious tradition which has its own peculiar resources, practices, and language. It involved a re-reading of the resources of their earlier faith. The New Testament bears ample witness to such comparative theological exercise. One such exercise is found in the Epistle to the Hebrews. "Long ago God spoke to our ancestors in many and various ways by the prophets, but in these last days he has spoken to us by a Son, whom he appointed heir of all things, through whom he also created the worlds." (Heb.1:1-2). Then the epistle goes on study the sacrificial traditions within Judaism and come up with a Christology which is rooted in the Jewish tradition but breaks new ground by proclaiming Jesus as both the High Priest who offers sacrifice and the lamb that is slain in sacrifice. The Fourth Gospel, for instance, comes up with presenting Christ as "Word-become-flesh"– a comparative theological exercise done in the context of Greek and Jewish philosophical traditions.(John 1:1-18). This was true of Protestant and Roman Catholic Christians in India. Most of them are products of the Western missionary enterprise. As converts to Christianity mostly from the Hindu tradition they had to negotiate and form their Christian identity with the dynamics of difference that I have mentioned.

Why engage in such comparative theological exercise at all? The answer to this question is multi-faceted and historically developmental. There have been varied purposes and intentions behind such a comparative theological exercise. We need to briefly survey this historical development to properly locate ourselves in the contemporary academic theological exercise called Comparative Theology promoted by Robert Neville, Francis Clooney, John Thattamanil, James Fredericks, Michelle V. Roberts, and others in the American theological scene.[3] Keith Ward, a British theologian, has been engaged in comparative theology for many years.[4]

Internalizing Intent

Comparative theology in relation to Christian identity formation has the intent of making sense of one's newly found faith to oneself. For example, a Tamil Christian like me cannot think through and articulate my faith without dealing with Tamil religious categories. Every word I utter in relation to my own religious faith is in the context of that word used in the Hindu tradition and there is an implicit comparative theological exercise involved in that. This is not always done at an explicit and unconscious level. My book, *The Crucified Guru: An Experiment in Cross-Cultural Christology,*[5]as an exercise in comparative theology, illustrates an intentional and conscious effort at my internalizing of Christian faith. During the early years of my theological teaching (1971-1974) I discovered that use of the term *avatara* (Hindu term for the idea of incarnation though literally meaning descent) for Christ often promoted docetic understandings of Christ both among my students and among Christian congregations around.The M. Th. Degree program at United Theological College at Bangalore (1974-76) offered me an opportunity to engage this issue and led me to the discovery and use of Spirit Christology expounded by Norman Hook in his book, *Christ in the Twentieth Century.*[6] One of my most respected teachers at that time, Roy Pape, encouraged me to pursue this. While a student at UTC I was working out my Christology in the English language and Spirit Christology made sense in that context. But when I returned to teach in Tamil, it was not easy to think in Tamil with Spirit Christology. Yet my internalizing intent would not allow me to be satisfied with thinking in English alone about Christ. To think in Tamil about Christ I needed a comparative engagement with Tamil Saivism and such engagement led me to the concept of guru in Tamil Saivism. Thus the vision of Christ as Crucified Guru opened the doors to my fuller internalization of my faith and to an increased adoration of Christ.

What I have described here is not something that happened to me alone. The translation of the Bible into Tamil language and the composing of Christian hymns in Tamil involved the same kind of internalizing intent. One of the first things that Protestant missionaries did in India was to translate the Bible in the local languages. The first Protestant missionary - Bartholomew Ziegenbalg - landed in Tranquebar on the eastern shores of Tamil Nadu in 1706, and he proceeded to translate the Bible into Tamil first. Translation of the Bible of course is a highly loaded theological activity. It is also a comparative theological exercise. First of all, one has to come up with a name for this book. One could transliterate it as Bibil. Yet, given the developed scriptural tradition of Hindu faith, one has to find a way to signify this book as scripture. Then only this new book can be internalized as Tamil Christian's scripture. Therefore, the term *veda* seemed appropriate. Starting with Roberto De Nobili who arrived in India in 1605 and Ziegenbalg in 1706, there have been attempts to use the word *vedam* in ways it would point to Christian scripture. Nobili used the phrase *Deva Vedam* (divine veda) or *saruvesvaranal aruliceyyapatta vedam*(the *veda* given by Lord God). Ziegenbalg used phrases such as *sutya vedam* (true veda) and *vedaposttgam* (veda book).[7] Given the flourishing Saivite tradition in Tamil Nadu, the bible was named in the later translation as *Parisutta Vedagamam* (Holy Veda and Agama).

The second area where comparative theological thinking can be found is in the matter of choosing the right word for *theos*. The word, *theos*, signifies a personal but one and only God of the whole universe and in Christian use of it refers to the Father of Lord Jesus Christ. Choosing the right word for *theos* has not been an easy task given the variety of names for God in the Hindu and Tamil traditions. None of the translators chose Brahman, given the supra-personal character of Brahman. Nobili and Zigenbalg opted for *isvara* and qualified it as *saruvesvaran* (the isvara of all or above all). The later translations of the Bible opted for *tevan* (since it is the closest to Deus in Latin). Various forms of the same word are available to Tamil Christians such as *deivam*, *devareer*, etc. Today the word *kadavul*(literally meaning transcendent + immanent) has gained popularity and is used in the latest inter-confessional translation of the Bible, called, *tiruviviliyam*.   All these comparative exercises were for internalizing one's new found faith.

Tamil Christian poets and hymn writers have been much freer in their "learning across religious borders." Some of our early Protestant hymn writers belonged to a sub-caste that had easy access to Saivite and Vaishnavite writings in Tamil and therefore they were proficient in them. Krishna Pillai and Vedanayagam Sastriyar used Hindu terms freely in their hymns. Krishna Pillai employs the three-fold exposition of ultimate reality – *sat* (Truth/Being), *cit* (Consciousness), and *ananda*(Bliss) – for adoring Trinity in one of his hymns. So does Vedanayagam Sastriar in his hymns.[8] He even praises God as *parabrama yekovah*, (combining Braham in Hindu thought and Yahweh in Christian tradition) in another hymn. Both these writers are very critical of the Hindu tradition in their apologetics; yet when it comes to praise God and asking for God's mercy they engage in comparative theological thinking.The intent behind all these comparative theological activities is the internalization of Christian faith.

Apologetic Intent

The internalizing intent often went hand in hand with an apologetic intent. During the Western missionary movements' involvement in India one sees a number of comparative theological works. Most of these writings were focused on arguing for and defending Christian faith over against Hindu faith. As H. M. Scudder, an American missionary in Tamil Nadu in the 19th century, acknowledges that his and other missionary writings "assume, as a starting point, some prominent falsity in Hinduism, which is exhibited and refuted as an introduction to the opposite truth," which is Christ who claimed to be the Truth.[9]The morality of such comparative theological work is rightly questioned and criticized both by Christians and Hindus in India.Most of the Indian Christian theologians as narrated by Robin Boyd in his book, *Introduction to Indian Christian Theology*[10] have engaged in comparative theological work either with internalizing intent or apologetic intent. Most of these works exhibit a careful and sympathetic study of Hindu tradition. H.A. Krishna Pillai's rendering of John Bunyan's *Pilgrim's Progress* as an epic-level Tamil poetical work is a supreme example. Krishna Pillai not only internalizes the Christian faith through the Hindu traditional categories but also recommends Christian faith to those outside the Christian community. Here is a coming together of internalizing intent and apologetic intent. Vengal Chakkarai's *Jesus the Avatar* examines the concept of *avatar* within the Hindu Vaishnavite tradition and presents a comparative Christology with both internalizing and apologetic intent.[11]

Dialogical Intent

From the middle of the 20th century there has been a shift in our comparative theological stance. There came a move from apologetics to dialogue – a genuine desire to know and understand the other so that various religious communities might live in peace and harmony. Such a dialogical intent aimed at loving one's religious neighbor with empathy and understanding. Once Christians were involved in such dialogical encounters with people of other traditions, it led to another kind of comparative theological exercise called theology of religions. Dialogical encounters cannot escape comparison between religions as such. Such comparison raises a fundamental theological question: How do we reconcile the fact of religious plurality within our picture of God? Most of the organized inter-religious dialogues face the question of comparison and thus cannot avoid comparative theological thinking. Yet theology of religions is not comparative theology as such in light of our recent understanding of comparative theology.

Transformative Intent

Comparative theology as we talk about it now has a different intent. As Francis Clooney suggests as a subtitle to his book, comparative theology is "deep learning across religious borders." It involves a careful reading of one's own religious tradition and that of the other and engaging in responsible comparison that leads to transformation on both sides. As John Thattamanil writes, "Comparative theology takes the content of other people's ideas seriously, seriously enough to challenge those ideas and seriously enough to be changed by those ideas."[12] It is this project of "challenging" and "being challenged" which determines the character of comparative theology. How do we keep affirming and challenging the other at the same time? How do we invite the other into our own Christian theological construction and thus allow it to transform our theological vision while maintaining the peculiarity of our own tradition? These are to be our guiding questions that will determine the fruitfulness and the effectiveness of comparative theology. Mutual transformation and mutual learning depends greatly on how we keep these two going at the same time. Robert Neville sees comparative theology as "both descriptive and normative at once."[13]

Let me return to the question: Is thinking theologically in Tamil a comparative theological exercise? It is becoming clearer to me that Tamil theological thinking is necessarily comparative. But the question is: what is the intent of such comparative engagement? My immediate ancestors come from a small town called Nazareth in South India. This town is located in the southern part of Tirunelveli district of the Tamil Nadu, India. It is only a couple of miles from Alwarthirunagari, a famous Vaishnavite center and not too far from Kayalpattinam, a Muslim town. In 1804, the whole village accepted Christian faith due to the work of local and English missionaries, and changed the name of the village from Canpattu to Nazareth.

In such a setting, thinking theologically is always in comparison to and over against the Hindus and Muslims on the one hand, and in comparison to the other denominational and caste Christians. We were Tamil Anglican Christians – different from Hindus and Muslims and different from the Western missionaries in our customs and rituals. Thus our theological thinking was for the most part done in this sort of comparative exercise. There are villages around Nazareth that came to Christian faith as villages and changed their names to Jerusalem, Megnanapuram, Mudalur, etc. There was a definite awareness about Tamil ways of thinking and doing things. One of the catechists in Nazareth, Arumainayagam, well-educated for his times, got into a controversy and conflict with the local Anglican missionary and walked out of the church to start a church of his own. It is called the Indian Church of the Only Savior, popularly known as Nattu Sabai or Hindu Christian Community.[14] He rejected the Western hymns translated into Tamil, composed his own hymns on the 150 psalms in South Indian classical music tradition, and titled it as Tehillim. Only those hymns are used by this community even today.

The four intents that I have described so far are not mutually exclusive options. We need to find ways of combining these four in creative ways depending on our context. Comparative theology within the Western Academy is mostly constructed in the context of curiosity about other religious traditions. Francis Clooney's interest in Hinduism and Robert Neville's fascination with Confucian thought have led them to engage in comparative theology. Therefore, their writings do not have an apologetic intent. On the other hand, comparative theologies in Tamil Nadu arise out of existential crisis in the face of religious plurality and thus will have both an internalizing intent and an apologetic intent. As we saw earlier, Tamil hymnic writings exhibit a combination of internalizing and apologetic intent. The process of naming the Tamil Bible began with a strong apologetic intent. But today there is willingness to move to a dialogical mode. In the most recent translation of the Bible in Tamil, the word *viviliyam* is used and the Bible is referred to as *Thiruviviliyam*. *Viviliyam* is an interesting transliteration of the Greek word *biblion* into Tamil. The very history of naming the Bible in Tamil points to an interesting progression of theological thinking that moves from apologetics to comparative theological mode of thinking. A deep learning across religious borders has happened here respecting the distinctive character of both religious traditions.

The future of comparative theology depends on how we deal with the emerging new religious identity. The early converts had to forge their identity on stark contrasts between their own faith and the faith of others. We today have to negotiate our identity in comparative engagement of both traditions. All comparative theologians in the Christian community are challenged to become not just Christians but Christians Plus. Of course Christian identity has always been hybrid; but the hybridity we are referring to here is an intentional and conscious hybridity that advances the possibilities for peace and harmony. Thus new identities are in the making and the future will reveal more. I am definitely not thinking of a universal religious identity forged out of an uncritical mixing of various religious traditions. What we are dealing with is a new form of religious identity that is carved out of a critical and careful reading of one another's religious traditions.

Comparative theology is worked out through a careful reading of each other's sacred texts in the case of Francis Clooney, John

Thattamanil, Michelle Roberts, and others. These theologians are also aware that comparative theology is not limited to texts. One needs to open oneself to other forms of practicing comparative theology. Exploring the layers of meaning that lie underneath the words used in Tamil Christian theology can enable one to think theologically in a comparative mode. Similarly, with the advent of Dalit theology, one is prompted to look at the various practices among Christians a text for comparative theological exercise. Such a discovery of Tamil Christian practices is not limited to Dalits alone; every jati among Christians has its own set of rituals and practices. Those provide a fertile ground for comparative theological reflection and action. In the latest volume on comparative theology edited by Francis Clooney, several theologians warn us against religious, cultural, and gender hegemony that creeps into comparative theology[15] and call us to widen the field to include practices and rituals.

Comparative theology leads also to "new forms of solidarity," to borrow James Fredericks' phrase.As he writes,

> Christians welcome the "other" in dialogue and see to develop new forms of social and religious solidarity with the "other. Instead of banishing or domesticating the "other," doing theology comparatively requires Christians to welcome the "other" as teacher and friend.[16]

This is not only in our minds, in our hearts, and in our joint forms of service; it should be expressed physically in the work of comparative theology that is undertaken in the presence of the religious other. In the present political climate of Tamil Nadu, there is a dire need for new forms of solidarity that can work across religious borders. Within the churches themselves, there is need for new forms of solidarity.

To conclude, the future of comparative theology depends on greater intra-religious dialogue and conversation. People in our churches and theological communities are becoming more and more aware of the implications religious plurality for Christian discipleship. They are also having access to the resources of other religious traditions. For them to engage in comparative theology, we need a lot of conversations among Christians themselves. Let me end with a story. Several years ago, I got an email from a pastor in Buford, Georgia inviting me to speak to his congregation on the issue of how Christians might relate to people of other religions. I agreed. A couple of weeks before the event came an email from the pastor with these words. "I read your book, Relating *to People of Other Religions: What Every Christian Needs to Know*[17]and therefore I am sorry we have to cancel our invitation." – in other words, we want to de-invite you! He gave two reasons for this de-inviting. First, he mentioned that it was easier for me as an Indian to say all these things; but his people in Buford could not. Second, he reiterated his commitment to ground his congregation in the Christian faith and that the pedagogical style of my book did not help toward such grounding. I replied expressing gratitude for his candor and mentioned two things. First, what all I say in that book is not because I am an *Indian* Christian but because I am a *Christian*. It is my commitment to Christ that demands of me to engage my religious neighbors in dialogue with humility and reverence. Second, as a minister I prefer to give options to my congregation so that they may choose their modes of discipleship and not feel regimented into one way of thinking. Even though this story comes from Buford, Georgia, it is very relevant for Tamil Christians as well. A lot of intra-religious conversation is needed among Tamil Christians. The future of Tamil Christian Comparative Theology desperately depends on such intra-religious conversations!

Endnotes

[1] Major parts of this essay were presented as "Irenic Invitations and Prophetic Protests: The Future of Comparative Theology" at a Symposium on "The Future of Christian Spirituality and Interreligious Interactions" in honor of Dr. Pyun, Sun Hwan of Korea held at Drew University Theological School, Madison, NJ during September 26 – 28, 2012.

[2] Francis Clooney, *Comparative Theology: Deep Learning Across Religious Borders*, Oxford, Wiley-Blackwell, 2010, p. 21.

[3] See: Francis Clooney (ed.)*The New Comparative Theology: Interreligious Insights from the Next Generation*, London, T&T Clark, 2010.

[4] Keith Ward's writings engage the various world religions in a comparative theological exercise. See: Keith Ward, *Religion and Revelation*, Oxford, Clarendon Press, 1994; *Religion and Creation*, Oxford Clarendon Press, 1996; *Religion and Human Nature*, Oxford Clarendon Press, 1998; and *Religion and Community*, Oxford, Clarendon Press, 2000.

[5] Nashville, TN, Abingdon Press, 1994.

[6] Norman Hook, *Christ in the Twentieth Century: A Spirit Christology*, London, Lutterworth Press, 1968.

[7] I am depending heavily on Bror Tiliander, *Christian and Hindu Terminology: A Study in Their Mutual Relations with Special Reference to the Tamil Area*, Uppsala, 1974, Soosai Arokiasamy, *Dharma, Hindu and Christian According to Roberto De*

Nobili: Analysis of its Meaning and its Use in Hinduism and Christianity, Rome, Editrice Pontificia Universita Gregoriana, 1986, and M. Thomas Thangaraj, "The Bible as Veda: Biblical Hermeneutics in Tamil Christianity," *Vernacular Hermeneutics*, edited by R. S. Sugirtharajah, Sheffield Academic Press, 1999, pp.133-143.

[8] See: *Christian Lyrics and Revival Songs*, enlarged and revised edition, Madras, Christian Literature Society, 1988.

[9] H. M. Scudder, *The Bazaar Book or Vernacular Preacher's Companion*, translated by J. W. Scudder, Madras, Graves, Cookson and Co., 1869.

[10] Robin H. Boyd, *An Introduction to Indian Christian Theology*, 2nd Rev. Edition, Madras: Christian Literature Society, 1979.

[11] P. T. Thomas, *The Theology of Chakkarai, with selections from his writings*, Bangalore, CISRS, 1968.

[12] John J. Thattamanil, *The Immanent Divine: God, Creation, and the Human Predicament*, Minneapolis, Fortress Press, 2006, p.xii.

[13] Robert Neville, *Behind the Masks of God: An Essay toward Comparative Theology*, New York, New York University Press, 1991, p.ix.

[14] See: "The History and Teachings of the Hindu Christian Community called Nattusabai in Tirunelveli," *Indian Church History Review*, Vol. 5, no. 1, 1971.

[15] See: Hugh Nicholson, "The New Comparative Theology and the Problem of Theological Hegemonism," in Francis Clooney (ed.) *The New Comparative Theology*, pp. 43-62; and Michelle Voss Roberts, "Gendering Comparative Theology" in Francis Clooney, *The New Comparative Theology*, pp. 109-128.

[16] James L. Fredericks, *Buddhists and Christians: Through Comparative Theology to Solidarity*, Maryknoll, NY, Orbis Books, 2004, p.112.

[17] Nashville, Abingdon Press, 1997.

Israel Selvanayagam and the Evangelical Arminian Tradition

Kenneth Cracknell

No volume of essays in honour of Israel Selvanayagam would be complete if there were not in it some mention of his connection with British Methodism. But his heritage within the Church of South India stemmed historically from the Congregationalist tradition. He began his ministry at the early age of eighteen when he was appointed as a 'probationer in pastoral ministry' of the CSI in his home village of Parakkanvilai, proceeding four years later to the Tamilnadu Theological Seminary in Madurai. Here, whether he knew it or not at that time, he became the inheritor of a remarkable set of attitudes formed by Congregationalist scholar-missionaries who worked in South India in the later part of the nineteenth century.[1] The most prominent of these were Englishmen, T. E. Slater (1840-1912) and Bernard Lucas (1860-1921), together with Scotsman J. N. Farquhar (1861-1929) and two Americans, John P. Jones (1847-1916) and Robert Allen Hume (1849-1929). Of these five Lucas and Jones worked in Madurai and it is not perhaps coincidental that in this city interfaith theological education was finding new paths in Israel's time as student and teacher.[2] This strong Congregationalist tradition has remained important to Israel's life and writings.

In what follows, though, I want to reflect on some extraordinary turns of events that have marked Israel's scholarly career. In 1988 Israel arrived in Wesley House, Cambridge (where I had just come to teach), in order to complete his researches into the Vedic doctrine of sacrifice. The theological shaping of his earlier years (see the editors' biographical Introduction) had been in colleges in South India where the Methodist tradition was very significant, with his supervising professors at Bangalore, Eric Lott and David Scott, both being Methodist. Then, from those Cambridge days, began a long and close association with British Methodism. Israel served the British Methodist Church with great distinction as a theological teacher at Wesley College Bristol, at Queen's College, Birmingham, as Principal of the College of the Ascension in Selly Oak, and lastly as Interfaith Consultant to the Methodist churches in and around Birmingham. What I want to do now is to celebrate some Wesleyan/Methodist themes that are central to Israel's thought.

The cruciality of Arminian Evangelicalism

A recent volume just published by the SCM Press in 2011 on some Christian theologies of religion indicates the continuing relevance of the Arminian form of evangelicalism. In *Only One Way: Three Christian responses on the Uniqueness of Christ in a Religiously Plural Word*, Gavin D'Costa, Paul Knitter and Daniel Strange set out their perspectives as to how theology of religion may be done. D'Costa writes as a conservative Roman Catholic, defending among other things the Roman Magisterium and in particular the document *Dominus Iesus* of 2000, very much associated with the name of Josef Ratzinger/ Pope Benedict XVI. Paul Knitter is a Roman Catholic of quite another tradition, namely that of Karl Rahner and Raimundo Panikkar. modified by Paul Tillich and process and liberation theologians. The third position presented in *Only One Way* is that of what is called 'Protestant Reformed orthodoxy' or 'conservative evangelicalism'. Daniel Strange of Oak Hill Theological College, London, presents a lucid and straightforward account of what he understands as the grammar of the Christian faith in this form. He sees this as derived from an 'epistemologically authoritative Biblical revelation', interpreted by the ecumenical creeds, the Reformation's five *solas* (*sola Scriptura, solus Christus, sola fide, sola gratia, sola Deo Gloria*), the creeds of the Reformation and some recent pan-evangelical statements and covenants. Daniel cites with approval two leading Dutch missiologists, Henrik Kraemer and J. H. Bavinck, as well as the Britishers, Lesslie Newbigin and John Stott. It will surprise no one that with such authorities Strange's theology of religion is negative and, from our point of view, singularly unhelpful. The religions of the world are seen as essentially idolatrous refashionings of divine revelation. The relationship of Christianity to other religions is that of 'subversive fulfillment', and the missionary task remains for Strange that we should engage in combative *elenchics* (Bavinck's chosen term): that is, in missionary challenge and apologetic.[3]

Yet the greatest difficulty with Strange's exposition of 'Protestant Reformed orthodoxy' is how the image of God is conceived. God is presented as one who is self-sufficient, unmoved and immovable, and therefore 'wholly other' from humanity. He (the masculine pronoun is wholly appropriate) is 'jealous' and 'wrathful', so much so that his divine anger needs to be appeased by the death of Christ on the cross as an act of propitiation. This presentation of the nature of God, as Knitter writes elsewhere in the discussion, is of 'a stereotypical father, who is always in charge, does not need any one, is jealous of any other male, controls by wrathful fulminations, is ready to love us but only if we do not offend him or are ready to pay the price and satisfy him if we do' (p.164).

Such an account makes me want to dwell on an alternative form of Evangelicalism. Associated primarily with the 'Wesleyan evangelicals',[4] that is, followers of John and Charles Wesley, this offers a diametrically different presentation of the Gospel, focused as it is on the grand themes of the Fatherly love of God, of salvation through faith alone, and of the free offer of salvation to all. For nearly sixty years in the eighteenth century these ideas were set forth by John and Charles Wesley in songs and sermons, as they resisted the restrictive Calvinist orthodoxy that surrounded them.

This ultimately limited version of the Gospel message stemmed from John Calvin (1509-64) who had been explicit that:

> The covenant of life is not preached equally to all, and among those to whom it is preached does not always meet with the same reception. This diversity displays the unsearchable depth of the divine judgment, and is without doubt subordinate to God's purpose of eternal election. (*Institutes of the Christian Religion*, 1559, in the Beveridge translation, vol. 2, p. 202)

The doctrine of the election of a few and the condemnation of the many took shape in English in such statements as the Lambeth Articles (1592) and the Westminster Confession (1647), and culminated in the hyper-

Calvinism of the eighteenth century that was so familiar to John and Charles Wesley. A summary of the Lambeth Articles highlights the contrast (I am using the version in Philip Schaff''s *The Creeds of Christendom Vol.3*).

> 1. God from eternity has predestinated certain persons unto life: certain persons he has reprobated. 2. The moving or efficient cause of predestination unto life is not the foresight of faith, or of perseverance, or of good works ... but only the good will and pleasure of God. 3. There is predetermined a certain number of the predestinate, which can neither be augmented nor diminished. 4. Those who are not predestinated to salvation shall be necessarily damned for their sins. 5. A true living and justifying faith, and a sanctifying by the Spirit of God is not extinguished ... it vanishes not away in the elect, either finally or totally. 6. A person. ..endued with justifying faith is certain, with the full assurance of faith, of the remission of his sins, and of his everlasting salvation by Christ. 7. Saving grace is ... not granted, not communicated to all persons by which they may be saved if they will. 8. No one can come unto Christ unless it shall be given unto him, and unless the Father shall draw him; and all persons are not drawn by the Father, that they may come to the Son. 9. It is not in the will or power of every one to be saved.

In the very earliest years of the Methodist revival, Charles Wesley published a volume of verse entitled *Hymns of Everlasting Love* (1741). He included among these a poem in seventeen verses and from its length this was plainly meant as something other than a congregational hymn. It is in fact a formidable creedal statement, functioning almost verse by verse as a refutation of the Lambeth Articles. Nearly forty years later the poem was reprinted without modification in the second issue of *The Arminian Magazine* (October 1778).[5]

Charles Wesley began with the fundamental insight of the Wesleyan revival that God is everlasting love, best denoted by the word 'Father'. Other key phrases run through the writings of John and Charles Wesley: 'Love divine, all loves excelling'; 'Thy nature and thy name is Love'; 'pure universal Love Thou art'; 'ceaseless, unexhausted love'; 'eternal depth of love divine'. For the Wesley brothers, the single source of salvation was love and the only content of salvation lay in the heart's being filled with God.

Such a vision of God made any talk of a restricted salvation, or of divine 'wrath' or 'punishment' truly anathema to the early Methodists. So this 'creedal hymn' starts right in on its main themes:

> Father whose everlasting love
> Thine only Son for sinners gave
> Whose grace to All did freely move
> And sent him down a World to save
>
> Help us thy mercy to extol
> Immense, unfathomed, unconfined,
> To praise the Lamb who died for All,
> The general Saviour of Mankind.

It immediately states its dominant concept:

> Thy undistinguishing Regard
> Was cast on Adam's fallen race,
> For All thou hast in Christ prepared
> Sufficient, sovereign, saving Grace.

Some eight times in twelve lines Charles asserts the 'all-ness', or universality of the grace of God (a quick count of the other stanzas shows the word 'all' used eleven times, and 'world' or 'ends of the earth' four times. In direct contradiction of Lambeth Article 8, Charles Wesley writes:

> Jesus hath said, 'we all shall hope,
> Preventing Grace for All is free:
> And I, if I be lifted up,
> I will draw All Men unto Me'.

The doctrine of the election of a chosen few Charles Wesley ascribed to human beings projecting their own diminished sympathies and lack of compassion onto God. This he describes as idolatrous and, indeed, blasphemous. Addressing God as 'Thou Universal love', Charles asked why any of us should 'of thy Grace despair'.

> 'Tis we, the wretched abjects, we,
> Our blasphemies on Thee translate;
> We think that Fury is in Thee,
> Horribly think, that God is hate!'

For such belief is inevitably the consequence of holding any kind of Calvinist view. It must lead to the extraordinary assertion (which Charles satirizes in a form of address to God) that if this were true

> Thou has compell'd the lost to die:
> Hath reprobated from thy face

> Hath others sav'd, by them past by,
> Or mocked with only *Damning Grace*.

In the original text *Damning Grace* was italicized and marked with an asterisk and then explicated as *Common Grace*, that is, the 'common operations of the Spirit' to which the Westminster Confession alludes, because, as we have seen Lambeth Article 7 assert: 'Saving grace is ... not granted, not communicated to all men, by which they may be saved if they will'. Such notions are to be seen as 'horrible decrees', and Charles Wesley voices his exasperation with the whole body of Calvinism in the sixteenth stanza;

> Still shall the Hellish Doctrine stand?
> And Thee for its dire Author claim?
> No - let it sink, at thy command,
> Down to the pit from whence it came.

From the premises of 'damning grace' and 'double predestination' (some to eternal life, some to damnation) it follows that the efficacy of the atonement is also limited and that therefore Jesus Christ did not die for all people, only for the elect. Thus as the climax of the poem its author pleads for God's speedy intervention in what was to the earliest Methodists a matter of supreme urgency:

> Arise O God, maintain thy Cause!
> The Fulness of the Gentiles call:
> Lift up the standard of thy cross,
> And All shall own Thou diedst for All.

Here we have a strong allusion, as in an earlier stanza, to the words of Jesus in John 12.32: 'I, when I am lifted up from the earth, will attract all people (or everything) to myself (*kagô ean hupsôthô ek tçs gçs, pantas helkusô pros emauton*). With this affirmation Charles Wesley brings to a close his declaration of the Armninian Evangelical position.

Arminian Evangelicalism won its way in the Nineteenth century
Evangelicalism in this mode was equally necessary to the evangelism of the increasingly non-churched masses who were arising as a result of the British industrial revolution, as well as to the world-wide mission of the church. As James Morrison, an early nineteenth century Scots minister who abandoned Presbyterianism, once commented:

> If it were not true that Christ died for the heathen, pray what gospel is the missionary to preach when he lands on a foreign shore? Is he to tell them that God loved a few men scattered somewhere or other through the world, and therefore for aught that he could know, there may happen to be some of the favoured ones among them, and for these Christ died?[6]

Writing as one Congregationalist missionary who had fought his way out of the Calvinist tradition, T. E. Slater, also noted

> If there are those who still believe that the heathen, as heathen, are exposed to endless torment, let them by all the terrors of such a vision devote themselves to their rescue with the most passionate energy; though we would offer the solemn warning that in teaching such a doctrine, they are taking away with one hand what they are offering on the other, and weighting the Gospel with an appalling burden, which, in the view of the fatalism and pantheism of the East it cannot bear.[7]

Such arguments found resonance in powerful theological movements in the nineteenth century that eroded the image of God as sovereign Will and supreme Judge. In the Scottish heartland of English-speaking Calvinism, Thomas Erskine of Linlathen (1788-1870) and John McLeod Campbell (1800-1972) removed the doctrine of the atonement from its connection with forensics and placed it firmly in the arena of personal relationships. For them God functioned as 'Father' rather than 'Judge. In this they were joined, in England, by Frederick Dennison Maurice (1803-1872), and in the United States, by Horace Bushnell (1802-1876). Added to these theological reconceptualizations rediscovery by Biblical scholars of the 'Jesus of history' in the mid-nineteenth century showed that 'the Fatherhood of God' was central to his teaching and that ethical commands centered upon 'justice' and 'brotherhood' as key themes. All these tendencies undermined the older systems where the work of Christ had been chiefly to propitiate the wrath of God. By 1879 the United Presbyterians in Scotland had passed a Declaratory Act profoundly modifying the sense of the Westminster Confession stating:

> While the outward and ordinary means of salvation for those capable of being called by the Word are the ordinances of the Gospel ... it is not required to be held that any who die in infancy are lost, or that God may not extend His grace to any who are without the pale of ordinary means, as may seem good in his sight.[8]

This move was followed by other Scottish Presbyterian bodies, so much so that two historians of the church in Scotland have commented that after three centuries 'the reign of Calvinism had ended'.[9]

That the Congregationalist churches had been on an identical path in this period can be seen from some remarks of David Simon (1830-1909) at the International Congregational Council in London in 1891. Referring to what he called 'the changing evangelical consciousness', Simon said that the positive result of the transformation of theology in the nineteenth century had been to substitute a 'Christocentric system' for a 'theocentric Calvinism'. The latter, he said had had its 'two co-ordinate foci, the Divinity and Atonement of Christ' replaced with the two foci of' the fatherhood of God and the living Personality of Jesus.[10] Such a far-reaching change in Congregationalist thought was to be profoundly consequential for the Church of South India. The Congregationalist missionaries we have already noted as profoundly influential, Slater, Lucas, Farquhar, Jones, Hume and their many colleagues, were all Evangelicals in the Arminian tradition, as were the later stalwarts of Congregationalism who become part of the Church of South India in 1947.

The centrality of faith and experience in Wesleyan evangelicalism
When Israel Selvanayagam came to the United Kingdom for the first time he and his family found themselves welcomed into British Methodism at Wesley House, Cambridge. They were immediately at home because they already shared the same kind of evangelical faith as these Methodists. Inevitably certain Wesleyan themes made themselves explicit, and Israel and I often commented on them in frequent conversations. I highlight two of them. Both derive from John Wesley.

1.   Faith as the universal basis of religion
From the time of his conversion experience in Aldersgate Street in the City of London on May the 24th in 1738, John Wesley would make a distinction between mere belief in Christian doctrines and the assurance of faith. As he wrote in his *Journal* 'I felt my heart strangely warmed. I felt I did trust in Christ, Christ alone for salvation, and an assurance was given me that he had taken away *my* sins even *mine* and saved *me* from the law of sin and death' (emphases in the original). Neither theology nor philosophy, neither asceticism nor devotional practices had brought about a profound sense of a new relationship to God: faith became, as Wesley wrote later, the door to real religion, to a sense of new birth and the real potentiality of holiness.[11]

Some wide-ranging consequences flowed from this fundamental reorientation. Since faith is no longer seen as an intellectual construction, doctrinal formulations become rather secondary. Wesley frequently affirmed this relative unimportance of what he called 'opinion', as for example in *The Character of a Methodist*, where he writes: 'all opinions that do not strike at the root of Christianity we think and let think'; and, going even further, in *A Plain Account of the People Called Methodists* he says 'orthodoxy, or right opinions is at best a slender part of religion, if it can be allowed any part at all'. In a sermon written against the background of Catholic-Protestant divisions in Ireland in 1749 and called simply *Catholic Spirit*, John Wesley asserted that differences of doctrinal opinion were the inevitable consequence of 'the present weakness and shortness of understanding' and 'different men will be of different minds in religion as well as in everyday life'. Consequently a certain agnosticism is called for because 'to be ignorant in many things and mistaken in some is the necessary condition of humanity.' This, says Wesley each person must recognize is his own case. 'He knows in general that he himself is mistaken; although in what particulars he mistakes, he does not, perhaps he cannot know.'

> Every wise man, therefore will allow others the same liberty of thinking which he desires they should allow him, and will no more insist on their embracing his opinions, than he would have them insist on his embracing theirs. He bears with those who differ from him, and only asks him with whom he desire to unite in love that single question, 'Is thy heart right, as my heart is right with thy heart?

Therefore we are not to be divided from one another about opinions, and even less about customs and ways of worship. This does not mean, Wesley insists, a free-for-all where any opinion goes: a person must cleave to what he or she thinks is the most rational and the most scriptural and be steadily fixed in deep religious principle at the same time

> his heart is enlarged towards all mankind, those he knows and those he does not; he embraces with strong and cordial affection neighbours and strangers, friends and enemies. This is catholic universal love. And he who has this is of a catholic spirit. For love alone gives the title to this character: catholic love is a catholic spirit.[12]

It did not take much effort for many of Wesley's spiritual heirs in the multifaith communities of Britain in the 1970s and 1980s to apply the notion of 'catholic universal love' to their new Hindu, Muslims, Sikh or Buddhist neighbours. Nor was it difficult for them to discover that despite outward differences of belief or opinion, they could meet these same neighbours on the level of faith. In this way they took up the great enterprise of interfaith dialogue, so different from the combatative judgmentalism associated with missionary *elenchics*. Here they were following the paths already trodden by Methodists in many other parts of the world.[13]

2.   John Wesley and the faith of other people

In this recognition that 'faith' rather than 'belief' was the point of contact with other men and women they had further support from John Wesley, specifically from Wesley's own recognition of the quality of faith in people other than Christians.

Wesley frequently said that 'true religion, in the very essence of it, is nothing short of holy tempers'. In Sermon 130, *On Living without God;* one of the last he ever wrote (in 1790), indicated forcefully that he believed that 'the merciful God regards the lives and tempers of men more than their ideas. I believe he respects the goodness of the heart and if the heart of a man be filled (by the grace of God and the power of his Spirit) with the humble, gentle patient love of God and man God will not cast him into everlasting fire...'[14] This sentiment matches John Wesley's striking commendation of Muslim faith in his 1788 Sermon 106, *On Faith.* Enterprising a typology of Faith in this sermon that could include Heathenism as well as Materialist and Deist, alongside Jewish and Roman Catholic forms of faith he refers to many individuals who were

> of quite another spirit; being taught of God, by His inward voice, all the essentials of true religion: Yea, so was that Mahometan, an Arabian, who, a century or two ago, wrote the life of Hai Ebn Yokton. The story seems to be feigned; but it contains all the principles of pure religion and undefiled.[15]

This reference to one of the notable stories of Islam (see R. A Nicholson's *The Literary History of the Arabs*) shows Wesley fully able to appreciate the faith of those from outside the Christian traditions.

These extraordinary insights were developed for adherents of Wesleyan evangelicalism in the late twentieth century by the comparative religionist and theoretician of interfaith dialogue Wilfred Cantwell Smith (1916-2000).[16] On his father's side he was the son of a staunch Canadian Presbyterian Elder who refused to join the United Church of Canada in 1925. But his mother was a Methodist who had once wanted to become a missionary. It was she who nurtured him in the values of the Arminian Evangelical tradition. Deep respect for his father led Smith to study in the English Presbyterian Westminster College in Cambridge and to become a lay missionary connected with the Canadian Presbyterian Church in pre-partition India. It was only after the death of his father that Smith felt able to be ordained in the United Church of Canada with its Arminian Evangelical tradition (the Methodist Church of Canada has become part of the UCC in 1925).

Beginning with a series of radio talks in 1962 called then *The Faith of Other Men*,[17] Smith tirelessly sought on the one hand to understand the fact of faith as 'a well-nigh human phenomenon immensely diversified in particular, remarkable persistent in general', and a corollary to this, to ask where God is in all this. When Smith formulated the problem back then, he pleaded that we must take the Christian doctrine of grace more seriously and asked: 'does God let Himself be known only to those to whom He has let Himself be known through Christ? Does God love only those who respond to Him in this tradition?'[18]

Though Smith never to my knowledge made his Arminian Evangelicalism explicit, running through all his writings are the sharp distinction between faith and belief and the equally sure conviction that God has spoken at all times and all places through his inward voice. As he wrote in *The Faith of Other Men* in 1963:

> The God whom we have come to know, so far as we can sense the divine action, reaches out to all persons everywhere, and speaks to all who will listen. In the Church, we listen all too dimly. Yet both within and without the Church, so far as we can see, God does somehow enter human hearts.

Nothing could be more Arminianly Evangelical, or more in tune with John Wesley, than this.

Closing remarks

A close reading of Israel Selvanayagam's major writings shows that he was fully conversant with the works of Wilfred Cantwell Smith as well as with those of Methodist writers who have been his contemporaries. I do most cordially invite readers to look again at Israel's writings to see how Israel's biblical exegesis and theological interpretations alike move in an Arminian Evangelical direction. The British Methodist Church owes him very considerable gratitude for his long period of preaching and teaching in its midst. At the same time we can confidently assert that Israel gained much from his close fellowship with those British Methodists who were committed to interfaith dialogue within the subtle framework of John Wesley's Arminianism.

Endnotes

[1] I have described the path-finding endeavours of these individuals to formulate positive attitudes towards Indian religion in *Justice Courtesy and Love: Theologians and Missionaries Encountering World Religions,* 1846-1914 (1995). Indeed the title of that book comes from Slater: 'we shall never gain the non-Christian world until we treat its religions with justice, courtesy and love'. Israel has since written with great respect about these scholar-pioneers in his *Being Evangelical and Dialogical: Healthy Balance in a Multi-faith Context* (2011).

[2] Advanced and sensitive instruction within the seminary itself was given in all the major world religious traditions. Israel had as his Christian mentors such people as Dayanandan Francis and Paul Sudhakar, and, significantly, he had a Hindu teacher as well, Professor S. Gangadaran, a Saivite devotee who chose to live on the T.T.S. campus.

[3] From the Greek verb *elenchein,* to reprove, to correct, and in particular to refute, see the usage in Matthew 18.15 'if your brother sins against you, go and tell him his fault.' NRSV).

[4] This phrase used by Strange on p.181 in a reference to the doctrine of prevenient grace, but otherwise this alternative evangelical tradition is not noted in the course of his remarks.

[5] Jacobus Arminius (1560-1609), a Leiden professor challenged the deterministic logic of Calvinism from within a Calvinistic framework. Wesley's own central doctrines of prevenient, justifying and sanctifying grace had much more in common with Catholicism than with Calvinism, but he was glad to honour the name of Arminius in the journal he founded in 1778 as *The Arminian Magazine.*

[6] James Morrison had been a minister of the United Succession Church until he was expelled from that body in1841. Two years later he founded the Evangelical Union, the Arminian denomination from which J. N. Farquhar went as a missionary to India.

[7] In *The Philosophy of Missions,* (1882), p. 41.

[8] Quoted in Kenneth Cracknell, *Justice Courtesy and Love* (1995), p. 25.

[9] Andrew L. Drummond and James Bulloch, *The Church in Late Victorian Scotland 1874-1900* (1978), p. 216.

[10] See Cracknell, *Justice Courtesy and Love,* note 140 on p. 301.

[11] A much fuller exposition of Wesley's theology may be found in Kenneth Cracknell and Susan White, *An Introduction to World Methodism,* pp 104.

[12] *Catholic Spirit* is Sermon 39 in *The Works of John Wesley*, (ed. by Albert C.Outler), vol. 2, pp 81-95, from which all these quotations are drawn.

[13] Methodist writers who made this move in the latter part of the twentieth century include Lynn de Silva, Wesley Ariarajah, from Sri Lanka; John B. Cobb, Jr.David Chappell, David Scott, Marston Speight, Diana L. Eck from the USA; Geoffrey Parrinder, Frank Whaling, Eric Lott, Roy Pape, Peter Bishop, Martin Forward, Elizabeth Harris, from the UK.

[14] *The Works of John Wesley* (ed. Outler), vol.4, p 175.

[15] *The Works of John Wesley* (ed. Outler), vol.3, pp 492-3. Outler says this sermon 'comes closer to an explicit statement of his vision of universal saving grace than anything else in the Wesley corpus.' p.491.

[16] I have briefly sketched Smith's life story in the Introduction to *Wilfred Cantwell Smith a Reader*, ed. Kenneth Cracknell (2001). Note there my account of Smith's encounter at Westminster College, Cambridge with Professor H. H. Farmer. Farmer had been at Tambaram in 1938 and had taken issue with Hendrik Kraemer, for whom, in Farmer's view, God's relationship with humanity was not thought of as 'Father love' but on the contrary as 'sovereign will'.

[17] *The Faith of Other Men* was republished with less gender specific language as *Patterns of Faith around the World* in 1998. It was followed by *The Meaning and End of Religion (1963), History and Belief (1977) Faith and Belief (1979)* and *Towards a World Theology* (1981).

[18] As presented in *Patterns of Faith around the World*, pp.144-5.

The Re-Forming Spirit:
The Mission of the Spirit and Reformed Theology[1]

Kirsteen Kim

It was my privilege to work with Israel at the United College of the Ascension, Selly Oak from 2001 to 2006 and to be challenged by his original and insightful approach to theology from an Asian perspective. This paper written, but not published, during those years, is indebted to dialogue with him and is an appeal to Western theologians to treat Asian theologies with greater seriousness and respect.

> Did not Jesus, according to John the Evangelist, say to Nicodemus: 'the Spirit (or wind) blows where it wills; you hear the sound of it. But you do not know where it comes from, or where it is going' (John 3.8)? The same Spirit must have been blowing where it wills in Asia as well as in the rest of the world, enabling men and women there to shape their own histories and empowering them to hope in the midst of suffering, pain, and death. To regain our faith in God as the Lord of history, we have learned to see how our people, empowered by the Spirit, rise from the ashes of destruction again and again from one generation to the next. Our theology of history is no longer a theological discourse on the 'divine economy' of salvation for the world with the Christian church playing the central and privileged role, but an account of the power of the Spirit

---

[1] This paper was part of a longer presentation at the 'Re-Forming Theology' Seminar, West Midlands Synod of the URC, Queen's Foundation, Birmingham, 30 April 2003.

at work in men and women of Asia who build their life and history for themselves and for generations to come.

C.S. Song, Presbyterian Church of Taiwan.[2]

The above quotation from C.S. Song, a leading Asian theologian of the Reformed tradition, displaces the church and sets the mission of the Holy Spirit at the heart of an Asian Christian understanding of history. Song argues that in the Asian context, where Christians are minority communities among the religions of Asia and the church is a recent arrival, there is a need for a radical re-forming of theology in Asia based on the conviction that the unbound Spirit has been at work there through the ages. Such a theology would allow Christians to cooperate with those of other faiths to tackle the overwhelming problems of Asia. Song challenges theologians who describe themselves as 'Reformed' to rise to this challenge.

Taking the challenge of Song as its starting point, this paper will attempt to show how theology of the Holy Spirit in Western tradition – and the Reformed tradition in particular – which has generally taken second place to the theology of the church and the theology of faith, is now coming into its own through a rediscovery of the mission of the Spirit in the world. This will help to explain where Song is coming from and act as a further challenge to re-form our theology of the Spirit in the light of the Spirit's re-forming role in Asian history.

The Holy Spirit in Reformed theology

Although we do not first associate the Reformation with the doctrine of the Holy Spirit, Alasdair Heron argues that the Reformers were well aware that fundamental insights of the Reformation: justification by faith and the authority of Scripture were all necessarily bound up with the Holy Spirit. As far as faith was concerned, Luther revolutionised the Medieval understanding of the historical outworking of God's grace through the church when he reinterpreted justification as the direct intervention of God on behalf of the sinner, mediated and appropriated only by the immediate activity of the Spirit of God. In other words, justification is accompanied by sanctification when God's Word comes

---

[2] C.S. Song, *Third Eye Theology: Theology in Formation in Asian Settings*. Revised edition (Maryknoll, NY: Orbis Books, 1979), 13.

to us through faith, which is itself a gift of the Spirit. For Calvin, the union between Christ and the believer, which lies at the heart of his theology, is brought about by the Spirit. Calvin gave a systematic priority to the activity of the Spirit in the individual Christian life and this was to set the tone for future Protestant thinking about the Spirit. Regarding Scripture, Luther gave a central role to the Spirit in conveying the Living Word through the reading of the Bible. On the one hand, the Bible cannot be understood without the Spirit and, on the other, the Spirit's 'inner witness' is to none other than the Word in Scripture. Calvin's perspective was similar but expressed in terms of his theology of unity: the Spirit that unites us to Christ also enables the reception and appropriation of the Bible. Therefore, in the emerging Protestant theology the Spirit was seen in two ways: as Enlightener, who inspires Scripture and interprets it, and Sanctifier, who brings about faith and empowers the new spiritual life. Later Protestant theology has not always preserved the explicit pneumatology of the Reformers. The emphasis on individual relationship with God has resulted in a tendency towards a trinity of God-Jesus-*my* faith. The reliance on *sola Scriptura* has led to a suspicion of later doctrines, including the Trinity, to a questioning of the personhood of the Holy Spirit, and to Unitarianism. In general where Catholicism focussed the presence and activity of the Spirit in the Church, Protestantism has concentrated the Spirit in the individual heart and life. And Reformed theology focussed this further on the appropriation of God's Word.[3]

In the modern period, there was a reinterpretation of the meaning of 'Spirit' in keeping with the thinking of the times. Heron has traced three different theologies of the Spirit which reflect the differing starting points of the great trio of Kant, Schleiermacher and Hegel, associating the Spirit with the practical, the psychological and the philosophical, respectively. The 'practical' or Kantian understanding sees the Spirit 'as a cipher for the realm of moral and spiritual values' begins with the ideal figure of Jesus Christ as re-constructed in the nineteenth century. 'Spirit' is understood primarily in relation to the human consciousness and the Spirit of God tends to be domesticated in the highest human religio-ethical ideals of the kingdom of God and 'the brotherhood of

---

[3] Heron, *The Holy Spirit*, 99-117.

man'.[4] The 'psychological' approach, which has its origins in the Reformation and in Schleiermacher's work, also owed much to Kierkegaard's reaction against idealism and viewed the Spirit from an interior, pietistic or subjective standpoint that connected the Spirit primarily with the self. This view has its origins in the New Testament experience of the Holy Spirit and its antecedents in the Old Testament prophetic tradition and identifies the Spirit with individual experience or the experience of the community.[5] The 'philosophical' interpretation originated in Hegel's use of the term 'Spirit' (or 'Mind', *Geist*) as the fundamental category of ultimate reality and offered a dynamic understanding which also linked the Spirit with the entire history of the universe. It picks up the Old Testament concept of the Spirit in creation and Greek philosophical ideas of *pneuma*. It related the Spirit to cosmic forces and issued in evolutionary and process theologies.[6] Each of these approaches represented a secularisation of the concept of 'Spirit' by identifying the Spirit's presence and activity irrespective of the boundaries of the church. However they also tended to tie the Spirit to Western civilisation as representing the best ethical standards, the most developed consciousness, and the highest reaches of development.[7]

Karl Barth's study of the doctrines of the Church Fathers led him to rediscover the doctrine of the Trinity and his concern to be christocentric caused him to defend the *filioque*. As in the rest of his theology, in his doctrine of the Trinity too Barth's starting point is the revelation in Jesus Christ. In this light Trinity is necessary because the Word is of God and it has an effect. That is revelation presupposes a Revealer and revealedness. Thus Barth reordered the Trinity as Son-Father-Spirit,

---

[4] The liberal theology of Ritschl, with its focus on love, popularly expressed by Adolf Harnack, is the chief example of this.

[5] As examples of the 'psychological', Wheeler Robinson understood the social or historical experience of the Spirit as a corollary of the individual experience, whereas Schleiermacher identified the Holy Spirit with the spirit of the community.

[6] 'Philosophical' theologies consider the Spirit in terms such as 'Being', 'Existence', 'Historical Dialectic', 'Life', or 'Process'.

[7] Heron, *The Holy Spirit*, 99-116, 137-40; H. Wheeler Robinson, *The Christian Experience of the Holy Spirit* (Digswell Place, Herts: James Nisbet & Co, 1928), 20-21.

representing also the order Good Friday-Easter-Pentecost. But despite his appreciation of the Trinity, Barth's defence of the *filioque* along traditional Western lines meant that the Spirit appeared as a mode of operation of Christ in the world rather than as a distinct person of the Trinity. His pneumatology was caged in by his christology to the extent that 'his achievement is not so much an original exposition of the third article of the creed as a detailed description of the Christian's subjective appropriation of the second article'[8] and he failed to produce a dynamic doctrine of the Spirit.[9] Furthermore, his interpretation of the *filioque* prevented him from appreciating any wider work of the Spirit in creation and so the application of his theology to the other religions, for example, was with decidedly negative effects.[10] In Barth's theology, the only other spirits at work in the world are opposed to the Spirit of God and of Jesus Christ. What is more, the reaction of Barth and other dialectical theologians against liberal optimism and self-righteousness meant that for much of the twentieth century Protestant pneumatology was caught in the perceived dichotomy between the Divine Spirit and the human spirit, the transcendence of the Spirit and the Spirit's immanence,[11] usually indicated by preference for the terms 'Holy Spirit' or simply 'spirit' (with a small 's' or a capital 'S'), respectively.

The Holy Spirit and mission

Apart from its theology of the Spirit, looked at from the perspective of mission history, the Reformation itself was a movement of the Spirit. The mission of the Spirit brought about the inculturation of the gospel in the cultures of northern Europe and liberation for its people from the imperialism of Rome. In the Reformation, the Spirit inspired a new confession of Jesus Christ as Lord and motivated believers to re-form their lives, their church and also their society.

---

[8] Philip J. Rosato, *The Spirit As Lord: The Pneumatology of Karl Barth* (Edinburgh: T & T Clark, 1981), 181,187.

[9] Dietrich Ritschl, 'Historical Development and Implications of the Filioque Controversy' in Vischer, *Spirit of God, Spirit of Christ*, 46-65.

[10] Hendrik Kraemer, *The Christian Message in a Non-Christian World* (London: Edinburgh House for the IMC, 1938).

[11] Jürgen Moltmann, *The Spirit of Life: A Universal Affirmation* (London: SCM Press, 1992; trans. Margaret Kohl), 5-8.

In his 1963-64 Warfield lectures, Hendrikus Berkhof attempted to move Western pneumatology forward beyond sanctification and ecclesiology toward an interest in the Spirit's wider work in the world. Berkhof gave priority to a discussion on the connection between the Holy Spirit and the Christian mission and linked the neglect of the Spirit to the neglect of mission in systematics. He complained that, due to the paucity of reflection on mission, that is its lack of orientation to the world, theology has been 'static and introverted' and missed 'the great movement of the Spirit' that is mission. His proposal that mission was the Spirit's primary work led Berkhof to broaden the scope of his study to include the Spirit in relation to creation, liberation and consummation.[12] However, without invalidating his perception of a close relationship between missiology and pneumatology, Heron points out that Berkhof, following the direction set by Barth, reduces the Spirit to 'the name of the exalted Christ acting in the world'.[13] Berkhof therefore fails to develop a true creation theology of the Spirit. As a result of this, his perception of the movement of the Spirit – that is of Christian mission – is limited to Christian activity in other parts of the world.

A similar phenomenon is apparent in the work of the Dutch Reformed missiologist, David Bosch, whose book *Transforming Mission* has become the dominant text book for mission studies. As in Barth, the Spirit is associated with Pentecost and, following Berkhof, with the church's mission which began then. Bosch develops the relationship of the Spirit and mission showing how the Spirit initiates mission, guides mission and empowers it.[14] Though Bosch's understanding of mission, and therefore of the Spirit's work in the world, is broader than Berkhof's, encompassing the whole witness of the local church in six continents, his theology of the Spirit is restricted by a lack of attention to the Old Testament and therefore to creation. This is related, in my opinion, to a failure to engage with African theologians and a restriction of the trajectory of God's work in history to the Christian

---

[12] Hendrikus Berkhof, *The Doctrine of the Holy Spirit: The Annie Kinkead Warfield Lectures 1963-64* (London: The Epworth Press, 1965), 30-41, 94-108.

[13] See Heron, *The Holy Spirit*, 167-70, 126-27.

[14] David J. Bosch, *Transforming Mission: Paradigm Shifts in Theology of Mission* (Maryknoll, NY: Orbis Books, 1991), 113-4.

– and predominantly Western – story.[15] Bosch's interest in the Spirit's work is directed toward the world, but its vision of the mission of the Spirit in the world is tied to Christian activity.

In his volume on pneumatology, *The Spirit of Life: A Universal Affirmation*, Jürgen Moltmann took up Orthodox concerns about Western pneumatology being 'christomonistic' and failing to recognise the economy of the Spirit as distinct from yet working together with the economy of the Son. After due consideration, he rejected the *filioque* as 'superfluous' and stressed the 'mutual relationship' of Word and Spirit, Son and Breath, in order to develop a trinitarian pneumatology. Moltmann was motivated to overcome the problem that Berkhof and Heron identified as central for Protestant pneumatology: the association of the Spirit with either divine revelation or with personal experience but not both. This was a corollary of the divide between 'theology from above' and 'theology from below' introduced by Barth and other dialectical theologians. Moltmann declared this to be a false antithesis and stressed the personhood of the Spirit as the one who connects the two, bringing about the experience of revelation and relating experience to revelation.

Moltmann argues that, logically, the restriction of 'the fellowship of the Holy Spirit' to the church 'makes it impossible for the church to communicate its experience of the Spirit to the world'.[16] Furthermore, unless the Spirit is recognised outside the church, says Moltmann, the church cannot learn and so he believed the ecumenical movement had to be helped to 'rediscover the immanence of the Creator in the creation'.[17] Moltmann drew ecumenical attention to the mission of the Spirit which preceded the incarnation and the possibility that the work of the Son could be seen as taking place within this, as opposed to the work of the Spirit being viewed as entirely within the mission of the Son. That is, he advocated a spirit christology to complement the more traditional logos christology. He presupposed that 'the redeeming

---

[15] Kirsteen Kim, 'Post-Modern Mission: A Paradigm Shift in David Bosch's Theology of Mission?', *International Review of Mission* 89/353 (Apr 2000), 172-79.

[16] Moltmann, *The Spirit of Life*, 8.

[17] Jürgen Moltmann, 'The Scope of Renewal in the Spirit' in Emilio Castro (comp.), *To the Wind of God's Spirit: Reflections on the Canberra Theme* (Geneva: WCC, 1990), 31-39.

Spirit of Christ and the creative and life-giving Spirit of God are one and the same'. This led him to recognise a wider field of the Spirit's action outside the church, rediscovering the Spirit's cosmic breadth. Moltmann attributed his theology of the immanence of God's spirit in all creatures to Calvin and therefore saw it as one of the focal points of Reformed theology. This makes it – like the church – a theology which is reformed and yet always reforming, particularly in the sense that it concerns the re-formation of the world, and no area of life is outside its scope.[18] Moltmann insists that appreciating the Spirit in all creatures is fully compatible with the close relationship characteristic of Reformed theology between Word and Spirit: 'for where the Word is, there the Spirit is too – otherwise the Word is not the Word of God; and where the Spirit is, the Spirit shines from the Word and illumines the understanding of faith – otherwise it is not God's Spirit'.[19]

The worldwide church and the mission of the Spirit

'The future of Reformed theology' was a subject much under discussion in the closing years of the twentieth century. The volume edited by David Willis and Michael Welker on this subject rightly recognises that the future may well lie with churches outside the historical heartlands of Europe and even North America.[20] Reformed theologians are nowadays just as likely to come from Africa, Asia or Latin America. They are not just Swiss and Scottish, they may be Taiwanese like Song, or another part of Asia, or from almost any other part of the globe. In attempting to do theology Reformed theologians from Asia, for example, are caught in an impossible situation vis-à-vis the still dominant Western tradition. If they draw on their indigenous traditions to re-form theology, they are accused of syncretism. If, on the other hand, they read and reinterpret Calvin and Barth, they are accused of copying the West. Those theologians who explicitly utilise Asian spirituality in their theology are appreciated in the West for their exoticism but their theology is not invested with scholarly weight. It goes under the category of 'Third World Theology', 'Non-Western

---

[18] Moltmann, '*Theologia Reformata et Semper Reformanda*' in David Willis & Michael Welker (eds.), *Toward the Future of Reformed Theology: Tasks, Topics, Traditions* (Cambridge: Wm B. Eerdmans, 1999), 120-35.

[19] Moltmann, *The Spirit of Life*, 231.

[20] Willis & Welker, *Towards the Future of Reformed Theology*.

theology' or 'world Christianity' rather than theology proper. Whereas those who quote the Reformers and use the language of modern Korea are found to be lacking in originality and therefore of marginal interest to Western scholarship. Somehow a book on Calvin by an Asian scholar is regarded as necessarily less authoritative than one by a German. No wonder Asian theologians largely do their own thing and carry on regardless. There is a huge market for theology books in Asia, not only in English but in different Asian languages. What is needed is a more level playing field so that there can be a global conversation between theologians from different cultures and contexts. It is the nature of the Holy Spirit, who blows where she wills, to inspire and facilitate such developments.[21]

As far as Asian Christian theologians like C.S. Song are concerned, the weakness of most Western pneumatology, including Moltmann's, lies in his emphasis on 'the history of the Spirit' and his interpretation of this history as closely tied to the history of the church, particularly in its Western form. Moltmann recognises that John's portrayal of the Spirit as Paraclete dispenses with salvation-historical language, and he rightly argues that because the Spirit is the Spirit of Christ, there is necessarily a historical perspective.[22] However the question is with whose history is the Spirit associated, or where in the world in history has the Spirit been at work? Since creation, can we say that the Spirit been more active in Europe than in Asia? Just because modern Asian churches stepped into the apostolic succession only recently, does this mean they are any less endowed with the Spirit?

Asian challenges to Western pneumatology

Asian challenges to Western pneumatology hinge on this question of history. From the perspective of modern Europe, it possible to see the church as playing a central and decisive role in history. It is possible to say that the best in our culture and history is due to the influence of the Christian faith and Christian institutions. When the pre-Christian era is so very distant in our history, it is easy to forget that Christianity

---

[21] Kirsteen Kim, *The Holy Spirit in the World: A Global Conversation* (Maryknoll, NY: Orbis Books, 2007).

[22] Jürgen Moltmann, *The Church in the Power of the Spirit: A Contribution to Messianic Ecclesiology* (London: SCM Press, 1977; trans. Margaret Kohl), 33-37.

once came to us from West Asia. In our more optimistic moments we can even identify the history of the Spirit with our own history – as the liberal theology of the imperial age tended to do. For most of the Christians in Asia, however, history appears very differently. The Asian story is different. It is not possible to ascribe the best of most Asian cultures directly to the revelation of Jesus Christ. On the whole Asians cannot look back and say that obedience to the Word of God in Christ is responsible for moral progress or social transformation. (Though in many recent instances there are good arguments that this is an important factor.) Asians must tell a different story. The Christian church is not or has not been centre-stage in Asian history. If present at all it has been on the whole marginal to society and Christians have been a minority. What is more, in the colonial period, the church played an ambiguous role, sometimes supporting and sometimes working against the aspirations of Asian peoples for the liberation that the Spirit brings.

What happened in these societies before Christianity? Did the Creator Spirit pass Asia by? Was Spirit of truth and love absent from Asian thought and Asian society? In the light of the revelation that the Spirit of God is the Spirit of Jesus Christ, Asian theologians can look back over their history and see signs of the Spirit at work. The Spirit inspires not only the interpretation of the Bible but also the reinterpretation of history from a Christian point of view. For Asian theologians the Spirit of Christ is the Lord of history and defines history. Whereas in the Western church it has often appeared to be the other way round: the history of the church has defined the activity of the Spirit and confined it within Christendom. From an Asian historical perspective, the Spirit must be at work within cultures and religions that are very different. It is necessary for Asian Christians to affirm this if they are to be proud of their identity as Asians.

This is why dialogue has been a particular contribution of Asian theologians to international discussion. The origins of the Conciliar theology of dialogue lie in the experience of Indian theologians, and particularly in that of the late Dr Stanley Samartha, the first director of the WCC sub-unit for dialogue, who was Indian. India has provided a 'laboratory' for Western study of religions and their inter-relationship. Furthermore the Indian constitutional model of secularism as equal respect for all religions has provided the social framework for dialogue.

The theological basis for the World Council of Churches' guidelines for dialogue also owes much to Indian understanding of the God as the Universal Spirit. In arguing for dialogue as the way forward in interreligious relations, Samartha repeatedly drew attention to Jesus' saying that 'the Spirit will lead into all Truth' (John 16.13) as the pneumatological foundation for mission, meaning that in dialogue the Spirit could be speaking through any of the partners and not only through the Christian party.[23]

Does a creation theology of the Spirit from an Asian perspective mean that the Holy Spirit functions simply to endorse all things Asian as good? (And often conversely to declare all things Western bad?) It may sometimes appear so in the rarefied atmosphere of international theological debate but in the living realities of Asia it is clear that all is not well. In many respects the Christian churches of Asia are struggling against their culture and religions, as well as against economic exploitation and political oppression from within and without. A theology of dialogue in Asia does not mean being nice to one another, it means working for the salvation of our neighbours as well as ourselves and this involves challenging and confronting evil and injustice in the name of Christ. With this in mind, Israel Selvanayagam insists, dialogue cannot and should not be separated from evangelism. The Christian message is distinctive and different from that of any other faith.[24] In pneumatological terms, the Spirit of Christ is not the Spirit of Brahma, Vishnu or Siva. But the Spirit who descended and remained on Jesus Christ was not unknown to the Asians who beheld Jesus' baptism (John 1:29-34).

In his contribution to 'the future of Reformed theology', C.S. Song argues (against Wilfred Cantwell Smith) that it is impossible to conceive of a general or universal theology of religions (or of pluralism) but only of a Christian theology or a Buddhist one or a Hindu one.[25] In this respect some Christian scholars of religious pluralism have arrived

---

[23] S.J. Samartha, *Courage for Dialogue: Ecumenical Issues in Inter-Religious Relationships* (Geneva: WCC 1981).

[24] Israel Selvanayagam, *A Dialogue on Dialogue: Reflections on InterFaith Encounters* (Madras: CLS, 1995).

[25] C.S. Song, 'Christian Theology: Toward an Asian Reconstruction' in Willis & Welker, *Toward the Future of Reformed Theology*, 58-74.

at a theology that is closer to a Brahminic Hindu model than to an Indian Christian one. Hindu philosophy understands many religious paths to the same ultimate reality whereas most Indian Christian theologians of dialogue prefer to leave the question of ultimate reality on one side and discuss how the paths can run together at this point on the way. Since in India Christians, Hindus, Muslims and Sikhs must live together in this world the focus of dialogue is on shared values and hopes for today, on living together in the here and now. This does not amount to endorsing one another's religious beliefs; though neighbourliness implies we take an interest in those. The majority of Indian Christians are from out-caste backgrounds and for centuries have been excluded from mainstream society and political power by traditional Hindu beliefs about *karma* and reincarnation. They have found in Christianity a release from their predicament and are not about to allow themselves to be reincorporated into a Hindu social order.

An Asian Christian re-reading of history begins by discerning the signs of the Spirit, recognising implicitly or explicitly that there are other spirits at work in the world. It may be that the presence and activity of the Spirit in Asia can be discerned not only in the confessing Christian community but also where there is Christ-likeness in terms of lives that display the fruit of the Spirit and where people are empowered to speak out, teach, lead, heal, and exercise the gifts of the Spirit in a loving way. If, as is increasingly the case, mission is understood as discerning where the Spirit is at work and joining in, then discernment becomes the crux and starting point of any mission enterprise.[26] Though the Creator Spirit that Christians believe was focused in Jesus Christ can be discerned from a Christian perspective as present and active within Asian tradition and society over history, the Spirit also comes to Asia from outside as she speaks through the Word of God revealed in the Bible. Reformed theology in Asia will always draw attention to this dimension. Although in its origins, the Bible is an Asian book, the recent growth of the church in Asia has been due to the Word carried by missionaries from the West. The Christian missionary movement from the West has also had a wide

---

[26] Kirsteen Kim, *Joining in with the Spirit: Connecting World Church and Local Mission* (London: Epworth-SCM, 2009).

and positive impact on many Asian societies and cultures, as Asian theologians and political leaders have testified. In this way, and also by the faithful preaching of the Word of Asian pastors and theologians, the Spirit is experienced in Asia not only as affirming Asianness but also as challenging it. The Spirit speaks through the Word with a prophetic voice converting hearts and lives.

The Christian Gospel has been received by Asian Christians anew in recent centuries with great thankfulness. They may be more conscious than Europeans of a time before they knew the good news of Jesus Christ and before they experienced the Spirit in fullness. It was this sense of gratitude that motivated the early Christians to share the good news.[27] Asian Christians are motivated by the same Spirit of thanksgiving to mission to their own society and across cultural and geographical boundaries. However, due to the different historical circumstances in which the gospel is received, Asian theologies of mission may differ profoundly from Western ones. David Bosch's book points to a single emerging ecumenical paradigm, but what we may find is a number of distinct paradigms of mission arising from different contexts. Song argues that contemporary Asia demands a new re-formation in theology that deals with Asian issues and issues from Asian experience.

> Such a time calls for a self-understanding of the church that is different from the past. Is this not why the Reformation proved to be a revolutionary event in the history of Christianity? A season such as this challenges Christians to reflect critically on the faith they have inherited from their forebears. Is this not what the Reformers in the sixteenth century set out to do? And the era in which we find ourselves demands that Christian theologians be engaged in reshaping and reconstructing Christian theology that is open to what God is doing in the world, not of yesterday but of today. Is this not the way *Reformed* theologians should go about their theological task?
>
> C.S. Song[28]

Asian theologians challenge Western theologians not to impose their norms on others. C.S. Song expects that theologians of the Reformed tradition are best equipped to re-form theology in Asia. And if

---

[27] Bosch, *Transforming Mission*, 138-39.

[28] C.S. Song, 'Christian Theology: Toward an Asian Reconstruction' in Willis & Welker, *Toward the Future of Reformed Theology*, 58-59.

Reformed theology is truly always reforming, we can expect further challenges to traditional theologies in the coming years. The Re-forming Spirit will continue to broaden our horizons and open our eyes to the Spirit's presence and activity in unexpected places. When we get to where the Spirit wants us to be, we may find Asians were there before us.

The Theological Underpinnings of Interfaith Relations Promoted by Peace Trust Kanyakumari*

Gnana Robinson

1. Inter-faith Relationships and Dialogue in Pre-independent India

The Christian Approach to people of other Faiths was largely a one way traffic-monologue in pre-independent India. The Christians living in India under colonial rule, although a minority of 2.5% to 3.00%, had been living with a majority complex, because of the patronage of the British colonial rulers, who were known to represent a Christian nation. The Christian missionary-approach in those days had often been aggressive in nature. The evangelical exhortations of missionaries and church leaders to win *Bharat* (India) for Christ and to build up "the Kingdom of Christ" were understood politically. Any attempt on the part of Christians to study Indian religions was discouraged by Mission Boards. Thus, Bartholomew Zieganbalg, the first Protestant Missionary in India, was eager to learn Hinduism in some depth so that he could preach the Gospel meaningfully to the Hindus. He wrote to his mission board in Halle in Germany seeking their permission to study Hinduism. After long waiting, we are told, Zieganbalg got a reply saying that he was sent to India not to learn of Hinduism, but to destroy Hinduism. Walbert Buehlmann, a German scholar, describes this general attitude of Christianity towards other religions in those days as follows:

Christianity challenged world religions. It came out with the claim to be the only true religion and with the goal of destroying other religions totally.[1]

The following quotation from the Congress on World Mission at Chicago in 1960 reflects this general attitude:

In the years since the war, more than one billion souls have passed into eternity and more than half of these went to the torment of hell fire without even hearing of Jesus Christ, who He was, or why He died on the cross of Calvary.[2]

Once the decolonization process started, this favored position of Christians in India changed. The hitherto humiliated and oppressed non-Christian natives began to assert the identities of their Faiths/ Religions. Native shrines and temples, some of them for long forgotten and neglected, have been renovated or rebuilt. Scriptures that were lying unopened for years were dusted, studied and taught with renewed interest. Every native religion has been asserting its identity over against the identity of Christianity, and making almost every claim that Christianity has been making in the past.

This changed historical context demanded a fresh missionary approach. While the conservative missionary agencies were not in a mood to change their "one way traffic" traditional missionary approach, the ecumenically minded mission agencies tried to find new ways to meet people of other Faiths, and "inter-religious dialogue" was one of their new approaches.

"What is the goal of inter-faith dialogue?"
This was a basic question raised both by Christians and non-Christians. "Conversion of the non-Christian partner" was the answer of many. Because of this, many of the non-Christian partners were suspicious and sceptical, whenever Christians spoke of inter-faith dialogue. They charged the Christians of having a hidden agenda of conversion to Christianity. While many of them had great regard for the life and teachings of Jesus Christ, some even paying homage to him as one of the *avatars* (incarnations) in Hindu Faith, most of them were against proselytization (conversion).

Another emerging trend in the conflict-ridden Indian context we can identify is for minority groups such as Muslims, Christians and Communists, to be tempted to align together to fight against their alleged common enemy, the Hindus. Such a move, we have to point out, is unbecoming of our major Faiths such as Islam, which advocates Allah's mercy to all, and Christianity, which preaches God's love and forgiveness to enemies. Also from a rational point of view such a move will be suicidal for the minorities in India, because any immoral militant move taken by minority groups will only help the militant Hindus to legitimize the immoral militant activities of the majority Hindu group. It was in this context that Peace Trust Kanyakumari started its interfaith activities by promoting harmony among people of all Faiths and working together for peace with justice.

2. Peace Trust's Inter-faith Initiatives have a threefold Theological Underpinning

a. *Theological Underpinning: The First Step for Clearing Mistrust and Suspicion in a Multi religious and Multicultural Community*

By "theological underpinning" we mean our understanding of God on which our relationship with our fellow humans and the creation rests. Peace Trust Kanyakumari saw the importance of laying a solid theological foundation for people of different Faiths to be free from their mistrust and suspicion.

> As the first step towards this, we called for a National Consultation on **"The Uniqueness of Religions and their Relatedness to other Faiths"** held for four days from 23-26 July 1986. Eminent leaders such as Swami Agnivesh, Evangelist Paul Sudhakar, Haji Ahmed Khan. Bishop C. Selvamony, Dr. Gnana Robinson,etc. participated in this consultation. The consultation came out with an agreed common statement known as **Kanyakumari Declaration I.**

The first part, *the Matters of Belief,* dealt with the doctrinal basis on which Peace Trust has been carrying out its inter-faith relationships and dialogue all these twenty-six years. This is what the declaration says:

> "We affirm that God is one. He is the Creator of the Universe and that God is Love, Justice and Truth, and this God has been concerned about all people. Therefore, it is not right to assume that any people have been left without the guidance and care of God."

It was also agreed that all religions affirm that the only way open for the humans is to be sustained by God through total surrender to God's perfect will. They are thereby enabled to reflect on the qualities of Love, Justice and Truth in their human relationships and actions.

All were humble enough to admit that the history of each religious tradition has suffered in the past because of distorted and partial perceptions of Truth, namely God. Sometimes certain blatant contradictions, which negated and refuted the original insights and values, had been allowed to dominate the thinking of religious people and thus injustice and inequality began to be seen as ordered by God's will.

It was also unanimously affirmed "that God is against accumulation of wealth in the hands of a few and that a just distribution of wealth, resources and opportunities is mandatory" on God's people.

Secondly, on matters regarding *Inter-faith Relationships* the following seven steps were accepted:

i. Accept people of other faiths also as children of God and respect their particular convictions.

ii. Promote better understanding at all levels between people of different faiths. This may be done by encouraging participation in each other's festivals and in each other's worships.

iii. Refrain from pressurizing others to change their religious allegiance by exploiting situations of predicament and weakness, or by capitalizing on fear or by inducements.

iv. Refrain from abusing and misusing the Minority rights granted under the Constitution of India.

v. Desist from involving religion in situations of conflict between individuals or groups.

vi. Refrain from spreading rumors and to resist the temptation to believe that the people of other Faiths to be in the wrong with out caring to verify the truth.

vii. Seek reconciliation rather than aggravating situations of communal tension.

Thirdly, on *Matters of Joint Action* for Social Change, all are exhorted to come together to work for the welfare of all focusing their attention on the following four fronts:

First in the economic front to fight against the unequal distribution of wealth, **secondly** in the social front to fight against injustice at all levels—child labor, bonded-labor, disparity between men and women, unemployment, illiteracy, etc., **thirdly,** to reduce defence expenditure in favor of improving the living conditions of the poor in the country, and **fourthly,** to bring pressure to bear upon all those involved in the proliferation of nuclear armament so that a total ban of nuclear weapons may be effected.

This consultation helped people of other Faiths to remove from their minds the suspicion and fear of Peace Trust Kanyakumari having a hidden agenda in its call for communal harmony and inter-faith co-operation. This was evident from the change of attitude of one of the participants, Mr. K. Chandrasekharan Pillai, a leading Advocate in the district and a hard core Hindu under the influence of the conservative Hindu movement known as *Rashtriya Swayam Sevaksangh (R.S.S.)*, which is behind the *Hindutva* movement in India.[3] He hailed the Kanyakumari Declaration as a great step-forward in inter-faith relationship, and immediately started a support organization by name **"Religious Amity Service Association" (RASA)** in Kanyakumari in December, 1986, having him as its president, "giving ample representation to the various religions for the specific purpose of propagating and implementing the Kanyakumari Declaration".

b.   *Christological Underpinning*

Peace Trust being a Christian initiative, we wanted to be clear for ourselves as well as for our fellow Christians as to the Christological basis on which we enter into inter-faith relationships and dialogue. For this purpose we called a meeting in1986 at Peace Trust Kanyakumari. Bishops, clergy and laypersons participated in this consultation with great interest.

It was significant that the Most Revd. Dr. I Jesudhasan, the then Moderator of the Church of South India and the Bishop of the South Kerala Diocese of the C.S.I. stayed throughout and gave leadership to the Consultation. The Rt. Rev. C. Selvamony, the former Bishop of the Kanyakumari Diocese, assisted us as the Co-ordinator of our programs. After four days of serious deliberations, the group was able to come out with an agreement on vital issues of Christian Faith and prepared a statement which is known as **Kanyakumari Declaration II**. The salient features of this Declaration are given below:

i. India being a multi-religious country, Christian Communication must take place only in a spirit of Openness.

ii. This Spirit of Openness compels us to recognize that people who adhere to other Faiths also are people of God and in their own ways are being used by God in carrying out God's ultimate purpose.

iii. This recognition of other Faiths, however, does not rule out the distinctiveness of every Faith nor their distinctive insights, self-understanding, sacraments, traditions, value perceptions and cultural modes of expressions. Therefore there is a great deal of opportunity for mutual enrichment as well as for mutual challenge.

iv. Within the Bible itself and in the subsequent Church history, it was observed, a variety of Christologies have emerged. This variety arose as a result of attempts to present Christ in a meaningful way in different cultural, religious, socio-economic and political contexts.

v. It was noted, in the present day, except for the religious perception that Christ as the mediator between God and the believers, all other aspects have been lost sight of, for we have failed to contextualize Christ. Nevertheless several attempts at understanding the significance of Christ have been made by a few people and groups.

In this respect the Consultation looked at three different models of indigenous Christology emerging, namely, Reception Model, Re-interpretation Model and the Hindu Model:

a. **Reception Model:** In this model the *Advaita* categories (Non-dual philosophical system) are accepted and used as they are understood by Hindus, e.*g.*: The interpretation of Jesus' words "I and my Father are One" in the light of the Hindu saying *"Aham Brahmasmi"*, meaning " I am Brahman". This paves the way to overcome the age-long rigid distinction maintained between divinity and humanity.

b. **Reinterpretation Model:** In this Model Advaita categories are reinterpreted to suit Christian understanding of God as a personal Being. For example, the concept of Trinity is interpreted with the help of the Hindu concept of God as *Sat-cit-ananda* , meaning "Being - awareness- bliss", the threefold qualities of the all inclusive ultimate reality.

c. **Hindu Model:** In this Model Hindu scholars' attempts to understand Christ are taken note of. Many faithful Hindu believers have no difficulty in accepting Jesus as one of the many *Avatars* in their Hindu Faith. It is a common scene in the homes and business centers of Hindus a portrait of Jesus hanging along with the portraits of other Hindu deities with equal floral and incense homage done. There have also been attempts to work out Christologies on the basis of different lines of thought revealed in Hindu scriptures such as *Saiva Siddhanta,* a Saivite scripture in Tamil.

The models mentioned here are mere pointers. Still more in-depth studies in Hindu scriptures have to be done to present Christ to Hindu intellectuals.

In its attempt to formulate a comprehensive Christology, Peace Trust Kanyakumari affirmed categorically the belief that in and through the life, death and resurrection of Jesus, God is involved in human history in the most decisive and normative way, expressing God's two-fold specific purpose for human history with its religious dimension and its secular dimension.

> "The religious perception would need to be conceptualized and interpreted using available indigenous, philosophical categories. We need to have no fear regarding this…. In no other way could we speak meaningfully with people who think using these categories."[4]

Members felt that the secular dimension of the divine purpose has been the most neglected in Christian mission, and hence resolved to point out the imperatives before us in this regard. The Gospels give us ample guidance to show that Jesus through his life, death and resurrection did away with the separation of the sacred and the secular, faith and politics, male-chauvinism, religious exclusion, etc. His radical understanding of the Sabbath (e.g.: Mark 2:27; 3:4), his treatment of men and women as equals, his consistent concern for the poor and his uncompromising stand against *Mammon,* the idol of worldly riches, his friendship with the so called sinners and the outcasts, of the religious elites are evidences enough to show the holistic mission of Jesus. Thus, the Declaration affirms,

> "The sinful, exploitative and oppressive ways are decisively reversed in and through Jesus. This event of renunciation of the self in the service of others and the resultant conviction that this event has initiated the process of bringing into fruition a new humanity marked with justice, love, peace and harmony, is the central core of the Christian faith."[5]

It has therefore been Peace Trust's firm belief,

> "That the Church has been and will continue to be an important instrument of change. It has to play an important role in communicating the counter-culture values of the New Humanity manifested in Jesus."[6]

These counter-culture values have to do primarily with inequality and injustice:

> "Therefore, there is an urgent need for the Church to rediscover its true identity as the Body of the One who was put to death because of his concern for justice and equality. The same fate awaits all those who find their identity in the crucified one."[7]

All those who participated in the Consultation were convinced that the above declaration "sets a definite direction" for people to act, though it is not exhaustive or complete. All believers in Christ are therefore urged to examine carefully "whether the direction set forth is in accordance with the portrayal of Jesus in the Bible, and if so convinced, then to seek ways and means of setting the course for the Church in that direction.."[8] Towards this the following six recommendations are made:

i. All member of the Church are urged to make a systematic study of the life and teachings of Jesus and the meaning and the significance of his death and resurrection

ii. To make a serious study of the society analyzing its socio-economic, socio-political and socio-cultural forces at work.

iii. To study the scriptures of the religions of our neighbors seriously, because this will help us to understand our neighbors better and enable us to see the common traits among all religions, the distinctiveness of the Christian Faith and its relationship to people of other Faiths.

iv. The Synods and the Leaders of churches are urged to give top priority to the preparation and distribution of study materials useful for inter-faith relation and dialogue.

v. To start dialogue groups with a view to engaging in common action for social change.

vi. To make the best use of Theological Institutions and Centers like Peace Trust Kanyakumari to equip the churches in initiating interfaith studies leading to joint programs of action for social change with justice and equity.

Following these two major ground-breaking consultations with their declarations, Peace Trust Kanyakumari carried out a number of programs following the action-reflection model. Some of these action programs are mentioned below.

c. *Humanistic Theological Underpinning*

I have always understood "People of God" in the wider ecumenical perspective inclusive of all the inhabitants of this *Oikoumene*, the Household of God. As such, as a theological educator for more than forty years, I have always been talking about the **"Trifrontal Theological Education"**, the first two fronts being the Ordinands for Ministry in theological institutions, and the laity, the members of the Christian Community, and the third front being the people of God outside the ecclesiastical community, the members of the wider-*oikoumene*, people belonging to other Faiths or no Faith[9] A holistic theological education should cater to the people of God in all these three fronts.

Biblical Theology, as well as Christology, affirms that God is at work among these people of the third front as well. Since, according to our Christian faith, there is no God other than the only God revealed in Jesus, I firmly believe, all the prayers and supplications offered by these people outside the church, to whichever name the prayers are addressed, reach this only true God revealed in Jesus, as affirmed by the experience of the Italian Cohort Cornelius (see Acts 10:4). As such the experiences of such people in the wider *oikoumene* become a source for our study of God's purpose and God's activities among people of other Faiths. Such a study of God I call the "Humanistic Theology".[10]

Gandhiji, Vinoba Bhave, Jeyaprakash Narayanan, A.P.J. Abdul Kalam and Anna Hazare at the national level and P. Kamaraj, E.V.R. Periyar. C.N. Annadurai and P. Kakkan at the Tamil Nadu level, are a few among the Indian leaders who have been carrying out the life-giving ministry initiated by Jesus Christ, who come under the category of people about whom Jesus said, "He that is not against us is for us" (Mark 9:40). These are indeed people who are with Jesus, but not "Christians", members in the role of any church. An earnest study of the experiences of such leaders will help us to formulate a Humanistic Theology.

What I mean by Humanistic Theology is a reflection on God from the experiences of humans, the children of God, because Jesus saw **"the holistic welfare of the humans"** as the only criterion for his ministry and mission (see Mark 2:27; 3:1-4). If the Good Shepherd, who leaves behind the 99 sheep in the fold and goes after the one lost sheep can be an image of God (Luke 15:3-7), and if the Father, who runs toward and embraces the returning prodigal son, who squandered the father's wealth and ruined his life, can be another image of God (Luke 15:11-13), can this God of Life revealed in Jesus Christ be indifferent to and unconcerned about God's children who are outside the religion called "Christianity"?

My fellow-Christians, who are members of the religion Christianity, may ask me "Those who are outside Christianity are people who have not accepted Jesus Christ as Lord and Saviour. How can they be "with Christ" in their life and witness? They may further point out that the person who cast out the evil spirit in Luke 9:50 did so **"in the name of Christ"**. But the persons we have mentioned above, Gandhiji, Kamaraj and others, have not done anything in the name of Christ.

To those friends, who raise such questions, I wish to point out a couple of facts on the basis of the Bible. The revelation the author of John's Gospel in the Bible had is that Jesus Christ is "the word of God which was in the beginning" (John 1:14). **The Word of God** that is from the beginning is the Medium of Revelation that reveals God's will to the world (see Isaiah 55:11). As St. Paul mentions in Romans 1:20, God, the Word, has been from the beginning revealing God's will to humanity through God's creation. That even after the earthly time of Christ, God has been speaking to people, who have not heard about

Jesus Christ, through God's Spirit, is evident from the story of Cornelius mentioned above (Acts 10: 1ff).

Jesus Christ described those who were with him as "the salt of the earth" (Mathew 5:13). The working of the salt is not visible to physical eyes, but salt is capable of making its impact on objects with which it comes into contact. Likewise the words of Jesus, which his faithful followers take with, are capable of making their impact on people among whom these followers live and work. Jesus made it clear that not all those who make verbal confessions without corresponding actions, but only those who work in accordance with the will of God, though with no verbal confession, will find their way into the reign of God:

> "Not everyone who says to me, 'Lord, Lord', shall enter the Kingdom of heaven, But he who does the will of my Father Who is in heaven" (Matthew 7:21).

All those who thus fulfill God's will in this world, belong to the family of Jesus (Matthew 12:50).

3.   Joint Inter-faith Actions

From its inception in 1986, Peace Trust Kanyakumari has been promoting joint interfaith actions along with the promotion of inter-faith relations and studies. Joint actions for the common welfare of humanity can foster and strengthen inter-faith relations and studies. Space does not permit us to list down all its activities for the last 26 years. Still I will mention a few to show Peace Trust's multifaceted activities.

Inter-faith Seminars, Consultations and Study Programs

For the purpose of educating the rural village population on the importance of the theological maxim "One God, one Human Family", Peace Trust Kanyakumari organized **Inter-faith Celebration of Important Religious Festivals** such as *Deepavali* (Festival of Light) of the Hindus, *Ramzan* (Festival of Sharing) of the Muslims and the Christmas (Festival of Salvation /Redemption of life) of Christians – all on the same stage in one multi-religious village almost every year. Believers of every religion interpreted the meanings of their respective Faiths in the form of dances, songs and skits. Scholars of different Faiths explained through their lectures how the core message of their festival contributed to the common welfare of all people crossing the boundaries of religion. All these joint celebrations took place in a joyful atmosphere, where people of different religions could experience and feel their common humanity.

Under its action motto **"Unite to Serve"**, Peace Trust Kanyakumari has all along been involved in a number of joint action programs. We may briefly mention the following:

1.   **Seminar on "Religion and Human Solidarity" in 1990**
Peace Trust Kanyakumari organized a Seminar on "Religion and Human Solidarity". In this Seminar papers on the theme were presented by leaders from the three major religions in the region. These papers were published as a booklet. The cover design of this booklet — a busy road is blocked by a fallen tree, and the people on the road are put to great difficulty. Seeing this, a group of people — Hindus, Muslims and Christians – come forward and jointly roll that hurdle (tree) out of the way. This design illustrates powerfully what inter-faith solidarity means.[11]

2.   **Solidarity with the suffering people in Sri Lanka**

3.   **A Year Long Justice and Peace Awareness Campaign in 1986**

4.   **A year long campaign against the menace of dowry**

5.   **A Year long Campaign Against the Adverse effects of Tourism in India**

6.   **An action oriented Study on the pattern of Land-holding and the plight of landless agricultural laborers in India.**

7.   **A Path Finding National Consultation on Communal Harmony on August 25-28, 2000.**

8.   **Nationwide Campaign for Communal Harmony from 2001-2006 – covering almost all the Provinces of India. [12]**

9.   **Integrated Rehabilitation for the Victims of Tsunami (2004-2008).**

Following the Great Tsunami of December 26, 2004, Peace Trust in partnership with the Global Ministries in Cleveland in USA and some more overseas partners was involved in a program of Integrated

Rehabilitation of the Victims of Tsunami (IRVT) in which educational helps were offered to the students affected by tsunami, houses damaged by tsunami were repaired, new houses were built for fishing folk who lost their houses, new boats, nets and engines were given to fishermen who lost their belongings, medical aid was given to thousands of victims, vocational training leading to job opportunities was offered to widows and young women who lost their husbands and parents in tsunami, etc.[13]

Further programmes have included

Educational Help to the Poor and the marginalized

A large number of poor students with no discrimination have been offered educational helps all through the years.

Empowerment of Women

A number of seminars and meetings have been organized on issues related to women's liberation.[14]

Empowerment of the Dalits

Madhikas are the lowest among the *Dalits*, and they still suffer under double exploitation and oppression, exploited by the general public as well as by the other Dalit groups, who consider themselves superior. Responding to the cries coming from this community, Peace Trust picked up twenty men and women from among them, brought them to Peace Trust, and offered a four days training to them, giving them awareness on their fundamental human rights and teaching them the methods of organizing themselves to fight for their rights. These leaders went back and started organizing their people. Today the Madhika liberation Movement has become strong in Tamil Nadu. Seeing that "education" is fundamental for their liberation, Peace Trust offered educational helps to around three hundred students every year for nearly five years.

National Consultation on the Working of the Constitution

When we heard that the BJP Government, which was supported by the *Hindutva* movement, had a secret plan to change the Secular Constitution of India to suit their objective of creating a theocratic Hindu state, Peace Trust Kanyakumari organized in 2002 a National Constitution on the Working of the Constitution of India in New Delhi under the Chairmanship of Justice Ranganath Misra, the former Chief Justice of India. The Consultation concluded, there was no need for any change in the constitution, but what needed was its effective working.[15]

Kanyakumari Justice and Peace Publications

In order to disseminate its inter-faith messages and values, Peace Trust started its own publication program known as Kanyakumari Justice and Peace Publications (KJPP).

Iniyavar Illam: The Inter-faith Care for the Aged

The need for a decent home for the care of the aged in the Kanyakumari region has been brought to the attention of Dr. Gnana Robinson by people in the region as early as the late nineties. After a long time of waiting and praying, a Home for the Care of the Aged has become a reality. *Iniyavar Illam (INIL)* is the name given to the home. The words in Tamil means "the home for loving and lovable people." This is an Inter-faith Home. The common worshipping/meditating place (Chapel) is known as **"House of Prayer for All"**. The only symbol on the altar is a light with a red mark at the centre—light being the common symbol of God in all religions, God as the dispeller of darkness/pain in life, and red indicating the self-giving, sacrificial nature of God's love, whose example every believer is asked to emulate. INIL is ready for occupation from June 1, 2012.

Conclusion

Peace Trust Kanyakumari understands inter-faith dialog not as an academic exercise, but as an inner-life exercise involving inter-personal relationships, study and action, underpinned by its threefold understanding of God, theologically, christologically, and humanistically. Therefore, Peace Trust sees its life in a multi-religious society as a dialogical living, dialogue at all levels—in religion, culture, politics and business. The values of the faith relation with God, the Supreme One, should therefore permeate into our relationships with our fellow humans at all the levels mentioned above. If our Faith relationship to God does not contribute to fostering our relationships with our humans, something is wrong with our Faith relationship to God. In such a case, members of every religion should examine themselves and their Faith, and try to correct themselves and their Faith.

Endnotes

[1] Von Walbert Buelmann, *Jesus, Buddha, Krishna und der eine Gott*, Publik Forum, Nr 24, 29th November 1991, p.16; Gnana Robinson, *Dialogue with People of Other Faiths and the Question of the Uniqueness of Christ*, KJPP, India, 2006, p.1.

[2] J.Percy (ed), *Facing the Unfinished Task: Messages delivered at the Congress on World Mission*, 1961, p.9.

[3] Gnana Robinson, *Hindutva at the Cross Roads*, p.13.

[4] *Christology in the Context*, Kanyakumari Declaration 11, 1986, pp.3ff.

[5] *Ibid.*, p.5.

[6] *Ibid.*

[7] *Ibid.*, p.5ff.

[8] *Ibid*, p.6.

[9] Gnana Robinson, *A journey through Theological Education*, CLS, Madras, 1989, p.64.

[10] See my article in Tamil, and then in English, 'Towards a Spirituality beyond the boundaries of religion, in Nonviolence', *Oct-Dec 2011, Vol VII, no 4, pp 166-173.*

[11] *Religion and Human Solidarity*, Centre for Peace and Justice, Kanyakumari, 1990.

[12] For details on reports on the seventeen nation-wide consultations and papers presented, see our publication, *Harmony Flame spreads across India*, ed by Gnana Robinson, KJPP, Kanyakumari, 2009.

[13] For some details on the Peace Trust's Tsunami rehabilitation activities, see Gnana Robinson, *Tsunami and the Providence of God*, KJPP, Kanyakumari, 2005, and Gnana Robinson (Edt) *Tsunami and Afterwards: What have we learnt from it?*, KJPP, Kanyakumari, 2011.

[14] G.Pankajam, Florence FRobinson, Evangeline Rajkumar, Wiston Somervell and Gnana Robinson (Edts), *Women in India Today: their status*, KJPP, 2008.

[15] Gnana Robinson (edt), *The Working of the Constitution of India*, KJPP, *Kanyakumari, 2003.*

Devoted to the Lord

The *parama-prema bhakti* of
Nârada *Bhakti-sûtra*

David C. Scott

Introduction

"**A**nother (essay) on interfaith dialogue! Some might view this as contributing to a satanic movement shaking the foundations of Christian faith. Others might see this as an important source of material for encouraging Christians to have dialogue with people of other faiths-now a growing concern all over the world." Thus, a decade and a half ago, wrote the one to whom this *Festschrift* is heartily dedicated, the Revd Dr Israel Selvanayagam.[1] Obviously, the latter, i.e. to provide significant source materials to encourage and facilitate Christians in interfaith dialogue, is our intention here.

There is no gainsaying that the devotional *bhakti* streams of the Hindu religious tradition have been, and continue to be, a natural point of contact for Indian Christian theologians,[2] as also for ordinary Christians. As a contribution to the ongoing dialogue, we shall consider the *Bhakti-sûtra* of Narada,[3] one of two classical texts[4] that have seldom, if ever, been brought into the interfaith conversation, despite the fact that they are widely considered to present an authoritative explication of *bhakti*.[5]

Acutely aware of the danger that an examination of the *Bhakti-sûtra's* text, qua text, could easily become a tedious and lifeless affair, we propose to consider the contents of the Nârada *Bhakti-sûtra* in the light of the *premâ-bhakti sâdhana*, the spiritual discipline, of a well known Hindu *bhakta*, Mirabai. This will provide a significant personal human perspective to our discussion. Not that Mirabai was specifically acquainted with or specially influenced by Narada's *Bhakti-sûtra*; there was no conscious effort to embody its teaching in her *sâdhana*, her spiritual discipline. Rather, our intent is to indicate a major factor in the shaping of her religious milieu, which may be of assistance in understanding the *Bhakti-sûtra*. Further, such an exercise helps to show the extent of the influence and authority of these aphorisms for many of the *bhakti* streams within the larger Hindu religious tradition.[6] This will be done by showing how the principles and practices detailed in them were evident in the religious environment of one *premâ-sâdhika*, an accomplished *bhakta*. Indeed, the Nârada *Bhakti-sûtra* deals with the need, nature and benefits of unceasing loving devotion for the Lord[7] with such authentic authority that their centrality for *bhakti* religion has been widely recognized throughout India.

Before proceeding, it is important to remind ourselves that in this *bhakti* stream of the Hindu religious tradition significant stress is laid on divine grace; for human beings, by their own accomplishments or merits, can never acquire fitness for communion with the Lord. The divine vision is to be had only when the Lord chooses to reveal Himself. However, the Lord is eternally fond of those who are devoted to Him, and is gracefully disposed to those who worship Him with singleness of heart.[8]

Nârada *Bhakti-sûtra*

The *sûtra-kartr*, the author of the Nârada *Bhakti-sûtra*, defines *bhakti* as *parama-premâ-rûpa* (su.2), i.e. it is of the nature of love which reaches the highest perfection. The adjective *parama* indicates that this most perfect of loves is solely for the Lord and is free from the slightest taint of worldly imperfection. It is the highest end; not a means to any other goal (su. 2-6, 26, 30, 33, 59-60, 66, 81). Indeed, this love is of the nature of *amrta*, the celestial elixir of immortality. Not only is the supreme loving devotion of the *bhakta* akin to the nectar of the gods, but it also partakes of the nature of the freedom and bliss of immortality. Indeed, it is the cure for human suffering in that it liberates the *bhakta* from *samsâra*, the cycle of birth and death (su. 3-4)..

Further, *bhakti* is of the nature of renunciation (*nirodha-rûpavat*), hence free from lust (*na kâma-yamana*) (su. 7). However it is not the extinction of all desires, but the consecration of these desires, emotions and actions to the Lord (su. 65). Renunciation also means undivided or whole-hearted devotion to the Lord, indifference to all that is antagonistic to Him, and giving up all other dependencies (su. 7-10). The *bhakta* is instructed to take refuge solely in the Lord (*kevalam-vicchinn-anurâgam labhate*) (su. 19, 49, 61, 65, 79, 82). This we shall see well illustrated in the life of Mirabai.

Continuing in the realistic and practical vein, the *sûtras* expand on the teaching that the life of devotion does not necessarily involve a life of inaction (BG. 3:4-24, su. 62). Indeed, actions that preserve life, such as eating and drinking, are to be carried on "as long as the body exists" (su. 14). It is the attachment to the fruits of action that is to be renounced; a related understanding central to the *Bhagavad-gîtâ*. The person who dedicates all action to the Lord rises above pleasure and pain, craving and aversion, and realizes everlasting peace (su. 48). Social and religious obligations are to be fulfilled, but dedicated to the Lord. The injunctions of the Vedas and other scriptures are to be observed until spiritual realization is sufficiently deep to prevent a "fall from grace". Social rules also are to be observed while attaining *bhakti* (su. 12-14. But none of these religious or social practices must be allowed to hinder the pursuit of *bhakti* for fear of public or private censure or derision (su. 83). This certainly turned out to be a major issue in Mira's life, one which we shall find referred to in many of her *padas*.[9] The *Bhakti-sûtra* so strongly presses single-hearted *bhakti* that even the scriptures, Vedic, Puranic, etc., are to be laid aside if they in any way obstruct the perfection of love for the Lord (su. 49).

Two kinds of *bhakti* are distinguished in the *Bhakti-sûtra*, secondary (su. 56) and primary (su. 67). Secondary devotion is born of desire and is threefold, depending on the predominance of *sattva, rajas* or *tamas* in the personality of the devotee (su. 56). The *bhakti* characterized by each of these *gunas*[10] is, as one would expect, superior to each succeeding one, culminating in "those primary devotees who are single-hearted in loving devotion to the Lord, for its/his own sake" (su. 67).

The *sûtra-kartr* describes eleven forms of devotion, for though *bhakti* is unique, it appears in differing forms. It is found in the *bhakta's* concentration on the attributes and greatness of the Lord, His beauty, His worship, His recollection; as in love for the Lord as servant, as master, as friend, as parent, as child, as lover for the beloved; or in love of consecration to Him; love of absorption in Him; and love expressed in pangs of separation from Him (su. 82).

This *sûtra* nicely describes the different grades of religious consciousness. At first the devotee is overwhelmed with the sense of finitude in the face of the infinity and majesty of the Divine, which is then venerated as a superhuman power. A more intimate relationship is fostered through remembrance and adoration that, in turn, matures into a personal devotion, beginning with the service of the Lord. There are the closer ties of a friend, which deepen into those of parent and child, and finally reach the intense intimacy of man and woman. But even this is transcended as the last vestiges of remoteness disappear, and the *bhakta* gives him/herself completely to the Lord. This, due to human nature, results in *viraha* the painful pangs of separation,[11] the highest consummation of love. But even in separation, a more profound union is experienced and the devotee is eternally united with God. The *sûtras* stress constant servitude and unswerving conjugal love for the Lord. The devotee is to cultivate radically singular loving devotion for the Lord, rising above the three prior forms of secondary love (su. 66) This theme, too, we shall pick up in our consideration of Mirabai's *bhakti*.

As aids to the realization of this "supreme love" a number of practices are listed in the *sûtras*. First, those **to be avoided**: (i) Evil company should be shunned by all means as it excites lust, anger, infatuation, lapse of memory, all of which finally lead to ruin. While these emotions are natural enough to human beings, it is contended that they are excited and exaggerated by the company of evil persons until the emotions and desires take on overwhelming proportions (su. 43-45). (ii) Money and sex have been universally viewed as detrimental to spiritual well being, as have atheists been perceived as a threat to faith in God. Hence, the seeker should not give ear to chatter about wealth, women or atheists (su. 63). (iii) At the same time, the *sûtra-kartr* seems constructively ambivalent about "pride, vanity and other urges of the mind". On the one hand, the devotee is urged to give them up (su. 64), but the means for such renunciation is a religious sublimation of them by dedicating them to the Lord (su. 65). (iv) Vain disputation and discussion about God are useless because they can only be inconclusive, and hence they should be avoided by the *bhakta* as a waste of time and energy (su. 74, 75). (v) *Bhakti* is facilitated by the ultimate renunciation of all objects of the senses and the accompanying attachment to them (su. 35). The person who renounces everything worldly, even the Vedas, will be filled in return with an abundant and continuous flow of *bhakti* that will transport the *bhakta* "across the ocean of this world" and enable her/him to assist others along the way (su. 47-50).

So much for the proverbial 'negative' means of preparing the mind and heart for *bhakti*. The *Bhakti-sûtra* also prescribes a number of **positive means** for the fostering of *bhakti*.

(i) Various discourses on *bhakti*, such as the *Bhagavad-gîtâ* and the *Ûrîmad Bhâgavatam (Bhâgavata Purâṇa)* are to be studied and faithfully followed.[12] The *sûtras* have their own list among which are non-injury to living beings, truthfulness, purity of body and mind, kindness and faith in God and other related strengths of character (su. 78). (ii) Another critical means of facilitating perfect love for the Lord is hearing and singing His glories. This can be done even while the *bhakta* is engaged in the daily round of duties and activities, perceiving the Lord in all activities. (iii) Indeed, every moment of the *bhakta*'s life is to be permeated with loving devotion to the Lord (su. 36, 37). No time ought to be wasted waiting for the propitious moment; hence the seeker is urged to begin the quest immediately (su. 77). (iv) God's grace is seen not only as the initiator but also the instrument, urging and enabling the *bhakta* to pursue perfection of the *paramprema* by association with great souls *(mahâtmâs)* and great teachers (su. 38 - 40). This is explained by the fact that in reality there is no difference between the devotee and his/her Lord (su. 41).[13] (v) The love of the Lord is the supreme and sole objective of all that the devotee says and does and thinks, waking or sleeping (su. 42 & 79). The means which the *sûtra-kartṛ* has specified for the realization of this goal are to be exclusively central in the life of one who enters on the *bhakti-mârga*. Indeed, this conclusion is emphatically stated by twice reiterating it in a single *sûtra* (su. 42). (vi) There is, however, the further assurance that, being invoked, the Lord will quickly reveal Himself to the seeker, who will thereby be filled with the realization of divinity (su. 80).

The **results** of developing this *parama-prema* in the *sûtras* are described in glowing language. The reader (hearer) is assured that by arriving at the perfection of *bhakti* a person realizes fulfillment and immortality (su. 4).

It is not the ambition of the *bhakta* to achieve *mokṣa*; this he/she realizes effortlessly. The *bhakta* is freed from the cycles of *samsâra* because the root cause, desire, has been removed by the Lord, who utterly satisfies. The *bhakta* does not lament the loss of anything; he/she does not hate anything or delight in anything, especially his/her own achievements (su. 5). Rather, there is a spiritual (*âtmika*) ecstasy resulting from the joy that is utterly silent in complete self- integrity (su. 6). The *bhakta* becomes God-intoxicated as the clamor of passion and craving are drowned in the overwhelming inner silence of self-realization. Having reached that *parama-premâ*, the *bhakta* sees nothing else, hears nothing else and speaks nothing else, because finally he/she thinks nothing else (su. 55). Nor is this surprising, for the devotee is filled with the presence of the Lord (su. 70). The *bhakta* and everything else belong to the Lord (su. 73).

In brief, then, the Nârada *Bhakti-sûtra* maintains that *bhakti*, which is described as *parama-premâ*, is the ultimate in the spiritual life, higher than knowledge or *jñâna*, and more excellent than *yoga*, it is the culmination of both, its own reward. It is not a means to any other end; it is the *summum bonum* of all life (su. 26, 30, 33, 59, 60, 66, 81). One who would experience the Divine should throw oneself entirely on the mercy of the Lord, allowing His grace to fill their lives. They would do well to tread the *bhakti-mârga* to the exclusion of all others. It is the easiest of all paths and superior to all. It does not require any self-verification; it is self evident. The *bhakti-mârga* is to be desired above all else because it fills the soul with peace and the ecstasy of divine joy, to the exclusion of all else.

Mirabai's *bhakti*

Such certainly was the experience of the 16th century Krishna *bhakta* poetess whose life situation did not provide much occasion or cause for peace and joy. Despite the paucity of verifiable historical information, all seem to agree that the circumstances of Mirabai's life were anything but happy.[14] Even a cursory glance at her life indicates that two sets of circumstances dominated: her several bereavements in her own and her husband's families and their continuing opposition, and her deeply experienced conjugal love for Krishna. She finally died in the solitude of her intense love for Krishna.[15]

Mirabai, along with a number of other religious poets of medieval North India,[16] is well known throughout the land, at least among the *bhajan* singers.[17] Indeed, Wendy Doniger describes Mira as the *bhakta* whose poems are the most quoted and whose life story is the best known of all the North Indian saints.[18] She is best remembered for her special relationship with Krishna,[19] and the rich devotional feelings so poignantly expressed in her poetry. In spite of the fame which she rightly enjoyed, however, we know very little about her life and compositions. Perhaps her singular devotion to Krishna, with resulting self-effacing renunciation, is partly responsible for the paucity of autobiographical information. As a result, questions regarding her life – when she was born, to whom she was married, who was her guru, and when she died – remain uncertainly answered. Because of the aura of popular reverence that accumulated around her, many legends about her are currently in circulation, but these assist us little in reconstructing an authentic biography.[20]

Matters are equally unclear regarding her compositions. Though there have been a number of collections attributed to her, none has been left unassailed by scholars.[21] For our present purpose, however, it is Mirabai's *padas* which are of immediate concern. Indeed, we have already suggested that it is for her *padas* that Mirabai is best known. These are most often found in anthologies, together with works of other poets.

However, as we have already said, these matters are not of immediate concern to us in our present endeavor, nor could we, at this juncture, add anything substantial to what has already been written in this area. The task we have set for ourselves is more modest and hence more readily amenable to fulfillment.

Devotees and students of Mirabai, alike, are unanimous in their agreement that her special relationship with her chosen deity, her *iṣṭa-deva*, Krishna, whom she considered her husband and lover, caused her *bhakti* to be particularly infused with love, *premâ*.[22] Mira showed inclinations of religious devotion early in her life, fostered by her grandfather and his Vaishnavite family. In fact it is highly probable these were the only ones who understood or empathized with her tender spirit. Mira is said to have been given a small image of Giridharlal[23] (Krishna) by a *sâdhu* who spent a couple of days with the family. Apparently she became deeply attached to the image, which in turn increased her love for Krishna. Tradition has it that she kept the image with her all through her marriage ceremony and later took it with her to Cittaur, where she refused to worship her husband's patron goddess, Kali, much to the annoyance of her husband's family.

With the death of her husband, some five years after their marriage, Mira was plunged into a period of persecution by her in-laws, who were greatly incensed that she did not commit *satî* in true *kṣatriya* fashion, and who also vigorously opposed her religious practices. It seems very likely that this served only to strengthen her spiritual ardour. She could now devote all her time and energy to the service and worship of her beloved Giridharlal, accepting him as her lover and husband. Indeed, a great deal of Mira's time was spent in the temple composing and singing songs devoted to Krishna, and providing hospitality for saints and *sâdhus* in return for the opportunity of listening to their religious discourses. Such activities, of course, were considered by her in-laws to be a gross contravention of the strict and rigid codes of behavior set for women of the royal household. Quite naturally, all this incurred the extreme displeasure of her husband's family, especially the new king who took the local throne after her husband and father-in-law died. Mira complained constantly of a certain Rana who gave her all sorts of trouble.[24] Many of her poems mention these trials (pd. 37 – 42, 50, etc.).[25] But Mira seems never to have been subdued.

In view of these circumstances and events it is hardly surprising that Mira sought personal comfort and fulfillment in single-hearted love for Krishna. Her lover was the fullness of youth, who wears a peacock feather crown, earrings, a garland of jasmine, a bright yellow garment, and holds a flute to his lips. He was the object of Mira's love and there can be little doubt about the centrality of this relationship for the Rajput princess.

Dwell in my eyes, O Nandlal.
The peacock feather crown,
   the fish-shaped earrings,
   the red *tilak* embellishing your lovely brow.
Your figure is charming,
   dark face, large eyes,
A flute is at your nectar-filled lips,
   Vishnu's garland adorns your chest.
Mira says, the Lord gives joy to saints,
   Gopal loves his devotees. (pd. 3)

Returning to the *Bhakti-sûtra* of Narada, we recall that those who would follow the *bhakti-mârga* are enjoined "going beyond the three universal characteristics of existence (*sattva, rajas, tamas*), develop love expressed in constant service of a devoted servant or wife; that love alone should be practiced" (su. 66). It is important to remember, however, that though the *sûtra-kartṛ* advocates a love for the Lord which is of the same nature as the g*opîs* [26] of Vraja (su. 21) he does not believe that erotic love, *kâma* plays any part in *bhakti* (su. 7). Mira's poems also reflect this understanding, for although she sometimes considers herself an ideal *gopî* (pd. 5, 176 – 178) we do not sense any of the emotions or other aspects of erotic love such as are found in the *Ŝrîmad Bhâgavatam or* the *Gîtâ Govinda*. Rather she seems to experience the emotions and reactions of a befuddled young girl falling in love.

Taking the earthen pot on her head, the *gopî* sets off,
   on the way she meets Prince Nandji (Krishna).
Forgetting the word for *dâhi* (yogurt),
   she cries 'Come buy my handsome Shyâm'.
In the creeper covered lanes of Vrindavan,
   she wanders bewitched by the charmer of hearts.
Mira's Lord is Giridhar Nagar,
   handsome and vigorous Shyâm. (pd. 177)

Indeed, some of Mira's most powerful poems are those in which she experiences Krishna as her husband and describes her profound and single-hearted loving devotion to him (pd. 13-17, 22-24, 46, 56). This is the wifely devotion, *kânta-âsakti* referred to in *Bhakti-sûtra* number 82. In at least one poem Mira describes her marriage to Krishna. Though a spiritual union that takes place in a dream, this is nevertheless important for her formal acceptance of Krishna as her husband.

In all of this, the point rightly stressed by Chaturvedi[27] is that the distinction between 'gopî love' and 'wife love' finally pales into insignificance in the profound intensity of the emotion Mira herself speaks of as *prem-bhakti* (pd. 46, 56). It is this to which she refers when she speaks of Krishna as beloved, *prîtam*, bridegroom, *dulha*, loved one, *sajan*, wife, *kânta*, etc. (pds. 17, 27, 31, 50) She also uses traditional love imagery, such as lamp and moth, water and fish, and *chakor*[28] (pds. 174, 191) to express her love for Krishna. She also tells us that she is the servant of Krishna's "lotus feet" (pds. 1, 35, 49, 161).

This is certainly the kind of *bhakti* expounded in the *Bhakti-sûtra*, defined as *parampremâ* (su. 2). Referring to the same intense devotion, Chaturvedi[29] speaks of *mâdhurya bhâva*[30] which he understands to include the initial infatuation of a young girl as well as the mature love of wife and lover. Certainly, we shall not go far wrong if we "classify" Mira's *bhakti* as being permeated with *mâdhurya bhâva*, a love full of joys and sorrows, between a man and a woman, which is the highest human expression of the *bhakti-mârga*.

Practical Aspects of *bhakti sâdhana*

But we must turn our attention to the practical aspects of the path of devotion mentioned above. *Sûtra* 82 explains, as we have indicated that though *bhakti* is one, it manifests itself through eleven diverse forms.

1.   "Intent[31] on glorifying the Lord's marvelous qualities." Without a doubt Mira never tired of praising the virtues of her Lord.

O heart, cling to the feet of Hari.
Beautiful, cool, soft as lotus,
    overcoming the heated passions of this world.
These feet cause the devotee to be firm,
    protect the helpless.
These feet pervade the universe from top to bottom,
    fill it with beauty.
These feet conquered Kâliya,[32]
    played games with the *gopîs*.

These feet upheld the Govardana mountain,
> removed the pride of Indra.
Mira is the slave of Lal Giridhar,
> who delivers one across the ocean of life. (pd. 1)

2. "Enthralled by the Lord's enchanting beauty." We have already spoken of the manner in which Mira sings of the beautiful youth, Krishna; we do not need to dwell on this point.

3. "Constant in worship." It seems inconceivable that one who kept a small image of Krishna with her day and night, and whose lyrical expressions of love for and devotion to her Lord we have seen, would not spend a sizeable portion of her time in worship.

4. "Absorbed in the perpetual remembrance of the Lord." A number of Mira's *padas* give evidence of the bitter-sweet joy of remembering her beloved Krishna.

On the banks of the Yamuna,
> he plays his flute.
The flute has stolen my heart,
> there is no peace in my mind.
Krishna is dark with a dark wrap,
> dark is the water of the Yamuna.
At the sound of the flute my sense leaves me,
> my body trembles.
Mira (says): O Lord, Giridhar Nagar,
> quickly take away my pain. (pd. 166)

5. "Devotion to the Lord as of a servant." Even in the poems where the emotions of conjugal love are central, Mira never forgot the divine identity of her lover, and frequently concludes the *pada* with the assertion that "Mira's Lord is Giridhar Nagar" and she is the servile supplicant, as in *pada* 166 above.

6. "Devotion to the Lord as of a friend." Though Mira addresses Krishna as "Friend" from time to time, it seems difficult to distinguish between *sâkhya* and *mâdhurya bhâvas*, intermingled as these two emotions are.

7. "Devotion to the Lord as of a child." There is a section entitled *Bâl Lîlâ* in Caturvedi's collection of Mira's *padas*, but they number only three and are primarily reminiscent in character, so they probably should be understood more in terms of being absorbed in perpetual remembrance, *smaraṇâsakti* than child-like devotion, *vâtsalyâsakti*.

8. "Passion for the Lord as of wife for husband." There is plenty of evidence in other parts of this paper to preclude the necessity of presenting more here to indicate the central importance of this element, the *mâdhurya bhâva*, in Mira's life.

9. "Intent on self-surrender." What else but surrender of one's self could result from the intensity of love for Krishna that was so poignantly expressed by one who understood herself as the wife of God?

> Come to that place where the beloved is to be found,
>> come to that place.
> If ordered I will color my sari saffron,
>> if ordered I will go naked.
> If ordered I will fill my hair-part with pearls,
>> if ordered I will tousle my hair.
> Mira's Lord is Giridhar Nagar,
>> listen to the praise of the Lord. (pd. 153)

10. "Obsessed with complete absorption in the Lord." There seems to be no indication in Mira's poems that she understood or expected the soul to be utterly absorbed in the Divine. There are, of course, as we shall soon see many poems telling of the extreme pain Mira suffered due to her sense of separation from her lover, Krishna. The majority of *padas* concerning union with Krishna seem to indicate a desire to see him, be with him. On the other hand there are references to the *ântaryâmin* or "indwelling controller" (pds 85, 101) and to the "physician who dwells in the heart" (pd. 73). Of course, there is the story of Mira's final assumption into the image of Ranchod (Krishna), but that probably says more about her followers' perception of her than her own understanding.

11. "Gripped by the pain of separation from the Lord." The poignancy of Mira's *bhakti* is, perhaps nowhere more apparent than in the poems dealing with *viraha*, the pain of separation which is the experience, at

one time or another, of every person seriously engaged in the spiritual quest. It is likely, for example, that the experience of *viraha* is very much akin to the "dark night of the soul" of which Christian mystics speak. Even while the lover sees the beauty and is overwhelmed by the ecstasy of union she realizes that it is fleeting. Krishna has already left her. She feels herself continually forsaken and pleads with Krishna to return to her. She senses that her Lord loved her initially but did not remain true to her. In most of her *viraha* poems Mira powerfully describes the acute pain of her separation from Krishna, drawing on the traditional imagery of *viraha* so common in Indian prose, poetry and painting. She hears rumors of his coming. She asks her friends to sing auspicious songs to attract him. But again and again he breaks his promise. Friends bring word of his dalliance with other women and she grows pale and weak, but no physician can diagnose or treat her condition. Finally she feels so deeply grieved at loving such a fickle man that she blames herself for being too weak.

Things that were once the source of joy and anticipation are no longer so. The beauties of nature no longer give any pleasure. The birds do not please; rather they only add fuel to the fire of *viraha* roaring inside her. Every season, every festival, which once was joyous and jovial now, only adds to her loneliness. With the change of the seasons, the pain of separation increases and decreases, heightening her sense of expectation and then dashing her hopes. The monsoon is the most difficult time for her to be alone, while all around her lovers are united. With the approach of the dark clouds the delighted peacock begins to dance. The *catak's*[33] thirst is quenched; the dry earth is thoroughly drenched; only the separated lover yearns in her darkened room. The thunder and lightning sometimes frighten the lonely one and sometimes awaken erotic desires in her. She waits, but it seems her lover will never come.[34]

We have seen, then, how the *prem bhakti* of this extraordinarily sensitive spirit well exemplifies in human life what the Nârada *Bhakti-sûtra* describes in ideal theory. Without doubt, the *parama-premâ* of the *sûtras* is to be discerned in this saintly woman. She certainly did not travel the *bhakti-mârga* as a means to a further end. It was the *summum bonum* of her life, enabling her, finally, to live that life in peace and the ecstasy of profound joy. Having experienced that "supreme love", she could, indeed, see nothing else, hear nothing else, speak of nothing else, think of nothing else. She was filled with the presence of her divine lover, Krishna in the manner of the *sûtra-kartr̩*, the significant difference being that Mira did so in and through her life, while the latter was limited to words. Because of the utter centrality of her relationship with her Lord and lover, Giridhar Nagar, she felt the pangs of separation most keenly and described them in many of her poems. In short, she exhibited the marks of the "supreme love" which the *Bhakti-sûtra* defined and helped to establish in the Hindu religious tradition.

Mira's *prem bhakti* was indeed akin to that multifaceted *parama-premâ* that levels all spiritual disciplines, and in whose fullness there is no need for physical penance or renunciation. It is distinguished by *tad-arpita-akhila-charita*, the dedication of all actions to him (su 19), or as Mira puts it *tan man dhan giridhar par waron, charan kamal mîran bilamani*, surrendering body, mind and wealth to Giridhar, Mira clings to the lotus feet (pd 11).

What does it all matter?

But ultimately what does all this matter? What does it have to say to and/or about the spiritual quest of women and men of faith in all religious traditions? In the final analysis religious experience is ineffable and can be described only in terms of symbols, myths and rituals, a matter not merely of intelligence, but rather of the heart.[35] We have of necessity been forced to speak all too inadequately merely of the outward expressions, not the heart and soul of the *Bhakti-sûtra's parama-premâ* as experienced by Mira's *prem bhakti*. But somehow in and through it all there breaks forth, with direct intensity, a genuine, deeply felt religious experience, an immersion into and a surrender to the Divine, broadminded, beyond the boundaries of creed or sect, indeed, beyond all human limitations and frailties and yet profoundly human. A great poetess? No, much more, a *mahâtmâ*, a great spirit, a beautiful human being, living in this world yet shrouded in the invisible presence of her divine lover and Lord.

Finally, in the ensuing dialogue of the Hindu and Christian religious traditions, there will, of course, be those, primarily Christians, who will contend that all this is unacceptably distant from the political and ethical demands on the life of faith. What good is all this God-centeredness if it cannot turn toward the welfare of human beings and the life of the cosmos? Must God-intoxication not turn to de-toxifying human privation and earthly pollution? Perhaps the Gospel of Jesus Christ is a counter-passion that demands that love of God and love for creation cannot be severed? There are, of course, Christians that only accent God as lover and there is much in Hinduism too that empties God into humanity and the cosmos. So this Gospel even if manifested in Jesus is seen clearly in many other religious places. The task, then, is to discover and explore them. For if there is no legitimate place for a beautiful and passionate love of God in the life of faith, are we not left with an arid and tedious theology of works, exacerbated by indications that our modern world is snuffing out passion in our pursuit and expression of religious truth?

End Notes

[1] Israel Selvanayagam (ed.). *Biblical Insights on Inter-faith Dialogue.* Bangalore: The Board for Theological Textbooks Programme of South Asia, 1995. p. xi

[2] See, for example, Robin Boyd, *An Introduction to Indian Christian Theology,* Madras: C.L.S., 1975 rev. ed.; A.J. Appasamy, *Christianity as Bhakti Marga,* Madras: CLS. 1928; Dhanjibhai Fakirbhai, *The Philosophy of Love,* Delhi: ISPCK, 1966; S. Kulandran. *Grace: A Comparative Study of the Doctrine in Christianity and Hinduism.* London: Lutterworth Press, 1964. Though not technically a theologian, as Boyd notes, Sundar Singh's works and recorded sayings – *At the Master's Feet* (1923), Vision *of the Spiritual World* (1926), The *Real Pearl* (1966) - are thoroughly theological and his influence on Indian Christendom was significant. Note also Klaus Klostermaier's "*Hrdayavidyâ* — A Sketch of a Hindu-Christian Theology of Love" in Klaus Klostermaier, *Indian Theology in Dialogue.* Madras: CLS, 1986, pp. 36-65; and David C. Scott. "Hindu and Christian *Bhakti*: A Common Human Response to the Sacred" in *Indian Journal of Theology* XXX.1 (January – March, 1980), pp. 12-45.

[3] The Nârada *Bhakti-sûtra* is a brief compendium of the *bhakti* 'system', probably intended to be committed to memory by *bhaktas* It is clearly dependent on the *Bhâgavata Purâna* and was probably produced by the *Bhâgavatas* of South India at quite an early date of the Sangam Period, along with the *Bhâgavata Purâna.* The *Bhakti-sûtra's* relation to the sage Narada is traditional, if apocryphal. However, he is mentioned in the *Vedas* and *Puranas* with some frequency and his depiction in the latter texts is such as not to rule out his experience as being basic to that of the eponymous author of the *Bhakti-sûtra.* Textual references in the present study are to Swami Chinmayananda, *Narada Bhakti-sûtra,* Bombay: Central Chinmaya Mission Trust, 2005 (First published 1976). (NB: names fairly commonly Anglicised in general have no diacritics in this essay, though complete uniformity is difficult – Ed.)

[4] The Shandilya *Bhakti-sûtra* is the other,. Though the Narada compendium is more popular, the Shandilya *Bhakti-sûtra* is considered to be to *bhakti* what the *Bhakti-sûtras* is to Vedanta. While Narada's collection of aphorisms are *sâdhana* oriented, those of Shandilya are of a more academic and polemic nature. Indeed,

the *Bhakti-sûtra*, especially that of Shandilya quite openly emulates the style of the *Bhakti-sûtras*, possibly to impress those for whom the latter were the supreme authority. Thus Shandilya begins *athato-bhakti- jijñâsa* - "Now, therefore, the enquiry into *bhakti*".

[5] Swami Prabhavananda. *Narada's Way of Divine Love*, Hollywood, CA: Vedanta Press, 1971, p. 18.   Swami Chinmayananda, *op. cit.*, p. 5.

[6] This is particularly true among the Vaishnava streams.

[7] The term 'Lord' is used to emphasize the deeply personal character of *bhakti* devotion.

[8] *Bhagavadgîtâ* 9:22-34.

[9] Mirabai's poems are in the *pada* form, a small spiritual song, usually composed in simple rhythms with a repeating refrain. John Hawley says of the *pada* "probably the most influential medium for expression of devotion (*bhakti*) in North India" John Stratton Hawley. "Author and Authority in the *Bhakti* Poetry of North India", *Journal of Asian* Studies, 47, No. 2 (May, 1988), p. 269.They are collected in her *Padâvali*. This was a popular style for singing devotional songs in the medieval period. Jayadeva and Vidyapati, both Krishna *bhaktas*, are considered to have perfected the *pada*

[10] The *guṇa* or mode of *sattva* is characterized by purity, illumination, order, stability, permanence, happiness, spirituality, and health; *rajas* is characterized by action, creation, desire, lust, attachment, movement, and striving; *tamas* is characterized by destruction, madness, disease, dissolution, ignorance, intoxication, heaviness, and sleep.

[11] Separation is a standard theme of court and folk literature In India. It is in separation that love is tested; if the love is real the pangs of separation will be strong. In a real sense *bhakti* is nothing but the feelings of sorrow in separation from God and the effort toward union with God.

[12] For example, the *Úrîmad Bhâgavatam* : "Devotion has nine marks: listening to the name of God, chanting his name, recollection of him, serving him, worshipping him, saluting him, servitude, friendship, and self-dedication to him." *Bhag. Pu* VII. 5. 23-24 as quoted by Swami Chinmayananda, *op. cit.*, p.149.

[13] For the purposes of this discussion we need not be concerned with the various possible interpretations of such a verse, e.g., from the perspective of *Advaita Vedanta*, or that of the *Tengalai* or *Vadagalai* schools of Ramanuja's followers.

[14] My primary sources of biographical information on Mirabai are: Pandit Chaturvedi *Mirabai ki Padavali*. Prayag: Hindi Sahitya Sammelan, 1966., Usha Nilsson. *Mirabai.* New Delhi: Sahitya Akademi, 1969, Hermann Goetz, *Mira Bai: Her Life and Times*, Bombay: Bharatiya Vidya Bhavan, 1966.

[15] There is a rather poignant legend about Mira's death, referred to by both Nilsson and Chaturvedi. It seems that the royal families of Mewar and Merta had sent an impressive deputation of *brahmans* to plead with Mira to return home. Reluctant to go back where she had suffered so much she put the *brahmans*

off by asking permission to enter the temple of Ranchodji (Krishna) in Dwarka, where she had finally settled. There, in the ecstasy of supreme love, Mira was assumed into the image of her Lover and Lord, never to be seen again. One is reminded of the marriage of Andal several centuries earlier in South India.

[16] Mirabai was more or less contemporaneous with Kabir, Surdas, Malik Muhammad Jayasi, Tulsidas and Tukaram.

[17] There are a number of North Indian *bhaktas* who are famous for their *bhajans*. Tulsidas, Surdas, Kabir, Tukaram and Mirabai are particularly well known.

[18] Doniger, *op. cit.*, p. 569. This in no way ignores the ancient and robust *bhakti* tradition in South India. See *Ibid.* ch. 13.

[19] Her experience of Krishna as husband and lover is unusual, if not unique, among well known North Indian *bhaktas*.

[20] Herman Goetz suggests an interesting hypothesis that the distortion of Mirabai's biography resulted from the political scene of her times as from veneration of her by admirers and followers. Goetz, Hermann, *Mira Bai: Her Life and Times*, Bombay: Bharatiya Vidya Bhavan, 1966.

[21] For a useful discussion of questions related to Mirabai's poetic output see Pandit Chaturvedi *Mirabai ki Padâvali*, Prayag: Hindi Sahitya Sammelan, 1966., pp. 26 ff.

[22] Mirabai conceived of the relationship between the worshipper and God in familiar human terms (e.g., the lover and beloved), while more abstract poets such as Kabir and his contemporary Nanak, the first Sikh Guru, portrayed the Divine as singular and ineffable.

[23] The epithet "Giridhar" (mountain bearer) relates to a legend found in *Bhâgavata Purâṇa* to the effect that Indra had been the deity worshipped among the pastoral people of Vraja. Krishna persuaded them to stop such worship. Indra enraged, sent a deluge of rain to overwhelm them, but Krishna lifted Mt. Govardhana and held it for seven days and nights as a shelter until Indra relented and paid homage to him.

[24] Possibly Rana Sanga, Mira's brother-in-law. See Goetz, *op. cit.*, p. 18.

[25] Unfortunately, there is no critical edition of Mirabai's *padas*. For the purposes of the present study we rely on Pandit Chaturvedi's collection of 202 *padas* in *Mira ki Padâvali*. References to *padas* are taken from Pandit Chaturvedi , *Ibid.* Translations are mine unless otherwise stated.

[26] *Gopîs*, wives of cowherd men, are depicted in the *Purânas* as dancing with Krishna in the great moonlit circle dance, in which he replicates himself so that each *gopî* thinks Krishna is with her. Similarly, the *gopîs* double themselves, leaving shadow images of themselves with their unsuspecting husbands. The *gopis* are both Krishna's wives and lovers.

[27] *Ibid.*, pp. 44-45.

[28] A mythical bird that is supposed to feed only on moonbeams.

[29] Chaturvedi, *op. cit.*, p.45.

[30] Vallabhacharya has described four kinds of possible relationships between a devotee and God: *vâtsalya* (child and parent), *dâsya* (servant and master), *sâkhya* (friend and friend), and *mâdhurya* (lover and beloved).

[31] The Sanskrit term *âsakti*, which is part of the descriptive title of each of the eleven manifestations of *bhakti*, has the basic sense of "attachment" or "addiction". Its frequent translation as "love of" is confusing, especially in the context of speaking of *bhakti*.

[32] An immense legendary serpent, with five heads all breathing fire, which lived in a pool of the Yamuna River and menaced the cowherds in the area.

[33] According to tradition, the *catak* bird drinks and lives only on raindrops.

[34] This is not only the case in the monsoon. In *pada* 115 Mira tells how all twelve months inflict pain on her in her separation from Krishna. The twelve month (*bârahmâsa*) theme was very common in portraying *viraha* during the medieval period.

[35] For an excellent discussion of the nature of religious language see Sally McFague, *Metaphorical Theology*, Minneapolis: Fortress Press, 1982.

Hindu Theology and Faithful Discipleship

Eric J Lott

'Why Hindu Theological Systems?'

To have shared the journey of faith with Israel Selvanayagam has been for me a great privilege. With Israel as a fellow-traveller, naturally there have also been moments of critical challenge! Not long after becoming my student well over 30 years ago, in his usual direct, even blunt, style Israel questioned the focus of my thinking: 'Why do you spend so much time on elitist issues like the Hindu Vedantic systems? What have such philosophical concerns to do with the heart of Christian discipleship, or even with getting to the heart of Hindu faith?' That was the gist of his critique.

My response at the time – a little animated I recall – affirmed my particular sense of personal vocation: 'If there is to be dialogue with Hindu theologians, entering their thought-world is a necessary part of such dialogue. Vedantic theology dominates that "thought-world". Engaging as deeply as possible with this theology is, I believe, essential to my missionary vocation in India'. In spite of the defensiveness of this response to young Israel, in what follows the discerning may well be able to trace the impact of the disciple on the mind of the teacher!

Are Belief-Systems Important – in Hindu Tradition?

Issues of belief - what sort of world, what sort of God, what sort of human being and human community and global destiny we envisage, and how we formulate such visionary beliefs - are issues of ultimate importance. We are surely right in rejecting the fundamentalist's absolutising of particular faith-statements. We are, though, wrong if we then assume, as many do today, that belief-systems and doctrines either matter very little, or even necessarily distort the reality of faith.

In a recent popular book, for example, Harvey Cox (2009) argues, rather like - Wilfred Cantwell Smith (1987), though with less subtlety, that 'beliefs' should be sharply distinguished from 'faith'. He condemns, rightly, as a fatal flaw in Christian history the Church's absolutising of credal statements of its faith. In reality, this assent to a tightly drawn up *set of beliefs* as the test of true Christianity was as much a political ploy (led by Constantine) as concerned with theological truth. However, to give absolute authority to particular faith statements is very different from the recognition that beliefs - especially what is believed about God and world - are of ultimate importance in the life of faith.

This discounting of belief-systems is especially common today among the large number of westerners dabbling on the edges of Eastern religions. Cox, along with many others, claims that 'Hindus' give little importance to 'beliefs' (*op. cit.*, p.221). The most recent reliable studies of Hindu tradition, such as by Israel's Cambridge professor, Julius Lipner (2010) and by another outstanding scholar in this field, Gavin Flood (1996; 2003), may well agree that earlier western 'orientalists' wrongly ascribed to 'Hinduism' the creed-based orthodoxy they believed to be essential to all respectable religion; but these recent scholars in Hindu religious life also assert the crucial role of 'theology' in a wide range of Hindu tradition (cf. E.Lott, 'Hindu Theology', in G.A.Oddie (edit.), *A Handbook of Hinduism in Asia*, Sage forthcoming).

It is quite true, of course, that 'theologies' function differently in Hindu religious traditions; certainly none gives precisely the same status to credal statements of 'faith' that we see in Christian tradition. Yet, Hindu symbol-systems (e.g. that underlying the sacred structure of a Hoysala temple, with its meaning-infused symbolic layers)are inextricably related to belief-systems.

It is also true that in the end none of our thought-systems, Christian or Hindu, suffice to *express fully the heart of faith*. Theologians of both traditions agree on this, though in very different ways. There *is* a sense, then, in which 'faith' goes 'beyond belief'. Our belief-systems, our credal statements, cannot be absolutised, cannot be taken as final expressions of our faith in God. Mystery is at the heart of that faith. Doctrinal statements, therefore, will always be in one sense *provisional*.

Nor is 'theology' always *systematic*. Indeed, the vital springs of most intellectually well-ordered doctrinal systems, Christian and Hindu, Vaiṣṇava and Śaiva, may well be the dis-orderly world of ecstatic dance, mythic story, mystic symbol, poetic and visual imagery, i.e. the visionary world of the religiously inspired. Israel's own earlier research into the Tamil Śaiva mystic poet, Mâṇikka Vâcagar, with his vision of the 'heart-melting' love of his Lord, is just one striking example of this. That kind of ecstatic experience lies at the core of systematic Śaiva Theology (Siddhânta).

Indeed, our great Apostle rightly claims that we are to be '*fools* for Christ's sake', taking even further the word of Jesus about becoming child-like in our attitude. Intellectual attainment does not enable us to 'enter God's realm'; our worldly 'wisdom' becomes useless 'foolishness'. Yet, the 'first commandment' Jesus pointed to enjoins loving God with 'all your mind', as well as with heart and soul. So, even if there will always be tension between faith and reason (as well as between the faith-reasoning process and self-giving praxis), deeply engaging reflection on the *meaning* of faith is part of our human response to God. And this must necessarily include reflection on the *meaning of the faith of others, and the significance of that faith for our own.*

To take this one step further: Any sustained empathetic engagement with those Hindus who have struggled through the ages with the meaning of their faith, has to entail *dialogical engagement within their intellectual world*. I remain convinced that this particular form of dialogical engagement is an urgently needed strand of true Christian witness, and has been crucial to my own missionary vocation. It remains part of my aiming to love God 'with heart, mind and soul/ strength'. Whether my own dialoguing has always been a form of *faithful* discipleship is another question. At least the challenge to such intellectual engagement is inescapable.

For, no matter how much we nuance the role of belief in Hindu religious life, faith expressed through very specific beliefs and doctrines, and often worked out in impressive theological systems, is a deeply embedded part of Hindu tradition. In all this, the *process* of systematising is as important as the *content* of our belief-systems.

Misunderstanding 'Hindu Theology'

As there are still many misconceptions about 'Hindu Theology', let me briefly list some basic features of those theological traditions:

(1). We have to affirm the *diversity and plurality* inherent to Hindu religious life, including its intellectual life during the centuries. Very clearly there is not just *one* theology, one *darśana* or visionary viewpoint. We need not take up the question as to what extent there is – culturally and theologically - 'unity in diversity'. This is the contention of the neo-Hindu apologetic that now so thoroughly dominates popular interpretation of 'Hinduism', Indian and western. Sometimes this is expressed as 'Many paths, one goal', a slogan that obviously assumes far too much concerning the nature of that 'one goal'.

(2) Without question it is *Vedantic Theology* that for about a millennium, and (in the form of 'Neo-Vedanta') increasingly in the past 125 years, has dominated Hindu 'systematic' articulation of faith. None of the 'Six Visionary Positions' should be disregarded altogether, for each is worked out with remarkable intellectual rigour and vigour. It is, though, the 'Later Exegesis' (the 'End of Vedic Revelation': *Veda-anta*) that very clearly deserves its position of pre-eminence; it was Vedânta that most successfully articulated the widest range of faith-experience found within 'Hinduism'.

(3) The frequent assumption that 'Vedânta means Advaita (as represented pre-eminently by Úaṃkara)', is clearly based on bias, on a particular choice between variant Vedantic positions (though it is Úaṃkara who proved increasingly successful among India's intelligentsia, to some extent no doubt, for political reasons. At critical periods such as the time of the Vijayanagar Empire and later in defining the most inclusive possible 'Hindu' identity when struggling against foreign rule, a non-dualist stance seemed far less internally divisive and more nationally inclusive.

The reality is, though, that there are serious differences on crucial faith-issues, as Vedantins themselves declared with great vigour. For example:

Is the created world, is our socio-cultural life, the material objects within our universe, *real* in an ultimate sense? Is there, or is there not, an ultimate *distinction* to be made between the Highest Self and the inner Âtman, or are we to see that *all* such difference is, ultimately, illusory? Is *relationship*, however 'inseparable' (Râmânuja's often-used term), the relationship of *dependence and devout love*, ultimately significant, or not?

In spite of what Neo-Vedantins claim, reconciling - theologically - these and other differences of faith-perception can be done only by making (in each case) one position first-order and the other second-order and thus lacking in ultimacy. There has been a fierce struggle within this tradition concerning 'the End (Meaning) of Vedic Revelation'.

In all our theological debates, there are, invariably, shared positions as well as points of crucial difference. Within Vedânta too there are a number of such shared features. In a publication just before Israel became my student (1980:10-19) I described ten such. Here I merely mention without further comment four core doctrines: (a) Vedanta's one great concern must be to find a true vision of 'Brahman' ('the expanding one'), the Great Being, the Highest Person; (b) to understand how that Great Being is the sole source of all things; (c) to find self-liberation through this vision; (d) and belief that such a vision is dependent on the Revelation of scripture rather than on reason (there being 'three foundation-sources' (*prasthâna-traya*) for doing theology – i.e. Vedanta is exegesis of Upaniṣads, Bhagavad Gîtâ, and the (555) Brahma Sûtras; in this theological process there is a dialectic between 'Hearing (i.e. listening to the revelatory word of scripture and guru), reflecting/reasoning, and interiorising').

Again, we need to note how different were the styles of exegesis of, say, Śaṃkara, Râmânuja and Madhva. Śaṃkara's very sophisticated view of the words of scripture as 'indirect pointers' was very different from the more realist approaches of the other two (Lott 1980:173ff). Yet, all witness to the great importance of the commentarial tradition in Vedantic history. Not only do they interpret the Word given from the past; in turn each great teacher's commentary, though taken as authoritative, is further interpreted, its meaning pushed further. This is all part of a thoroughly theological process, and those Christian theologians – Catholics such a R.V.De Smet and F.Clooney (1993) in particular – are correct in seeing the *theological* process (and at some points content too) between Hindu and Christian traditions as very similar.

Critical Questions for Vedantic Theology

Some readers may well feel how justified young Israel was with his critical question 30 years ago! Is this Vedantic theology, and the attempt to engage dialogically with it, actually an elitist *dis-engagement* from the ground realities in Indian society that face those who follow the way of a suffering Lord? Does it lessen any such elitism to claim remarkable analogies between this deep-rooted Hindu theological process and the ways in which Christian theologies have been worked out? At least for myself this engagement has led not only to deeper understanding of crucial paths of Hindu faith, but even to a sharpening both of my theological *self-understanding* as a minister of Christ in India and of my calling to share the suffering of that Servant-Christ. (What I mean by that will have to wait for another occasion).

Even so, I freely acknowledge there are critical questions raised by talk of engaging with Vedantic theologies. Yes, it *is* elitist, in the sense that few Indian Christians can be expected to share actively this particular form of 'engagement'. That, however, applies to most of our theologising. And I for one do not feel the need therefore to do away with all intellectual discourse in relation to faith, especially in relating to people of other faith. We must not forget: 'Love God with all your heart, *mind* and strength'.

The key question here, though is: What are the *dynamics* underlying and interwoven with Vedantic theology? To see this outstanding strand of Hindu religious life solely as expressive of 'Brahmanism' (because the *Brahman* – the neuter form - is its focus), or as an intellectual cover to hide a 'sacred' Dharma irrevocably Brahmin-dominated and therefore oppressive of all those deemed 'polluted', is to miss key factors, historical, experiential factors, lying behind Vedantic theology's emergence. That 'Brahminism' is hegemonic in character is undeniable, just as various power-centres in Christian history have aimed for 'hegemonic' dominance. Yet, the 'struggles' within the development of 'Hinduism' through the ages, struggles to break free from dominance by any but the Great One beyond, beneath and begetting all else, are struggles that we need both to reckon with as much as with the 'Brahmanising'. Empathising with those 'struggles' within Hindu history is also needed, as I have discussed elsewhere (in Selvanayagam 2002:76-83).

In particular, (a) whether we translate *Veda-anta* as the 'end' of the Vedas, or as their 'meaning', it is clear that here we have a movement (often led by *non-Brahmins*) that seeks to take us beyond Vedic/ Brahmanic ritual, in crucial ways even beyond adherence to the Dharma. Clearly, this movement takes up aspects of the 'Struggler', or 'Striver' (*Úramaṇa*) movements (Selvanayagam 1996:144-162), for whom the priestly ritual and dharmic observance were deemed useless for the soul's true destiny.

(b) Even more significant, the dynamic roots for many Vedantic theologians can be found, as noted earlier above, in the passionate devotion, in the ecstatic singing and dancing of many of the *Bhakti* movements. The Tamil Âḷvârs (those 'drowned' in love), and equally the Úaiva God-lovers such as Mâṇikka Vâcagar, may have been the principal early examples of this *bhakti*-passion; but many more such movements were to follow. Many of them were essentially counter-cultural in spirit, yet many also went on to find intellectual expression in either a form of Vedânta or a Siddhânta of similar style.

True, there are other streams within Vedânta for whom this ecstatic religiosity is either absent or plays little part. Úaṃkara's non-dualist Advaita Vedânta is no doubt extremely important in the history of this theological tradition. But, even if Úaṃkara did write a few devotional songs, they remain very secondary to the main thrust of his theology. God as the personal Being to be adored and loved with passion is far from a dominant theme for Advaita. Admittedly, this Advaitic position also entails a less serious view of sacral life: only the One is Absolute.

(c) There are, however, other key-themes found in those love-based belief-systems that are equally significant. Four features (especially prominent in the theology of Râmânuja) should be noted:

(i) There is the conviction – an extraordinary contradiction of the Advaitic view - that *all creation is utterly real*. Yes, we humans may often be deluded, in e.g. seeing the material, mortal, changeable body as the true and eternal self within that body; but our misguided perceiving, and the body's mortality, in no way diminish its reality. It is not an illusion, nor does it lack ultimacy. And this is because everything is the creation of the Great One, and, even in their materiality, all beings share in the reality of that Being's life. God's creativity is the basis for the realism of this worldview. Again, we note a problem: this 'realism' can also lead to not only an unprotesting acceptance of inequalities and suchlike, but even to their 'sacralising', especially when linked to the view that karmic law, operated by the Creator, accounts for such unpleasantries. Such, though, is not an intrinsic outcome to Hindu theistic realism.

(ii) Linked with this realism, there is belief in the *ultimate reality of the divine embodiment* (and although multiple Avatars were part of the Hindu worldview, in practice one compellingly divine 'Descent' – especially Krishna – was the special Focus of South Indian Vaiṣṇava devotion. In the North, for some God-sects it was Rama). In almost every case, the theists repudiated an 'as if' view of their Lord's embodiment.

This Avatâra doctrine, again, had to reckon with the question of *karma*, seen as the power determining each body's particularities. Râmânuja argued that in the case of God's embodiment, he is in no way subject to karma's power. For Christians, obviously aspects of this Hindu (and Buddhist) worldview are seriously problematic. In particular, the idea that our present birth, whether to a life of pleasure or pain, is the result of deeds, good or bad, committed in previous births. The thought – surely well-grounded – that we do inherit a burden from the past, that we do experience the consequences of our fathers' actions, is hardly the same as a full-blown karma-doctrine.

Briefly, we should also note the tendency in this Vaiṣṇava tradition to see divine embodiment, Avatâra-power-points, in the image-forms central to sacred temples. This too poses problems, especially for Protestant Christians – though the experience of divine glory, a sense of the Sacred, as present at many points of our earthly existence is surely one that Indian Christians are far more likely to find resonance with than will modern secularised western Christians. Along with love-possessed Hindu *bhaktas* who focussed their devotion on a recognised sacred shrine, quite a few sang scathingly of blind faith in such pilgrim-centres and even in Vedic scripture without inner vision.

(iii) Leading on from this, there is the outstandingly fruitful teaching of Râmânuja's (which he found deeply embedded in Vedic and Vaishnava scriptures) that the whole universe is to be seen as the *body of the Great Self* on which that 'body' is utterly dependent. God's life is thus seen as pervading, animating, sustaining all creaturely life. And this self-body, or God-world, relationship is one of 'inseparability'.

As I have written at great length on this theme in many other places (1980; and even in an earlier work first written in 1970, *God and Universe in the Vedantic Theology of Ramanuja*, Ramanuja Research Society, Chennai), here I merely reiterate that such a cosmology can be remarkably fruitful in re-visioning our eco-bound existence as part of creation. While this idea of a divine 'body' tends to be vigorously rejected by exponents of *Dalit* ideology (especially because of the Rig-vedic passage that speaks of Brahmins as the mouth, and finally of the low-caste as the feet), several *women* Christian theologians have with equal vigour espoused this image of the world as God's 'body'. They have, though, rarely referred to the prominent place it has in this Hindu tradition.

(iv) What we see in great swathes of these theistic Vedantins' writings is the *ultimacy of the love-relationship*, 'love's absolute response to love' (in Selvanayagam 2002:81) that is at the centre of *bhakti*-life. And divine *grace* - the undeserved love of God that draws a love-response, sometimes wildly extravagant, from the *bhakta* - is invariably at the centre of a serious 'love-based-faith. Theologically we find metaphors for divine grace such as the Tengaḷai idea of the mother cat picking up the loved one; the devotee's destiny does not depend on hanging on like a young monkey, which was the picture depicted by more restrained interpreters who insisted divine grace had to be matched by human effort. (Very close to the debate found in early Christian theology). And throughout the *bhakti* movements, the 'extravagance' of love for God is expressed in various exuberant forms - especially in singing and dancing to the rhythms of the Lord's heartbeat, even confessing the 'madness' of being seduced by the Divine Lover.

Clearly, in these God-love movements that lie behind many formal and systematic Hindu theologies there are elements of a counter-cultural, sometimes wildly untamed, and socially inclusive religiosity that is very different from the *dharma*-dominated religious formalism we find in Hinduism's developed communities. Vedanta has roots as much in the untamed inclusiveness as in domesticating dharma; yet, the constraints often show. Even with the great Râmânuja, in order to be an acceptable Exegete (a Vedantin), though he never loses sight of the 'overwhelming' love of God, and that God's many other wonder-evoking qualities, we do see a diminishing of the spontaneity of his Ālvâr predecessors and the danger of a dominance of dharmic formalities. He had become a respectable Âchârya and the Establishment had proved powerful. We noted above even the danger of an absolutising of given sacral structures (not necessarily Vedic as it happens; Pañcarâtra sacral tradition was clearly prominent too, though the possible significance of this is too complex to dwell on here). A non-dualist like Úaṃkara, in spite of a very weak role for divine grace, was able to sit more lightly to those given sacral structures, as nothing but his all-transcending Brahman, the '*Nir-Guṇa*', is absolutely and ultimately real. At this point a challenge to Râmânuja's worldview by Úaṃkara has to be recognised, though I see the former's counter challenge as the stronger.

Theistic 'realism', then, can bring its own dangers, but it is surely within those *bhakti*-related religious streams that Indian Christians will usually be far more at home, especially if presenting a challenge either to dharmic orthodoxy on the one hand or to a spirituality of other-worldly transcendence on the other. Irrevocably central was *relationality at every level*, based on the primary relationship with a thoroughly personal God. The theo-logic of seeing the whole universe in relational terms is that all creatures are irrevocably part of that relational life.

A *Dalit*-Indian-Christian Theology ?

With the emergence of Dalit Theology, a huge question-mark now looms over any talk of 'Indian-Christian Theology'. Up to the 1970s, so muted were Dalit, Tribal and other Subaltern voices in recognised theological and ecclesial circles, that none were taken to represent 'Indian-Christian' faith-talk. And this was despite being, by the 1920s, a substantial majority of the Christian community. The burgeoning and vibrant new Dalit consciousness tends, understandably, to eschew all attempts at Indian Christian self-discovery and faith-expression through exploration of any form of Hindu-related religious consciousness and spiritual imagery.

Within Catholic circles also there has been a rigorous turning back from those vigorous expressions of 'inculturation' - theological, liturgical, ecclesial - following Vatican II. Add to this the accusations by militant nationalist Hindutva that any such inculturation is 'stealing the clothes' of sacred Hindu tradition merely for proselytising purposes, and we see a further reason for the growing *polarising* of opposed positions.

As we saw, even within Hindu theological history for many centuries there were vigorous 'struggles' in the shaping of Hindu theologies. The bland 'inclusivism' of Neo-Vedanta has greatly blunted this vibrant theological process. And any inclusivism now tends to be seen as inevitably 'hegemonic' - the dominant group co-opting, incorporating and thus emasculating less powerful bodies. Even Marxism seems to have been incorporated into the Market! Yet, exclusive polarity is not the only alternative. For, even as a polar ideology, there is the danger of being shaped by globally dominant ways of envisioning reality. Strands of these globalist forces – both fundamentalist and secularising – are as dangerous to the spiritual life and theological visioning of Indian Christians as 'Brahmanism' has been. Any 'inclusive' indigeneity must not lose its critical vision.

Is such a 'critical, yet inclusive, indigeneity' possible? Perhaps with the new-found confidence of theologians within Dalit, Tribal and Women's movements, we might here find the enabling inspiration for new forms of indigenous Indian-Christian theology. For, it is those peculiarly 'inborn' ways of experiencing the world and all others, as an essential part of experiencing God-in-Christ, that we need in authentic theologising in India today. To see such ways of relating to God as having an organic link with crucially important strands of Hindu Theology is not as far-fetched as it first seems! Thankyou Israel, for having further stimulated my struggle to be faithful to Christ in my Indian ministry.

Bibliography

Clooney, Francis SJ, *Theology after Vedanta: An Exercise in Comparative Theology*, SUNY 1993.

Cox, Harvey, *Faith for the Future*, Harper Collins 2009.

Flood, Gavin, *Introduction to Hinduism*, Cambridge 1996.

Flood, Gavin (ed.), *Blackwell Companion to Hinduism*, Blackwell 2003.

Lott, Eric, *Vedantic Approaches to God*, Macmillan 1980.

Oddie, Geoff (ed.), *A Handbook of Hinduism in Asia*, Sage (forthcoming).

Selvanayayam, Israel (ed.), *Moving Forms of Theology*, ISPCK 2002.

Selvanayagam, Israel, *Vedic Sacrifice: Challenge and Response*, Manohar 1996.

Smith, W.Cantwell, *Faith and Belief*, Princeton 1987.

Thangaraj, Thomas, *The Crucified Guru: An Experiment in Cross-Cultural Christology*, Abingdon 1994.

Should Theology be at the
Heart of the Study of Religion?

P. Pratap Kumar

As a tribute to my friend and post-graduate classmate in Bangalore in the early 1980s, the Revd Dr Israel Selvanayagam, it seems fitting to offer this review of the substantive proposal that our then professor, Eric Lott, made in his work *Vision, Tradition, Interpretation: Theology, Religion and the Study of Religion* (1988). I have chosen to address a central proposal that Lott makes for greater 'mutual dependence' between Theology and Religious Studies.

Greater Role for Theology in Religious Studies?

Much of this book is an analysis of the nature of theology and the inner dynamics of the theological process. In addition, Lott not only offers a comprehensive review of the works of numerous scholars in the fields of both theology and religious studies, he also argues for a more comprehensive and sustained role for theology in the study of religion. He sets out to demonstrate how by giving priority to the 'self understanding of each tradition', and by 'integrating the sacred Focus which participants in religious traditions see as of crucial significance', there can be mutual interdependence between the two fields (Lott 1988: 254). In the three decades since this, various theologians interested in a meaningful relationship between Theology and Religious Studies have made similar proposals, particularly highlighting the enhanced place of Theology in the Study of Religion. It is for this reason Lott's work is worthwhile examining in some detail.

What is interesting since Lott made this proposal (actually written in 1981) is that not only Christian theologians but also scholars of religion who consider themselves as insiders, be they ethnic insiders or converts from a previously western background (largely Christian), have made this call to give greater priority to the insider's views and interpretations in the study of religion. Especially in many western countries, particularly in North America, there has been a significant growth among insider scholars who now study and teach their religions in western universities, and this new phenomenon has given impetus to the call for greater sensitivity to the insider's views in the study of religion.

This tendency needs to be placed in the perspective of varied responses, often negative, from the first generation immigrants who have settled in western countries for career reasons and who are mostly from a middle class background. They have often expressed their angst about perceived misrepresentations of their religions by western scholars. With the second generation ethnic communities beginning to take up study of their own religions and entering the academy, the emphasis on teaching and interpreting religions with insider voices and interpretations as the basis for the study of religion began to become more and more pronounced. The present trends in the American Academy of Religion conferences and the various articles often published in this regard in the *Journal of the American Academy of Religion* are good demonstrations of this phenomenon. For instance, the *JAAR* 69:4 (2000) produced a Special Issue on "Who Speaks for Hinduism." Scholars who wrote essays for the Special Issue, both western scholars as well as ethnic Hindus, emphasized the need for insiders to speak for the tradition. So, it is obvious that Lott is not alone in making his proposal for a significant role for theology in the Scientific Study of Religion.

'Theology' in Other Religions?

But, before we address this broader issue, let us first take care of some related and perhaps significant issues. First, Lott deploys the category 'theology' across religions while at the same time demanding conceptual integrity and coherence within each religious tradition. When he uses expressions like, "...the diverse theologies in our religious traditions", "theological process in any religious tradition"

(Lott 1988: 1), he seems to take for granted that 'theology' is a universal category. Not that he is unaware of the particular history of theology in the western Christian tradition and its one time judgmental attitude to other religions. And he defines 'theology' as "any mode of approach to religious phenomena that is thought to be determined *a priori* by some particular or esoteric presupposition of what religion is" (Lott 1988: 6). In this sense even Theravada Buddhism is included. However, this way of extending 'theology' and 'theologians' to include other religions does obfuscate the fact that the terms lose not only cultural integrity in the context of other cultural traditions, but there is also an implicit hegemonic tendency in trying to deploy terms beyond their cultural context. Besides, there is no evidence of interpreters and commentators in other religions thinking of their work as 'theology' and themselves as 'theologians'. Even present day Swamis, Gurus, and Babas don't seem to see themselves doing theology. The idea of Christian theologians thinking of the interpretive task in other religions as 'theology' might at best be seen as self-reflection of their own work.

Additionally, what is important to remember is that Christian theology, in the last two hundred years in particular, developed a highly complex academic discourse that is absent in other religions, particularly in the East. For instance, in Hinduism we do not find commentarial tradition since the time of the medieval period. Even though the medieval commentarial tradition undertaken by such eminent *bhâṣyâkâras* as Shankara and Ramanuja was characterized by their primary task of proving their particular religious point of view, that commentarial tradition is hard to be found since almost the time of the Mogul period. And today the many Swamis, Gurus and Babas who go around the West speaking about Hinduism are not to be considered commentarians but rather presenters of a watered down Vedanta Hinduism; certainly not doing what can be termed 'academic theology'.

In the absence of any western model of academic theological discourse in the East, it is highly misleading to speak of 'theology' even in the writings of Hindu medieval commentators. Conflating Indian theistic traditions with western Christian 'God' traditions is also misleading as it obfuscates the real differences in the way Indian thinkers conceptualized god, gods and goddesses. In the Vedic tradition, gods were no more than guests who came down to receive offerings and bestow gifts on their human counterparts (humans too could become gods and the Mahabharata heroes were once gods). And in the later mythological traditions, even the notion of a supreme God is much more about highly diverse regional manifestations than unified notions of Vishnu or Shiva or Shakti, as these mythological traditions cannot be disconnected from the local cultic temples. Even Ramanuja (of whom Lott has written widely) had to seek permission from Ranganatha to go to Varadaraja's temple, an episode that is well known in the Srivaishnava tradition. Even though one might think that both are Vishnu, to the people at the respective temples, it did not seem to matter. And the Ishvara of classical Yoga is nothing more than an instrumental arrangement between Purusha and Prakriti. With such diverse conceptions of god, gods and goddesses in the Indian tradition, it is misleading to subsume them under the broad category of theism and then conflate it with theology. Such conflations do no greater service than assist a Christian theologian to seek out 'theologies' elsewhere and offer misleading comparisons.

The main difficulty with extending the category of 'theology' in the service of comparative study, however, is its inability to go beyond a particular 'religious commitment'. Lott sees 'religious commitment' as central to the theological task, and even questions whether "all faith-commitment has to be suspended in a properly systematic approach to religions" (Lott 1988: 4). I have discussed this issue at some length in a forthcoming article.[1] It is understandable for 'religious commitment' to be central to the theological task. Even in the context of theology, it has to be in some broader sense beyond denominational and sectarian boundaries. But it presents serious methodological and epistemological problems if we wish such commitment to be part of, possibly even central to, the task of the study of religion.

W.C. Smith (1962, 1979), whom Lott refers to extensively, had previously demonstrated the difficulties in 'faith' being equated with 'belief'. Smith's main argument rested on the fact that faith is dynamic and changing and particular, whereas belief tends to reify religious commitment. However, the academic study of religion, whether done by insiders or outsiders, fundamentally depends on its methodological

---

[1] P. Pratap Kumar, "Does Comparative Theology have advantage over Religious Studies?" (*Journal of the American Academy of Religion*, forthcoming).

and hence its epistemological sagacity to make the data available to others who wish to undertake the study. If the data is solely generated on the basis of faith, then faith - being personal, subjective and lacking constancy - not only eludes the scholar's attention, it seriously inhibits careful and detailed documentation and comparison of the data. Besides, such faith-limited data becomes unavailable to scholars who may or may not be part of the tradition that is being studied, let alone those who have no religious commitment at all.

For this reason elsewhere I have argued in favour of studying Hinduism non-religiously (see Kumar 2008). What I am arguing for is that the data should be available to scholars whether they are insiders or outsiders and in this sense, religious commitment has no particular value in the study of religion.

Empathetic Value of Faith in Study of Religions?

Furthermore, the implication that religious commitment enables one to sympathize or empathize with a religious point of view has no real basis in one's ability and willingness to understand the other. This particular concern that non-religious people may not understand religious people has its deep-seated roots in the unfortunate division of society into secular and religious. Such notions have been championed by several earlier religious studies scholars, such as Mircea Eliade (1969) and others. In his quest of religious humanism, Eliade over-emphasized the religiosity of human beings to the extent that secular society is seen as an impediment in the search for religious meaning. However, one cannot ignore the fact that such a division of secular and religious in essence is deeply political rather than religious. One does not need to rehearse the whole of western history to understand the political underpinnings of such division in the West for control of political power by the state on the one side and the church on the other. Much theology in the western Christian societies was constructed in this context and therefore theological obsession for separating secular and the religious must be understood in this context.

Furthermore, to suggest that religious people may understand religions better, even if they are from another tradition, is not only to privilege religious people with some additional epistemological tools. More importantly, there is no evidence in society that this does really happen. There is perhaps more evidence to show that religious people are the ones who miss other religious people's point of view, by either not caring for other religions and being fundamentalist about their own religious convictions, or simply being ignorant of other religions. Here I applaud Lott's insistence that scholars should understand and engage in the study of religion as well as in the study of theology and thereby perhaps better understand their own religions. Nevertheless, it is important to recognize that privileging religious commitment for the study of religion denies our human ability to communicate in comprehensible language. We communicate across our differences in cultural backgrounds not because we share a common cultural commitment, but rather we share an ability to communicate in language that is translatable and objectifiable, albeit with conceptual difficulties.

Discerning Meaning and Possible 'Reductionism'

Lott, nevertheless, rightly emphasizes the importance of the *understanding of the meaning* of the religious tradition of the people one is attempting to study for the adequate account of that tradition (Lott 1988: 10-11). However, this is only the preliminary step in the methodological process in the study of religion. For, a scholar of religion then places such understanding comparatively alongside the data from other religions. Methodologically it is the scholar's theoretical intentions and goals that influence not only the choice of the data, but more importantly the meaning of that data. In other words, the comparative study of religion is not about merely discovering the internal meaning of the tradition, but more importantly it is for the purpose of explaining the social phenomenon that we call religion. The task is to offer a generalisable understanding that any scholar can possibly verify.

Lott's concern about the 'reductionism' (Lott 1988: 13, 160ff) by scholars of religion in attempting to explain religion is unwarranted. As he rightly agrees, fundamentally any description is in some sense reductionism; and this is true equally of theological studies. There is no such thing as pure description devoid of choice of what to describe. In other words, every description is implicitly a choice of data. There is always a point to that description and that point drives the process of choosing the data. However, Lott defines reductionism as "an account which attempts to explain the religious phenomena in terms that are intrinsically *not compatible* with the meaning expressed by the tradition's theologians." (Lott 1988:13). It is, thus, 'ontological compatibility' between the modes of interpretation from outside and a "tradition's own interpretation" that he argues for (*op. cit.*, 165). But the purpose of the behavioural sciences or academic studies of religion is to understand the empirical aspects of religion rather than engaging in debates about, for instance, the existence or the lack of a tradition's trans-empirical phenomena.

Here much depends on what is meant by 'compatibility'. But even with Lott's distinctive defining of 'reductionism', it has to be stated that the object of the academic study of religion seems to be lost. For, as mentioned above, its purpose, being comparative in nature, is to offer an explanation of the data, accessible to all, that is collected from different religions within the overall social context of those religions. And that explanation is not necessarily accepted as the intention of the theologians. But that does not make the explanation invalid or irrelevant to society. Take for example, the study of Ganesha by Paul Courtright, or studies of Shiva by Wendy Donniger. Although such studies became objects of vehement opposition by militant nationalist Hindus, as scholars we miss the point if we do not understand the theoretical background of such studies.

Priority of Empirical, Accessible Data

What one needs to understand is that in the hands of academic scholars of religion religious data cannot be sacrosanct or privileged. In so far as the data is part of human society, they are obligated to place such data alongside other data, and it is unfortunate and unnecessary to divide the data into 'religious' and hence privileged on the one hand, and 'secular', hence not privileged on the other. In other words, scholars of the academic study of religion need to explain religion in the context of everything else that goes on in the world, and this indeed calls for treating data with even-handedness. In order to explain the social significance of religion, scholars of religion have much more to say than that to which theologians wish to limit their data. Therefore, the data of scholars of religion is not merely religious, but a whole host of aspects of that society that might have some implicit or explicit connection. In other words, religion cannot be disconnected from other aspects of society.

For methodological and theoretical reasons, scholars of religion cannot be satisfied with data only from the theologian's systemic articulations or statements from religious texts such as scriptures, commentaries and so on. An example would be to consider the difference in interpreting the creation narrative or the flood narrative in the biblical texts between theologians of the tradition and the scholars of religion. There being several such narratives of creation and flood stories outside the Semitic world, scholars of religion are compelled to compare them to explain cross-cultural connections between these various narratives that may have some common home, or may not. Theologians on the other hand might be compelled to offer a theological interpretation of God's work in human history! But such is not the goal for the historian of religions.

It is true that Lott does not claim that 'theological' sources alone are to be the basis for studying religions, though his emphasis on empathy with distinctively 'religious' dimensions is marked. But, explaining religious data religiously is in fact impossible unless one is an insider and shares the same beliefs. Especially if one has to go with W.C. Smith's way of defining faith, there is really no way of explaining even if one is from within the same tradition, as faith is individual and hence changes from person to person. So, if that is the case, how does anyone access it and study it in order to explain it? At least on this point, Lott does not go as far as Smith did, but is willing to depend on linguistically available theological statements.

Significance of Symbol-Systems and 'Hidden Dynamics'?

While the interpretations of the theologians or participants may depend on their respective symbol systems that point to something beyond, the presence of symbol systems need not automatically assume, as Lott is anxious to claim, that "there is necessarily a dimension of life that is reflective, that is perceptive of meaning, that looks to a beyond dimension" (Lott 1988: 122). There may be some such 'beyond dimension', but it is not for the scholar of religion to vouch for this. This discipline has to be content to comment on what is mediated through language and is not privy to the internal meanings of the symbols, let alone intuitively capturing the meaning. Lott refers to how some scholars questionably rely upon intuition in their preliminary defining of religion (Lott 1988: 157). He does not make it clear enough that to ask scholars of religion to be intuitive in explaining religion is to ask for an unreliable and commonly inaccessible method. If intuition is let loose, then any explanation can get away on the claim that it is based on 'my intuition', even though the facts of the matter may vary. For this reason, obviously Lott considers another option that combines intuition with accounts of others and one's own observations (*Ibid*). But the important point is whether or not the explanation is available for subsequent verification and critique by other scholars.

Lott is concerned that behavioural sciences insist on privileging empirical investigation as able to decipher "the *hidden* dynamics of religious life", and thus is of 'decisive' importance in the study of religion (Lott 1988: 161-2). However, the point is that empirically available investigative tools and data are actually what we all can access and not mystically and intuitively available experiences. So, to argue that religion cannot be determined by anything other than itself (Lott 1988: 163) is rather illogical and romantic for the simple reason that religion exists in the empirical world, not in heaven! All that is possible to study is what it is possible to see and access through the epistemological tools that are commonly available to all. It is, furthermore, not true to assume that behavioural sciences make their empirical focus the "frame of reference" to understand religious life. Their theory is only to explain human behaviour and they have no further desire to speculate whether or not there is some "central, integrating Focus" beyond this world (Lott 1988: 165). Epistemologically speaking, there is no universal cognitive system that is available to all humans to confirm that there exists a "central, integrative Focus", unless one shares the beliefs of the tradition in which he or she is raised. This is not about ignoring the fact that for religious people who share in a common belief system there exists an integrative Focus beyond the empirical world. It is just that it cannot be the focus of the study of religion.

The Question of 'Truth-Claims' and their Evaluation

Linked to this question of critiquing religion is the question of 'truth-claims' which Lott contends are implicit within a religious stance. Thus, he queries the suggestion that "religious 'claims' are 'dispositional' rather than 'propositional', or perhaps 'indicative' rather than 'informative'." (Lott 1988: 177). Indeed, in the minds of believers, beliefs are not beliefs as such but are in some sense facts on which they build their lives. Lott recognizes that there is no way to evaluate these truth-claims of religions, but he allows that a comparative analysis of "ethical values and their consequences for human and cosmic life" may, with great sensitivity and within stringent limitations, be concerns of moral philosophers (*Ibid*). But – as Lott does concede with carefully expressed conditions - a critique of ethical values cannot be done without some critique of doctrinal aspects that are the basis on which such ethical stances are maintained in any religion. In a sense, therefore, critique of truth-claims is unavoidable in a pluralistic society and even scholars of religion cannot be immune to it.

Lott, therefore, concedes that philosophers of religion might engage in what might be seen as a form of apologetics. He argues, "[T]he line of demarcation here may not be very definite. Indeed, there is a sense in which just because philosophy of religion is in some respects close to various forms of theology, especially systematic, moral, and even apologetic theology, it must also work out its stance the more carefully and rigorously *independent* of any ultimate theological commitment" (Lott 1988: 178; emphasis in the original). Here Lott does clearly recognize a certain evaluatory role by philosophy of religion, but not to the extent that it becomes bipartisan. And he, therefore, reiterates that a philosopher of religion is to be "*independent* of any ultimate theological commitment." It is interesting that here Lott implicitly allows for the possibility of religious claims being critiqued, thus agreeing with scholars like Wiebe (1981).

Phenomenology of Religion

Coming to the crux of the matter, Lott gives considerable weight to phenomenology of religion among a range of approaches in the study of religion. After reviewing some of the classical phenomenologists of religion, including his own teacher Ninian Smart, Lott points out that "the basic concerns of phenomenology, i.e. *epoché* and *Einfühlung* (empathy) in particular, have been accepted in religious studies generally, certainly in comparative religion." Within this framework the "inner hermeneutical dimension" is to be part of comparative studies. In a sense, he sees phenomenology as offering useful methodological tools for comparative studies. And it is here he sees the interdependence of theology and religious studies (Lott 1988:191-192).

The problem with this proposal is that he seems to limit religious studies to the role of better expressing what the insider can inadequately express (notwithstanding his claim that religious studies should not be reduced to the status of handmaiden of theology) (Lott 1988: 185). Yet, religious studies is not able to refute the believer's stance on what he or she considers as the truth of their religion. Here to some extent he approves W.C. Smith's ideal stance: "[W]e cannot but admire the tenacity with which Wilfred Cantwell Smith has continued to affirm aspects of religious life which must surely be reckoned with: the unobjectifiable character of much of the *personal dimension in all religious histories in their everchanging historical dynamism*, and the corollary of this, the *dialogical nature of theological interpretation within a tradition* as it necessarily interacts with its context and with other traditions, are two of the constitutive factors in the process of understanding religious life" (Lott 1988: 201; emphasis mine).

However, what Lott, along with Smith, does not seem to be willing to concede is that the "personal dimension in all religious life" is *inaccessible* to an outside scholar of religion and hence poses a limitation for the study of religion. Unless this personal dimension is expressed in theological statements that are objectively accessible to outside scholars of religion, they serve no purpose for the comparative project in the study of religion. At some level they need to be objectifiable. Lott sees them on the one hand as 'unobjectifiable' and yet on the other hand wants them to be at the core of the comparative project in the study of religion.

An Integrated 'Science of Religion'?

It is therefore necessary to carefully examine Lott's comments concerning any 'Integral Science of Religion and Theology'. In general critical of attempts that establish a fully integrated system of theology and religion, he stresses both in Preface and Conclusion the essential distinction between Religious Studies and Theology. At the same time, there is the desire for much greater mutual interaction: it is this that we need to question. In considering the desirability of some kind of integrated 'Science of Religion', he quotes Wiebe's lament that there is no "methodological cohesiveness despite almost a century of discussion and debate" (Lott 1988: 203). But, given its diversity both in content and method and theory, as Lott himself recognizes, it is unavoidable for a field such as religious studies to lack such cohesiveness. He does reckon carefully with the various approaches to the study of religion – Historical, Behavioural Sciences, Philosophical Analysis, Comparative, Phenomenological, and what he calls 'Dialogical'. Yet, he tends to see religious studies as a 'discipline' (like theology?), though the wider consensus is to see it more as a 'field'.

In quoting Eliade's concern that "[T]he increasingly de-sacralised condition of the modern western world calls for its redirection away from its obsession with the profane and back to sacred reality" (Lott 1988: 205), Lott may not be endorsing this call for a 'unitive vision'. Yet, he is emphatic that "[I]t is to this essential core, the reality of the divine being, that the student of religion is to penetrate if there is to be an authentic understanding" (Lott 1988: 208). As this essay has argued throughout, it is unclear how methodologically and epistemologically one can ever figure out what that 'essential core' really is, given the vast amount of diversity that exists not only among different religions, but even within a single religion. In the absence of any consensus among religious people themselves on the reality of such divine being, how does anyone, let alone the scholar of religion, know what that 'essential core' really is. What methodological and epistemological tools are there that all scholars can deploy in the service of accessing such a goal?

Arguing that certain "peculiar qualities of scholarly sensitivity" are required, it seems that some form of 'religious' sensitivity is the foremost qualification in Lott's view. He suggests that just as musicians of one culture can appreciate the music of another culture, with empathy religious studies scholars may possibly have a more "authentic understanding of a[nother] religious tradition." (Lott 1988: 209). Yet, he does recognize that an inclusive theological vision cannot be itself the basis for an inclusive approach for all religions (Lott 1988: 210). Having surveyed a range of scholars from Georg Schmid, Charles Davis, John Hick, George Rupp, and Wolfhart Pannenburg, Lott recognizes the limits of their suggestions for an integral science of religion. Rightly he sees the difficulty of "systematic science of religion and the systematic theological process of any religious tradition" converging to such an extent that they become identical. He recognizes the imperative of the two cooperating, but realizes the complexity of such a task.

Thus, he calls for greater interdisciplinary interaction and "interfaith reflective level of theologizing" to "avoid either ungrounded theosophical syncretism, or merely constructing another 'theology of religions', in which the thought, faith and life of the other tradition is interpreted solely in terms of one's own doctrinal perspective" (Lott 1988: 231). However, he sees the possibility that the exposition of a tradition by the theologian of another tradition could possibly offer "an authentic contribution to interpretation of their faith" (Lott 1988: 232). These are positive suggestions. Yet, while he recognizes that theology depends on religious studies for "greater understanding of other traditions" (Lott 1988: 233), there is a tendency to see religious studies as a handmaiden of theology, even though he also quotes Joachim Wach with approval that "only by being independent of theology can the study of religion challenge and stimulate theology" (Lott 1988: 185).

Conclusion

No doubt it is a noble idea that theologians of one tradition can "gain clearer visionary perception within one's own tradition" in the light of the understanding they can gain from other religions through the work of the scholars of religion. But this self-understanding cannot be the primary task of religious studies, even if it might be an unanticipated consequence. It is clear that Lott's primary concern is the preservation of the theological agenda and how best the theological process can be assisted by the study of other religions.

Two important conclusions that he finally draws are important to note, namely:

1. The primacy of self-understanding of each tradition; 2. The primacy of the sacred Focus of each tradition. Without a doubt Lott wants to see a greater role for theology in the study of religion. But this is exactly the point that Jonathan Z Smith (2010) lamented when he pointed out that Tillichian theology continues to dominate the study of religion in North America, and by extension I might add the English speaking world in general. Making theology the centre of the study of religion only resulted in two rather unworkable options - in the hands of Eliade it resulted in some form of new universal humanism that has no followers; and in the hands of W.C. Smith it resulted in 'World Theology' that no one could own as it is devoid of social context. As much as it is idealistic and romantic to demand that "Theology and

Religion must be recognized as thoroughly interdependent" (Lott 1988: 256) such mutual cooperation cannot be based on a privileged position for theology. And as long as the 'sacred Focus', 'Transcendental reality' and the self-understanding of a tradition is the object of the study of religion, comparativism will only result in empirically unviable options.

So, to answer my question in the title, I reiterate that theological questions cannot be central to the study of religion, but can only form part of several other social, historical and geo-political considerations with which the phenomenon of religion is tied up. As Lott argues, that there should be mutual interdependence between theology and religion, and that religion should be independent of theology as a discipline is essential. But Lott's elaboration of this position undermines the fact that the study of religion has its object in a wider arena that encompasses all of human condition, and religion is but one aspect of that human condition that cannot be made its core. Any attempt to make such a claim is nothing less than ideological and political. In spite of my critique of Lott's theological position in relation to the study of religion, his is still one of the most astutely argued positions, compared to most theologians, that I have read in this debate.

References

Eliade, M. (1969) *The Quest: History and Meaning in Religion.* Chicago: University of Chicago Press.

Kumar, P. Pratap (2008) "Insiders and Outsiders: Studying Hinduism non-Religiously" in *Introducing Religion: Festschrift for Jonathan Z Smith,* edited by Russell McCutcheon and Willi Braun. London: Equinox, pp. 192-207.

Kumar, Pratap P. (2011) "Does Comparative Theology have advantage over Religious Studies?" (Forthcoming in *Journal of the American Academy of Religion*).

Lott, E. J. (1988) *Vision, Tradition, Interpretation: Theology, Religion and the Study of Religion.* Berlin: Mouton de Gruyter.

Smith, Jonathan Z. (2010) "Tillich('s) Remains", in *Journal of the American Academy of Religion,* December, Vol. 78, No. 4, pp. 1171–1181.

Smith, W.C. (1978) *Meaning and End of Religion.* London: SPCK.

Smith, W.C. (1979) *Faith and Belief.* Princeton: Princeton University Press.

Wiebe, Don. (1981) *Religion and Truth. Towards an Alternative Paradigm for the Study of Religion.* The Hague: Mouton.

Hindu-Christian Forums in Britain, National and in Leicester: Difficulties and Possibilities

Andrew Wingate

With decades of involvement with Hinduism, as theological educator, in practical dialogue, and academically (see the biographical essay) Israel rightly had hopes that his experience could be transferable, and that he could play a significant role in Hindu-Christian dialogue in Britain. This was never easy for him as an Indian Christian, as we shall see below. He was, however, able to take part in various dialogue evenings in Leicester, where we had established a Hindu-Christian group, the work of which I outline briefly here. We then look at the national forum, which I was invited to be part of, and where he served loyally for around 7 years.

Leicester Hindu-Christian Forum

This began in 2002, meeting several times a year. An example of agendas, in 2004, was: Living across faiths; How to use our scriptures; Our faith pilgrimages; The concept of sainthood. It was decided eventually to meet always in the same Hindu temple. Hospitality was normally better in temples, and Christians would more readily go to temples than vice versa. Attendance was varied, and in 2005, an attempt was made to ask people to sign up to the group, involving commitment to attend five meetings a year. It was decided to tackle tough themes intentionally in 2005/6: Terrorism; Conversion and mission; Caste and class; Reincarnation and resurrection; Religion, culture and citizenship - a fine and daring agenda.

Memorably, Israel was a speaker when we held an evening comparing the birth of Jesus and the birth of Krishna, where his depth of insight was much appreciated, and this was one of the best meetings of the forum. It also looked at ikons and deities, where we looked at deities in a temple, and at ikons on slides; and at mixed faith marriage and families, where a clergy spoke, married to a Hindu. We considered common ethical values, with special reference to non-violence and ecology; at living in contemporary society, and issues of secularism. This meeting was held in a church, and it was then I remember that a Hindu friend said how wonderful to be in such a holy place. We said Compline at the end of the evening. A group of Hindus began to attend the Midnight Mass at Christmas, and these became dozens. They hesitated whether to take their shoes off in church, on this most holy of nights.

Plans were also made to have outings, to St Albans Abbey, and to Bhakti Vedanta Manor. But want of organising capacity prevented this happening. The Teape foundation in Cambridge gave modest support to the group at this time, which was a great encouragement. The St Philip's Centre drew up a fund-raising proposal for a Hindu staff member to be sought, at least part time, but funds were never forthcoming.

Eventually the Forum declined and is not now operating for lack of leadership in both communities. The Christian expertise is now lacking. Hindu leadership was also affected when their key person lost his place as Secretary of a leading temple where we used to meet. Hopefully, there can be a second coming of this group, since my research now has shown me how much was done, and how promising it had been.

Hindu-Christian National Forum

I asked Israel to join the developing Hindu-Christian Forum UK, of which I had become one of the two co-chairs. It is on this that I wish to focus for the rest of this essay. This was much more complex in its dynamic, but also achieved much in the years Israel was involved, until 2009, when I finish my reflections here.

It was in late 2000 that the then National Inter Faith Adviser for the Church of England, Michael Ipgrave (now Bishop of Woolwich) approached me to join a small group of Hindus and Christians, to meet as an informal forum, with the agenda first of all of getting to know each other, and then to see whether we could initiate a national Hindu-Christian Forum. We were an interest group, hand picked by Michael with his wide networks. Before long Michael asked me to become joint chair with a prominent Hindu leader, Dr Bhan, a vice president of the Inter Faith Network, and Chair of the Vishwa Hindu Parishad, a powerful Hindu organisation in India linked with the at that time ruling BJP, and the militant activist movement, the RSS (the Rashtriya Sevak Sangh). I agreed to this, and we proceeded step by step.

The Context

The Council of Christians and Jews (CCJ) was formed at the time of the Holocaust (1942) to enable reconciliation and a new beginning in Christian-Jewish relations. A Christian-Muslim Forum was formed in 2004, after an extensive listening exercise, and it is now a settled part of English religious and public life.

The third religion of Britain, and indeed of the world, is Hinduism, with a global population of around one billion, and British numbers, in 2001, of 559,000 (equal to the population of Sheffield), and has risen considerably since then, with the coming of large numbers of Sri Lankan Tamils, the majority Hindu. The fast-growing importance of India economically, the significance of the Indian diaspora to life in Britain, and the great contribution made at local and national level of Hindus to Councils of Faiths, and bodies such as the Inter Faith Network UK, made it obvious that the next bilateral forum to be considered should be that of Christians and Hindus. Another fact was the geographical spread of Hindus, and their professional and educational contribution. So many had experienced Hindus as doctors, nurses, teachers, shopkeepers, and academics.

The early years of the Forum

There was no formal establishment of the Forum. The group called together by Michael Ipgrave included Anglicans, Roman Catholics, Methodist, United Reformed, and Indian Christians. Later a Baptist participated. On the Hindu side, there were members of ISKCON (Hare Krishna), Swaminarayan, British Hindu Council, British Hindu Forum, Vishwa Hindu Parishad, and National Council of Hindu Temples. There were never more than 25 included. By far the majority were men, and on the Hindu side almost exclusively so. On the Christian side, most of the members had a fair knowledge of Hinduism, and some a lifetime experience of it. The Hindus usually had a working knowledge of Christianity, though few were scholars in dialogue. A first agenda was set to consider the nature of the Hindu community in Britain, conversion issues, media representations, and secularising atheism in Britain.

Three or four meetings a year were held from 2001 until 2007. They were alternatively in Hindu and in Christian premises, in Leicester or in London, and lasted several hours on a Saturday. Topics for discussion varied between the theological and the practical. There was a degree of coming together, but also some hesitancy and suspicion pervading the atmosphere at times. Fear of Christian mission, and the dominance of conversion questions overshadowed meetings, and hindered progress. It became clear also that there was an unseen third party in the room, with considerable feelings usually unexpressed, but sometimes coming openly: this was the feeling that relating to Muslims was the primary Christian agenda, and that because Hindus did not cause disturbance, they could be largely ignored, or treated as of secondary importance.

A major issue from the beginning was whether questions relating to India could be addressed in the Forum. The general understanding was that India should not be the primary focus of attention, and that the Forum was about the UK. However, it was understood from the Christian side at least, that what happens in India does impact upon Hindu-Christian relations in Britain, and that the distinction neither could nor should be made absolute. A parallel is what we experienced in Leicester with a Jewish-Christian Forum. This had to be suspended for several months when misunderstandings arose about Israel/Palestine. It was agreed that the Forum would continue but avoid questions of the Holy Land. This was artificial, but was the only way forward.

Some fruitful meetings were held in these years. Memorable was the warmth of welcome at Bhaktivedanta Manor, Watford, and discussions about the ISKCON document on dialogue, a model of its kind. ISKCON's willingness to be seen as a missionary organisation, was often helpful in our dialogues, particularly about mission and conversion. Excellent day discussions were held on Grace, Suffering and Prayer.

A very significant meeting was held in the Sanatan Mandir in Leicester. This was within a day visit by Dr Rowan Williams, Archbishop of Canterbury, in 2003. At the beginning of this day, the Archbishop was shown round the temple by a local Hindu, and he showed great attention as he always does. He presented an Ikon to the temple, and the temple presented a statue of dancing Siva to the Archbishop. There was a major meal for large numbers of local people, and he was led through to the dining hall under a dedicated arch of flowers. I asked why they were putting so much effort and money into the day, and its detailed preparations. The answer was moving: they wished to honour a living saint. There then followed a meeting of the forum. At the beginning, he said how important it was to ask questions, in critical encounter. He spoke about how he hoped the forum would address issues of spirituality, theology and scripture, since this is what had happened in India at its best, and we now had an opportunity here. He spoke of Father Bede Griffiths as an example. The Archbishop endorsed the request that Hindus have people included when the House of Lords was reformed (still in process now 9 years later!), and he said he would be happy to consider their issues with sympathy meanwhile. Discussion followed on some of the media reporting of the killing of Graham Staines in Orissa, and assumptions of its being linked with Hindu extremists. The Archbishop also offered to consider issues related to attacks on temples, such as that seen in Wembley, within a concern for the protection of all religious buildings. At this point, Israel raised further questions related to India, including questions of religious freedom in Gujarat, and a regulation of conversion bill in Tamilnadu. This was indeed a highlight of the story of the Forum, and of the Archbishop's engagement with Hinduism.

This was followed by two open sessions, one where Hindus spoke of their faith journey, and the other around Christian stories. Hindu emphases varied. Bimal Krishna Das of ISKCON said he was concerned about Truth: questions such as who are we, from where do we come, what is the purpose of life, what is before birth and after life? Others looked at caste and class; at the origin of Hindu ethics; at what makes a Brahmin; at the guru concept, the one who helps others to move from darkness to life. Concern was expressed about chaplains of RC or Muslim faith who acted exclusively in their prisons.

Another meeting looked at stereotypes of each faith, and the danger of using these in the absence of people of the faith being stereotyped, and the need for members of the group to show an example by countering such stereotyping.

The most significant achievement by the Forum was *An agreed statement of goodwill.*

I quote this here in full:

1. We respect one another's faiths as sources of spirituality and of ethics, while acknowledging our differences of belief and practice.

2. We affirm the importance for both our communities of religious freedom:

    a. Freedom to worship according to the practices of one's won faith.

    b. Freedom to teach the tenets of either faith.

    c. Freedom for those who wish themselves to change their belief after due deliberation and thought, and as an expression of genuine spiritual commitment.

    d. Freedom for those who do not wish to change their faith to be left alone to practice either religion without further intrusion.

We recognise that the balancing of one another's interests in the exercise of these freedoms can be a sensitive matter. There is a fine line between laudable enthusiasm and destructive fanaticism, and anyone can cross that line, whether deliberately or unintentionally.

3. We believe that it is necessary to repudiate strategies for conversion which are coercive or manipulative. In particular:

    a. Medical, educational and social welfare services must not be misused to facilitate conversions.

    b. Conversions must not be sought through force, fraud, threat, illicit means, grant of financial or other aid, or exploiting a person's poverty, ill health, mental weakness or without due consideration.

    c. The methods employed to propagate either religion should be explicit and acceptable to the two communities. They must not

> be of such a kind as to encroach on the freedom of religion of citizens.
>
> d. Persons contemplating to change their faith should be advised to consider carefully the impact their decision may have on themselves, their family, and their community.
>
> 4. We unequivocally condemn all attacks on places of worship and on members of religious groups; we disown individuals or organisations responsible for such attacks, and we urge responsible and accurate reporting of these events by the media.
>
> We believe it is very important that Christians and Hindus should meet together to listen to one another's concerns and to affirm their respect for one another, and we invite our fellow believers of both faiths to engage together in dialogue, mutual learning, and service of the community.

Full agreement is here reached about full condemnation of attacks on places of worship and members of religious groups. This became very pertinent afterwards, with the attacks upon churches and Christians in Orissa, Karnataka and Gujarat. It did, however, become a grey area, since it was in India, but unequivocal voices of condemnation were few and far between from Britain. Much of the statement about conversion is perhaps more directly applicable in India than in Britain.

The comment in the statement about the media is also pertinent. Hindu members feel the media does not give them a fair hearing, unlike, in their view, Christians or Muslims. Examples are issues related to sacred cows in Britain falling ill, and clashes with the RSPCA who insist they should be slaughtered - which happened in Bhakti Vedanta, Watford, and in a temple in Wales.

What lacked clarity was – who was bound by the statement? Was it just the individuals of the forum? What of their parent bodies? It was clear, for example, with the VHP, that this could not bind the Indian VHP. It was unclear how far British organisations had agreed. And what of our churches? The statement never came to official circles, nor was it ever published.

Weaknesses

The forum never had any money, and hence depended entirely on the goodwill and voluntary labour of its members. There was no money even for travel expenses, and members had to bear this themselves, or draw down funds from their sponsoring organisations. Nor was there any paid administration, and dependence here was on the organisations employing the leaders. This limited the number of meetings that could be held, and activities that could be initiated. Ideas were not lacking, but the means to implement them were. The leaders themselves were involved only as an add-on to everything else they were doing, and members attended by grace.

Commitment to the idea of the forum was strong from some individuals, who kept things going. Others were only nominally members, and they were distinguished by their nonattendance. But there was no mechanism for dropping people, unless they so agreed. Women and young people were conspicuous by their absence.

Strengths

The strong feeling was that there was a need for this forum, and this was one of the fruits of these early years. It became clear that it was not about whether to go forward but *how* to go forward. There was also a growing commitment from the Inter Faith Network, and then the UK Government's Department of Communities and Local Government, that they wished to support and undergird a forum of some kind.

Important topics were discussed. These included the report *Connecting British Hindus*, published in 2006, introduced by Ramesh Kallidai of the Hindu Forum, now a major player amongst Hindus. He made the significant observation that 85% of respondents did not like to be named 'Asian'. They split 50:50 on being called 'Hindu' or 'Indian'. Respondents say there are multiple ways of expressing their identity, including British/Hindu/Indian/Asian. This is typical of diaspora communities. Dialogue was held at the Home Office in 2006 on the Incitement to Religious Hatred Bill. The resulting Bill was seen as a damp squib, and Israel quoted the words of St Paul, about 'speaking the truth in love', and that there needs to be more of a cutting edge in the legislation. Israel also took part in an open dialogue invited by South Asia Concern about their website. This is an evangelical organisation, and Israel suggested a sentence should be added about a commitment to good interfaith relations, and the need for Asian Christians to be educated to take part in dialogue. Gauri Das, an ISKCON representative, said clarity about commitment to Christ should not be seen as negative by Hindus, as long as this did not mean being derogatory about Hindus, something understandably they are very sensitive about.

Israel was one of three Christians who spoke of his faith journey at a meeting in 2004. He told how he had been brought up to feel himself superior to Hindus, as a Christian brought up in a remote village. But he had much broadened in his faith, as he helped to liberate his co-villagers from various oppressions, while studying to the highest level. On coming to Britain, in the 1990's, had been shocked by the lack of spiritual maturity of Christians here. His own faith centres on the love of God, which only comes alive when God shares in his suffering, as a mother cries with her child. He now feels his Christ-centred spirituality is integrated and inclusive.

I reported on two European conferences, one of the WCC in Rome about conversion, where I had drawn attention to the goodwill statement; and one major conference of the European Churches in Rumania, where my efforts to get Hinduism included on the agenda as well as Abrahamic faiths, failed.

Provision of Chaplaincy was another area we were involved in, and this meant expressing the need for Hindu as well as Muslim chaplains in a range of institutions. We raised with the Home Office the question of visa requirements for Hindu priests, in the light of increased English requirements for Imams and others. At that stage (Jan 2006), they were not included because their duties did not include counselling or preaching, or house visiting. Pujaris chant the rituals in Sanskrit.

The saga of the listening exercise

In 2006, the decision was made to initiate a listening exercise, modelled on the Muslim-Christian exercise above. It was felt that the forum needed some more energy, and to be more representative. It was decided to focus upon Leicester, London, and Lancashire. Dates were set for these to be completed in 2007, and to be undertaken by members of the group, and were to be organised by a steering group which was to meet at Lambeth Palace, at the invitation of Guy Wilkinson, Archbishop's Officer for Inter Faith Relations. There was some hope of getting a civil servant seconded to take the role that Julian Bond had taken most effectively in the Muslim-Christian exercise. This was a hopeful period, and the minutes of the time record how plans were to be made for a national conference to be held in 2008, which would be addressed by the Archbishop of Canterbury.

Things had progressed by April 2007, and there was now a grant from the Community Development Foundation, to help with finances. Guy Wilkinson commented, 'We need to do everything we can to demonstrate to the wider world that relationships between the Faith communities are not the source of conflict that they are too widely perceived to be.'

However, all juddered to a halt in April 2007. To the amazement of Guy Wilkinson and all the four Christians on the steering group, the four concerned Hindus withdrew from the listening exercise unilaterally. They were from the Hindu Forum, Hindu Council, VHP and National Council of Hindu Temples. This took place in a two line email sent by Jay Lakhani of the Hindu Council. A press release was promised about the reasons, though that was never published. It took several weeks for me to find out from my co-chair, Dr Bahn, himself not on the listening exercise group, what were the stated reasons. These were two: that the Archbishop had received at Lambeth a delegation of Dalits, through the Christian Solidarity Forum, and felt to implicitly have endorsed their demands, including the inclusion of the caste issue within the equalities legislation in Britain (an error of fact); and that research had shown that Christian organisations in India were involved in inappropriate methods of mission and inducing conversion, as reported in a document written by Anusha Prasad, of the Hindu Forum (later a report that was disowned by the Chair of the Forum, and of dubious academic validity). It was later clear also that there were rivalries and lack of trust amongst Hindu organisations involved.

Next stages
It was decided to leave a gap for all to take stock, and then to try again. There was a conviction from both Christians and Hindus, that to have this forum was important. This was encouraged by the interest now shown by the Inter Faith Network, which was concerned about what happened between two of its most significant members. With the Network's encouragement, it was decided to go to the Department of Communities and Local Government (of the then Labour government), to seek funding for a listening exercise to be facilitated by a paid

academic from a recognised university. At the same time, it was agreed to continue with meetings of the Forum, as before, and making sure that all the main Hindu organisations were represented, as above. Meetings continued in a peaceful way, around largely theological and spiritual themes. This felt like a holding time. And DCLG eventually came up with an adequate grant, which needed to be supplemented by small amounts from different churches and Hindu organisations. A researcher recognised in this field was engaged, from De Montfort University, and she worked hard in preparing a presentation about how she intended to go about the work, following the guidelines as drawn up for the previous aborted attempt.

It was then discovered that DCLG could only pay the money to a recognised charity known to them, and their suggestion was that the grant should be made to St Philip's. This would be an in/out transaction, and the exercise was ready to go, and dates pencilled. However, things foundered again, because the Hindu group overseeing the listening exercise said they were not happy for the money to go through an explicitly Christian organisation. There was a long further delay, and meanwhile the engaged researcher had moved to the far north of England, and her new employer did not agree to her secondment for this work. It should also be noted that St Philip's Trustees were not happy with the complicated quasi legal memorandum, drawn up by Hindu members, which they would be expected to sign. DCLG kindly did not impose a strict deadline, but allowed time for this latest stumbling block to be overcome.

Trust was very fragile, and the only way to overcome this was to form a new subcompany, to run the listening exercise. They engaged the Oxford Centre for Hindu Studies, and a researcher employed by them, Jessica Frazier

Indian Christian question

Indian Christians are 30 million, and there are growing numbers in Britain. As joint Chair, I involved them from the beginning with two representatives. Robin Thomson brought in Sivagopalan Kumar, a Baptist minister and Brahmin convert, who calls himself a Jesubhakter. Robin and I had also served as missionaries in India. My co-chair was not happy with an article I wrote on *Hindutva*, and I had a two hour meeting with him, which was very useful from both sides, in bringing clarification, if not agreement. This helped the knowledge of Hinduism in the group, but increased the suspicion, I am told, of hidden agendas, in view of the extreme sensitivities on conversion issues. Also we were clear that caste has not gone away, either in India, but also here. Softening does not mean abolition. This made someone of Israel's background uncomfortable at times in the forum, I felt.

Newly launched Forum

The report is entitled *Bridges and Barriers to Hindu-Christian Relations*, and was released in June 2011, and given a high profile at Lambeth Palace, with the Archbishop, and the head of Bhaktivedanta Manor making significant speeches, at a relaunch of the Forum. This seemed to many like a first launch, but the above narrative shows how much had already been done over the years, by a committed group from the two faiths, and this should not be overshadowed by the problems around the listening exercise.

There is no space here to summarise the well researched and balanced report. I feel it underestimates the problems, but may be this is a healthy balance after the three immediately preceding years. I just highlight one of the consequential aims of the Forum, to research models of good practice in local dialogue and shared service to the community. The Leicester Forum above shows there can be good models, if they can be sustained. Encouragement from a national body would be very helpful, and clusters of local models can be formed and sustained. What is important is that these are not about one-off events, but building up a group together.

In 2009 I had handed over the Chairmanship to Archdeacon of Leicester, Richard Atkinson, who has recently become Bishop of Bedford. Dr Bhan had ceased to be co-Chair at the same time, and Ramesh Pattni took over, someone deeply committed to the vision of a Forum. Some funds have been accessed from the Near Neighbours Fund of the Church Urban Fund, for conducting one-off events, such as a dialogue programme held in Leicester and, and a dance programme in Neasden Temple. But finance is still lacking for a paid worker, which I would see as essential for the work of the forum to develop as might be hoped. Various plans were made earlier which could not be implemented, amongst other reasons, for lack of staffing. Two examples were plans for a major residential conference, with

Rowan Williams booked to give a keynote address, which would have involved academics and practitioners. Another for a scriptural workshop, on the lines of the Muslim-Christian *Building Bridges* seminars, which was to lead to a publication. I drew up the plan with Bimal Krishna Das in early 2005, but he was then transferred to India, and the initiative went no further.

Another key need is in the training area. There are few clergy with adequate knowledge, and above all experience of Hinduism or Hindus. For this, some experience of India is not just desirable, but I feel essential. Perhaps Israel, now back in South India, could play a role here? Abrahamic Faiths dominate the learning agenda in theological colleges, and in local contexts. So also Hindus have focused on developing their structures and temples in our cities. Here the Oxford Centre has been a very helpful development. As British Hindus grow in their knowledge of their faith, hopefully they can grow also in what it can contribute in dialogue with Christians and others. This means them knowing something of these faiths. So mutual education should be a major focus of an ongoing Forum.

Hindu response from Ramesh Pattni, BSc (Hons), MBA,MA, MSt (Oxford), Doctoral student at Oxford Centre for Hindu Studies, *Joint Chair of Hindu-Christian Forum UK*

The HCF in its conception and development has gone through classic stages of formation of many groups, stages of 'forming, storming, norming and performing'. The added dimensions of a long history of Hindu Christian interactions and relations on the subcontinent of India and the backgrounds, experiences, hopes and aspirations of the participants sometimes made it a challenging and difficult journey. There were times when the storms of complex views and positions made the Forum dysfunctional and periods when we seem to be making substantial progress. In particular for the Hindu members, the topic of conversion seemed to lurk in the background as the 'ultimate Christian agenda' and at other times openly being discussed as a barrier to all Hindu Christian relations. There were periods when the Hindu mistrust of Christian personal and organisational agendas made things come to a standstill and other occasions when there was a feeling of understanding, camaraderie and a deeper understanding of each other as individuals and as the 'other'. The turning point came when through the shifting membership of the organisation, the appropriate people, energies and commitment came together to make HCF a performing group that went on to commission the Bridges and Barriers report. This well researched project by OCHS gave us the focus and objective to direct our energies. Not only did the report give us the context and the goals within which to work, but made the Forum a 'performing' entity which now has a vision and a programme including - a conference on Yoga , plans for further interactions of the members and communities through the Near Neighbours Programme, and setting up networks of Hindu Christian Groups through the country to create a network feeding into the national Forum. Challenges and difficulties especially funding, lie ahead but the HCF has at least the energy, commitment and the inner resources to move forward within the framework of deeper sincere relationships, resilient and sincere friendships and working within the communities to share our theologies and actions for the mutual benefit of the Hindu and Christian communities.

Pastoral Issues in an Inter-faith Situation

Suresh Kumar

Preamble

Full time pastoral ministry was my motivating vision when (in 1981) I committed myself to my diocese and throughout my theological studies. My whole aim was to become a 'good pastor'. God had other plans. Many others – my teachers, Bishop's and principals of theological colleges I was associated with, decided and led me into teaching ministry at Tamilnadu Theological Seminary (TTS) in the year 1986. I met Israel there (then a 'Revd') and, finding many similarities, we became friends. It was from him I learnt the way of continuing a passion for pastoral ministry from a seminary campus. Involvement at TTS with Prison ministry, Theological Education for Christian Commitment and Action (TECCA) and my ministry at the CSI Church of the Divine Patience in Madurai gave ample opportunity to offer pastoral ministry to the needy. Close pastoral connection with my own diocese continued, which gave me a great advantage when I took over the administrative responsibility there. When offered a pastoral role in the UK, I had no hesitation in accepting.

Introduction

I will be telling stories of issues in my pastoral ministry in two very different parishes. Both are Anglican churches served in the parish structure, popular for their nature and composition. I will be narrating stories from my experience, and will draw out issues peculiar to the context. For a person from the Indian subcontinent, both situations are new, and mine will be an Indian Christian view of the issues. For anyone interested in interfaith issues, some issues are familiar - though placed in a very different context; other issues are very different.

I. A British White 'Folk-Pagan' Context

My first posting was in a parish called Braunstone Park. As an associate priest I had a mentor to teach me 'the British way of doing things in parish ministry'. Conducting worship and preaching presented no problem, but understanding the people, their faith and expectations, their view of life and death, and their perceptions of clergy and the Church, was a challenge. Braunstone is a white, working class neighbourhood with all the social issues you can think of. It had the highest amount of vandalism and teenage pregnancies. People are poor and uneducated. Never in my life did I think that there are places in Britain where illiteracy existed. It was very difficult to ask someone in the church to do a bible reading. They need to be informed well in advance, and some need training and practice.

The very first thing which struck me was the apathy people had about God and Church. In the Indian context I had seen people clinging to God and seeking help from the church spiritually and pastorally in times of need, difficulties and crisis. In Britain I saw the opposite. The poor, needy and people in crisis hardly ever turned to God or to the church. Two reasons I found out in my parish ministry: They were depending on the state to solve all their problems, they were living in a situation of welfare – housing benefits, training, employment, healthcare, children's expenses and in some cases everything was provided by the state and people were happy recipients. Secondly, people have been receiving confused and conflicting reports about the nature of the church. The church in Britain also had changed most of its traditional mission initiatives.

In spite of state welfare, the British cultural emphasis on individual freedom and privatisation of religion makes the church and its workers hesitate to provide pastoral support. Here is a situation where even visiting the sick and praying for them needs careful negotiation and an unspoken process has to be gone through. Permissions need to be in place and the situation needs careful handling. All my theological education, ministerial training and 23 years of experience were not enough!

Braunstone is a place where not even a single Asian family lived. People from the Asian background are scared of living here. The only Asian shop keeper lived on the other side of the city and always asked me how I managed to live there. Yes, I did have some problems in the beginning. Racial abuse, vandalism and uncomfortable situations did occur. But I always thought it is part of ministry and kept going. Once people know that you are harmless, they become friendly and I gained many very good friends in the parish. This fear among the Asian community kept the Braunstone parish free from Muslims, Hindus, Jains and the Chinese. However, still the situation is not a single faith community. People are Christians (of different denominations), non Christians, atheists, secular people, Romas and people who are not clear what their faith is. In my opinion many people there had a faith resembling folk religion. Many Church of England clergy do not hesitate to call this 'paganism'.

Story 1

A middle aged woman came to our church one evening and requested me and my senior to visit her house to offer prayers and chase away the spirit in her house. She felt a presence of 'another being' in the house. Whenever she entered a room she saw 'it' sitting on the bed or in a chair and when she goes in, it leaves reluctantly, moving to a different room. This lady was never baptised, did not go to any church and was not ready to call herself a Christian. But she thought the church people could help her situation. We accepted the invitation, went to her house, prayed in all the rooms and sprinkled holy water (my mentor thought it was a good symbolic gesture which will give the woman some confidence) and left pictures of our church cross. I am sure the woman was supported pastorally. She never came back to the church but I have seen her in the streets and she waved to me twice and that is it.

In the first instance I thought it was funny. If someone from my congregation in Trichy came to me with a similar story how would I have reacted? Definitely not in the same way as I did in Braunstone. I had an immediate comparison to make. Many times in my pastoral ministry in India I had Hindus and Muslims seeking a prayer when visiting sick friends in hospital. I have prayed for people of other faiths in the jail and during our Carol rounds. In an interfaith situation this is a therapeutic ministry provided irrespective of the seeker's faith orientation. Here is a human being in need and I as a minister must support them pastorally. However, I have always struggled to think how this can also be an opportunity for more clear witness.

Story 2

Gill (55) and Sue (27) came to our church with three little children one evening. They wanted to baptise four young children on the next possible Sunday. They insisted that it must be done as soon as possible. We made them sit and relax. Slowly we got more information. Gill has two daughters, Sue and Chloe (25). Sue had two children aged four and one. Chloe had delivered the day before they came to us: a son on Friday the Thirteenth (April). The family was in great fear that a boy child born on Friday the 13th is going to do harm to the family and wanted to protect the children by baptising them and giving them the Christian protection! Chloe and the new born child were still in hospital, but the family felt the need for rapid action to protect them from evil. Again, these people were not known to us and they were not practicing Christians. I could only think of them as having a faith based on Horror films, which somehow they identify with Christian faith.

Whenever we consider interfaith situations, we immediately think of big established religions: people with a clear understanding of their faith and with a sense of belonging to a faith tradition. But in places like Braunstone we have people who are not sure of what faith tradition they belong to. They seem lost in the tussle between faiths in Leicester. Even though there are many criticisms about the parish system in Britain, these stories and many others I have experienced prove a point. People who think they do not belong to a faith tradition have pastoral needs and they see the church near them as a place to seek pastoral help, from people they think will help. They need a reliable and trustworthy picture of the church. Obviously they are filling the vacuum in their lives with a Christian paganism, or some media propagated faith, perhaps with some form of Christian dualism.

II. British Asian Faiths' Context

I am presently serving in a parish where the interfaith situation is very different. St. Philip's church was built in the year 1909. By 1949 this was an established church with 980 registered members in the electoral role. The church had pews for 500 worshippers. The halls and the other facilities housed the Sunday school, mothers union, scouts and guides.

Today the church has 53 on the electoral role and on average 30 for Sunday worship. The halls were sold in 2000 to fund the repair work of the church after a fire in 1996. The church grounds were sold to make room for flats and to give the church some financial stability. The vicarage was converted into the St Philip's Centre working for interfaith relations. What had happened?

After the Second World War, Many Asian people who came to Britain chose to live in Leicester and the Evington area was one of the preferred areas for Muslims. Today our parish consists of about 87% of people from other faiths. 84% of the people in the parish are Muslims. On Evington road just across the road from our church building stands a mosque and on a Friday at least 2500 Muslims pray in it. We have Muslims, Hindus, Sikhs and Jains in the parish. Within my parish boundary, we have one Methodist, one United Reform, One Baptist, One Roman Catholic and one Free Church. There is also a Jehovah Witness worship hall. White, aged Anglicans live in just one corner of the parish and many others have moved out to various other places. So what is the new role of a pastor? And what are the pastoral issues we face?

Understandings and Misunderstandings: A. Christians about people of other faiths

1. Miss Elizabeth is 70 and lived in the parish for the past 35 years. She never married and was a regular member of our church since she moved here. She has seen most of the changes that happened in the area. She has hardly any friends from other faiths. She thinks she is fortunate to have some white Christians living on her road and her friends in the church are valuable to her. Yet, she thinks her Hindu neighbours are OK to deal with. She says, "They are a bit noisy, but cheerful. They have large families and their faith is not very visible. They go to temples in nice dresses. I do not understand why Hindus make a lot of extensions to their homes after moving in. They put up a lot of extra structures to their homes. However it is not a problem and they do not interfere with you in any way." Elizabeth seems to have at least some factual information about Hindu religion: e.g. its

tolerance and their concept of family, which should help Elizabeth have better relations with her neighbours.

2. Mrs. Mary (90) has lived in the same house in the parish for the past 53 years. Her husband died and her children moved to other towns. She is not very healthy but would like to live alone independently. Cooked food is served to her and she is mobile to some extent. She cannot come to church but has a strong sense of belonging to the Church. She has two white friends who live on the same street as her. They are not Christians, but they help her which Mary appreciates. Otherwise, she is not inclined to relate to her neighbours, though she is not sure whether it is because of their ethnicity or because of their faith. There are people who find it difficult to come out of their comfort zone and traditional 'way of doing things'. It is not a wilful rejection of others, but merely finding it unnecessary to come out to meet strangers and those somewhat alien.

3. Miss Grace (60) is confined to her house. She is severely disabled and needs someone to check on her well-being regularly. Often she needs to be referred to the hospital and most of the help she needs is provided by her Muslim neighbours. Grace thinks her Muslim neighbours are very good people and she has no ill feelings about Muslims. Her case provides us with a good model of 'near neighbours' interfaith relations.

4. Mrs Janet is 90 but very active. She did very well in her life as a social worker and is living alone. She has Muslim neighbours and she says she is friendly with them and can accept them and their faith. However she thinks women are suppressed by men. She is angry about the women having to wear Niqab. She thinks even though she lives next door she has not seen any women properly in her neighbouring house. They are always seen in Niqab and for Janet speaking and relating to someone without seeing them is not possible. She just says hello occasionally and was not able to develop any close friendship. While she has a good understanding of, e.g. the use of the 'veil', and had some personal interaction with articulate Muslim women, Janet's own firm belief system and her orientation to her own culture is strong and is the cause of her concerns.

5. Mr. Robert (60) lives next door to a Sikh. Robert's experience of their neighbours is very positive. He thinks they are very hard working,

caring and wonderful people. The Sikhs are very religious and their faith makes them do good things. Robert thinks Sikhism is a good religion.

6. Mr. Joseph (70) lives with his family. His neighbours are Muslims. He thinks the Muslims are very patriarchal and they live and practice their faith in an archaic way. He thinks the men are dominant and authoritarian. He thinks the parents force their children into everything, including religion. He thinks the Madrasa type of education that young people are forced into by parents is real brainwashing. He is also worried about forced marriages and young women ending their careers abruptly for getting married. Joseph thinks having a close relationship with a Muslim is not possible. However he thinks his relationship with his neighbours is a good one. (Keeping them at a distance)

I think we need to ask a very critical question. What went horribly wrong with the church in Britain? Why is Christian understanding of people of other faiths, even after about 50 years of co-existence, so poor? How far is the church disoriented?

Joseph's case is a very clear example of seeing Muslims from a 'British White Christian' point of view. Given that background, his reactions are only natural. With many older people in this society, he believes: 'If you come to live in Britain, then live like the British', which seems quite logical from his perspective.

B. People of other faiths' Understanding of Christians

1. Mr. Mahmood (55) is a member of the mosque in our neighbourhood. His parents were born in India and migrated to Kenya. Mahmood was born in Kenya and moved to Britain with his family. He is married and his children were born in Britain. He is a religious Muslim and claims to practice a complete Muslim life. He thinks Christians in British society are lost. He thinks they no longer love or approve the authority of the Bible. The British Christians made too many concessions on their faith. The present day young Christians are not Christians at all.

2. Mrs. Fathima (35) is married and wears a Hijab. She is not happy relating with Christians because she thinks there is no discipline among the Christians of Britain. She thinks Christian parents do not take any responsibility in bringing up children in a Christian way. Parental responsibility is ignored and this has led to children growing as they

wish and as the media dictates to them. There is no Christian culture in this country. What we see is loose culture. There is no modesty among women and nobody is interested in talking about morality. British Christian neighbours do not exhibit any serious family or even bondage between husband and wife. They do not know what they believe and where their life is going to.

3. Mr. Sandhu (62) is a Sikh. He thinks Christians in Britain are very good. They are very broad minded and accommodative. They do not hesitate to relate to him and the national policy and practice is so good in respect of people like him. His relative married a British White girl and she is a very committed Christian. He thinks the church's contribution in Leicester to embrace people of other faiths is commendable. He would like to see the British Christians practice their religion in a more overt way. He has no hesitation in going into a church or talking to a Christian. He is more worried about secular British people and right wing politicians.

4. Mrs. Neha (70) is a Hindu widow. She is full of praise for her Christian neighbours and everything about Christians is positive. She thinks her present outlook on life itself is the result of her interaction with Christians. If she was just a Hindu she would have been lost in the house as a widow. She would have closed herself to life and to her neighbours. With friendship, encouragement from Christians, she is living a full life with a lot of responsibilities and her contributions to the society are very well acknowledged. She thinks British Christians definitely have a mission bias and are living their faith. Taking care of the wounded, liberating the oppressed and providing a hope for the hopeless are all happening. She thinks some people criticise Christians because of their British culture not because of their Christian faith.

5. Mr. Syed (35) is from Afghanistan and drives a taxi in Leicester. He thought there were only Hindus and Muslims in India. When he met me he was surprised to see a Christian priest from India. He came to Britain thinking that this is a Christian country. Now he thinks that was a mistake. He thinks this is an immoral place and he thinks religious leaders are responsible for so much of immorality in the society. He is scared of bringing up his children in this context and wants to go back as soon as possible. He thinks the Christian leaders themselves in Britain are immoral and that's why they cannot teach

any moral teaching to the public. Even a few good Christians he met are shy of their faith and do not have any courage to speak about it.

6. Mr. Khan (18) was born and brought up in Britain. He is a student and claims to be a religious Muslim. He fulfils all his religious duties and is studying to be an accountant. He says that he meets and relates to young people of different faiths in his school. He thinks young people of different faiths do not have any problem in accepting and relating to one another. However he feels that Christians need to be more religious. Even people he thought are Christians from their cross pendants seems to wear it for fashion and not for faith. He thinks British society is going to be far away from faith soon. According to him, Muslims will be the only credible and visible faith tradition in Britain.

All the above opinions were expressed by people living in my parish in a one to one conversation. To protect people's identity, all the names I used are imaginary.

The stories narrated pose some vital challenges to Christians and to people of other faiths. Christians are obviously not performing the 'lamp on the stand' and 'salt of the earth' role they are called to perform. Christians generally seem insensitive to their neighbours.

The modern exegetical interpretation of Pauline letters to infant Christians reflects changed attitudes and in turn effects such changes. Thus, academics and modern 'progressive' Christians would discard many Pauline teachings on daily life, domestic life and on matters like marriage, eating the food presented to idols, the role of women, the place of church elders etc., as culturally irrelevant for today. In a multi-faith and multi-cultural context this poses a problem. Other faith community clergy and laity are not going to accept this way of handling scripture. Altering the traditional meanings to suit a modern way of living is not approved of by Muslims and Hindus. Are those of us who take up these new biblical interpretations aware of the cost of this new wave, when living in an interfaith situation? Christians need to put in special efforts to understand the complexity of their neighbours, their ethnicity, their languages, their culture and their faith and how these all contribute to their life styles and value system.

People of other faiths also need to understand that their perception of Britain as a 'Christian country' is not true to the reality and that all Christians are not same. The existence of paganism, pseudo folk religious beliefs, traditional Victorian Christian systems, post modern Christianity and the new progressive Christian movements need to be explained to people who matter.

So, how do you provide pastoral care in a parish with such diversity? I have come across diverse views about other religions and about their own faith and practises. An Egyptian young woman's views on many social issues were very different from those of the Pakistani women I met. Two Muslim girls (friends of my daughter) – both from Srilanka and Tamil speaking have very different views on many faith issues. One is dressed in jeans and T-shirt and the other in a Hijab. Both come into our church for an interfaith youth meeting and are quite comfortable in talking to me in Tamil.

When we celebrated the Christian Muslim interfaith week, I was seated in a table in our church hall for dinner. Two Somali women joined me in my table and in few minutes we started conversations about weddings in Somalia and in India. They explained how weddings are viewed and celebrated in Somalia among Muslims and I explained how Tamil Christians' weddings are celebrated. In a very short time we found we had so much in common irrespective of our difference in faith traditions. At the same time one of the women commented. How similar we are (India and Somalia) and how different this country (Britain) is.

Interfaith dialogue in my parish
We have an organised Muslim-Christian interfaith dialogue group meeting in our church, organised by St. Philip's Centre. Persons representing the two faiths will give a presentation on a certain theme and the participants will divide into smaller groups (consisting of people from both faiths) and discuss the issue and come again for a plenary. Issues like faith, scripture and weddings were recently discussed. A selected few people attend, being those who have time and energy and are interested in interfaith matters. Only two people from my congregation attend this regularly. In a parish like ours it would be ideal for more people to be present.

However there are issues regarding this forum. I have been part of inter-religious dialogue groups before, mainly in Madurai, and have always thought they were great meetings. However the diversity is so complex an issue here. The Muslims who come here are from various nationalities, sects, ethnic origin and with very different cultural and linguistic backgrounds. There is no single Muslim view on anything. The same is true of the Christian participants. People are divided by denominations, origins, age and from different spectrum of theological positions. I think the meetings explain to us the diversity we have and for someone who aspires for unity, it seems a distant dream.

As a pastor, I am worried sometimes when Christians feel vulnerable and weak in the midst of Muslims who express strong faith and are very firm about it. In some meetings, I observed that some Christians felt pathetic about their lack of knowledge and information about their own faith and about the divisions that surfaced among Christians in the meeting. Some Muslims felt very sorry for their Christian counterparts because they were not sure of so many things. However it is a process of education and what is important is that it happens and we are able to speak and observe.

The second level of dialogue is less formal and happens at grass root level. As the parish streets have become multi-faith, people need to be able to meet and speak to people of other faiths. In a bus, in a post office, in the car park, in the library and in the roads you have to see and in emergencies need to interact with people of other faiths. From my experience, the misunderstandings and lack of understanding about people of other faiths is playing a very important role in dialogue or lack of it.

What do we do in this context? Most interfaith seminars and meetings take place in our church building and there is ample room for anyone to learn about other faiths and to relate to them. The church hall hosts a preschool and children and parents of different faiths use it. This provides a platform for people to meet each other. The building is rented out for community use and several social and domestic functions happen here. Last Christmas season, the crib service in our churches chancel included a nativity play staged by the Leicester Interfaith youth hub. I have taken it upon myself to use the Sunday sermons to inform my congregation on various interfaith issues. For example, on Christmas day I preached on Avatar in Hinduism and incarnation in Christian faith.

Marriage between people of different faiths?

The Evington area of Leicester is very different from other areas of multicultural Britain. The composition is very complex and getting chances of other pastoral situations like marriages, funerals, pastoral visits and others are rare. In spite of the presence of various religious groups, inter-religious marriages are rare. The large numbers of Muslims in the area make people of other faiths take a defensive mode and this is well expressed in a statement by a Hindu girl on her marriage. 'I want to fall in love and get married to a guy who will love me. However I am from a Hindu family and I have to consider my parent's and grandparent's wish. If I fall in love with a Hindu boy they will be very happy and immediately make all arrangements for my wedding. It will happen with many people's blessing. If I select a White Christian they will hesitate but they will go ahead and will approve of it. If I fall in love with a black guy they will oppose it and will try to stop it. If I am adamant they will leave me alone and will try to avoid me in future. But if I fall in love with a Muslim guy my parents will kill me'.

Conclusion

Providing pastoral care to a small Christian Anglican congregation of 30 people itself has become a challenge. People have diverse positions in faith matters. (I know people who do not want to say the creeds and do not believe in many things which the Anglican Church believes as its position). When this congregation lives in a road surrounded by people of Muslim, Hindu, Sikh, Jain, Pagan and Unnamed religious beliefs, the confusion becomes complex. Even a funeral sermon based on John 14: 1-6 giving a hope of 'Jesus as the way to the Father' is questioned! The current debate on allowing gay marriages is making life difficult for a Christian priest to talk to Hindus and Muslims about a Christian wedding. The present immigration policy of allowing Europeans to come into Britain and blocking people of the Subcontinent also has raised serious doubts and a rethinking of racial bias in people of other faiths. The Near-Neighbours' programme now initiated by St. Philip's, where people of different faiths can come together just for being together and to relate to one another is a good step forward, but much still needs to be done if we are to be truly faithful to our neighbours.

Indian Conservative Evangelicals and their Modern Market Expressions

Solomon Victus

I consider this a great honor to contribute an essay to the Festschrift for Dr. Israel Selvanayagam. He is both a mentor, and a friend to me. As one who was brought up in evangelical piety, Dr. Selvanayagam was able to recognize the trappings which evangelical piety can succumb to. In most of his writings he was quick to point out such trappings with both empathy and critical concern. In this essay I aim to expose the contradictions in and the complexity of some extreme Indian evangelical groups' relation to market economy, globalization processes and the development of media technology.

The evangelical or conservative rightist Christians when seen through the eyes of a common secular person present us a puzzling picture due to the new trends adopted by such sects in winning their adherents in a peculiar way.[1] Sometimes their strategies look enigmatic. On the one hand they project that they are not at all concerned about this world because it is all evil; on the other hand they have no hesitation in enjoying the fruits of modernity and capitalism. This group seems to be increasingly materialist by giving more importance to wealth

---

[1] I do not touch upon radical or leftist evangelical sects in this article for they are relatively more concerned about the earth. The term evangelical is used to denote the conservatives only within Christianity.

and prosperity while negating the spiritual matters.[2] Their otherworldly approaches go against any concern for ecological matters such as the conservation of nature. One can easily say they are very selective in their approach to this world. Their understanding of Jesus' words, '...you are not of this world' (Jn.15:19b) appears very strange. Therefore one has to study their cultural values which are deeply connected to economics. Pradeep N. Thomas, a scholar in communication studies, expresses the contradiction this way: "While I continue to remain critical and skeptical of the specific politics of these new Christian traditions, I do acknowledge that the spiritual yearnings of millions of Christians around the world are being fulfilled by these new Christian churches. It is, in other words, important to distinguish and respect the spiritualities and traditions of faith represented by these new churches".[3]

Mushrooming Evangelists

Conservative Christian sects are innumerous all over the world and are growing at a tremendous pace. Most Christians in the Third World countries are getting attracted to this new type of evangelical Christianity mainly because the traditional mainline churches failed to cater to the type of spirituality people wanted. The vast majority of the Christians, especially conservative middle class persons express their dissatisfaction with the emptiness, purposelessness and hopelessness of the bureaucratic, materialistic and secularized society.[4] The mainline churches such as Church of South India (CSI) and Church of North India (CNI) own huge million-dollar properties and in the last few decades conflicts over property and litigation in secular courts have become a major problem in these post-colonial churches. In contrast to this a growing number of charismatic churches seem to focus more on capturing the airwaves and mediating faith to the masses, rather than being encumbered by issues of physical location

---

[2] Prakash James, *Deconstructing Christian Fundamentalism in Televangelism,* Unpublished M.Th. Thesis at TTS, Arasaradi, Madurai, March 2011, p3.

[3] Thomas, Pradeep Ninan, *Strong Religion, Zealous Media: Christian Fundamentalism and Communication in India,* New Delhi: Sage Publication, 2008, pxvi.

[4] Leela D' Souza, *The Sociology of Religion: A Historical Review,* New Delhi: Rawat Publications, 2005, p298.

and territoriality.[5] Almost all charismatic programmes focus on prosperity theology, miracles of healing, and experiences like 'slaying in the spirit;' and these are things generally associated with the charismatic doctrine.[6]

Not only the congregation members of the mainline churches are leaning towards these new types of churches but also the pastors of evangelical churches are moving towards new forms of organizational patterns in line with the modern consumerist world. It is interesting to note that both the people and the pastors are in search of something new. Earlier these evangelical pastors were highly critical of organized form of churches and its approaches. The most recent trend among them is to change and adapt even the Episcopalian forms and practices, and designations such as Pastor, Reverend, Bishop, Moderator, Diocese and Synod and so on are used by them. Moreover the new evangelists try to attract people with their modern infrastructures, worshipping places such as air-conditioned auditoriums, close circuit TV, latest popular music played with drums of all kinds.

Fascination with glamour is another feature of these groups because some of their ministers wear flashy colorful ties, artful tie-clips and trendy shirts and suits. Some of them drive expensive cars and go for the more fashionable attires. They bring the glamour of cities to the rural towns and villages.[7] Recent evangelical meetings at Arasaradi in 2011 exhibited so much of ultra modern expressions. There were flood lights all over the open air auditorium. The background lighting as well as the preacher's lectern made him look like an angel to the viewers. Advanced and sophisticated communication technologies were used. Live telecast was arranged to more than fifty countries. Sound system was highly sophisticated. The music and songs led in the meeting sounded like modern movie songs. There were singing of choruses, emotional body movements to go with the fast and slow beats in the music. Varieties of electronic music devices, noise, clapping, drum beats, speaking in tongues (unknown languages), and the

---

[5] Jonathan D. James, *McDonaldisation, Masala McGospel and Om Economics: Televangelism in Contemporary India*, New Delhi: SAGE Publications, 2010, p18.

[6] Jonathan D. James, *Ibid.*, p106.

[7] Prakash James, *Ibid.*, p12.

freedom for women to publicly express their piety contributed to a feeling of empowerment for few hours.

There are clear differences between traditional Pentecostal people (Ceylon Pentecostal Mission -CPM / The Pentecostal Mission -TPM) and the modern conservative evangelical people in India. For instance in the CPM / TPM churches certain things are forbidden such as cinema, television, fashionable clothes, cosmetics, jewelry, smoking, alcohol, confidence in scientific education, depending on material riches, and pre-marital relations. But in other modern evangelical churches the separation from the world now is limited to abstention from smoking, drinking, cinema, sexual promiscuity and thus its radical hostility to the world is neutralized.[8] Thus there are competitions now among the new independent Pentecostals and conservative churches to give baptism to the people who wear jewelry, for fear of losing the modernized and rich middle class members.[9] The traditional Pentecostal pastors wore white simple dress and their congregations were also very simple in appearance and identifying themselves with the poor. But the modern Evangelical pastors are mostly in suits and the most of the women in the congregation are in colorful modern dresses and wear a large amount of jewellery. One can easily recognize them as people from middle and upper middle classes. Interestingly, there is also a steep increase in the number of Pentecostal and evangelical students who study in liberal theological colleges in India partly to do with the modernization of their theological thoughts.

Belief in Modern Market

Modern capitalist market mesmerizes common people in different ways whether they are religious or irreligious. Gabriele Dietrich describes that in the present phase of capitalism, the emphasis is less on accumulation and more on instrumentalization of consumerism.[10] We are witnessing this today in our context how the capitalist market identifies and captures religious symbols and sentiments, events,

---

[8] Michael Bergunder, *The South Indian Pentecostal Movement in the Twentieth Century*, Michigan: William B.Eerdmans Publishing Company, 2008, p183, 189.

[9] *Ibid.*, p187-188.

[10] Praveen P.S. Perumalla, *No to Trodden Path: A Response to Network Marketing*, New Delhi: ISPCK, 2007, pxiv.

celebrations for its business. For instance *Adi* sale, new year sale, *akshaya thriti, akshaya aavani* are some of the auspicious religious days attached to gold or the buying of new clothes in Tamilnadu. These are now exploited by the market economy to its maximum. This phenomenon is slowly creeping into the churches as well through various forms of consumerism. Auction of gold coins in the churches have become a prevalent practice and is linked with the blessing of one's wealth. One can easily see what kind of a new market spirituality is emerging here. In many ways Indian conservatives and so called otherworldly churches are very vibrant in engaging modern media. Many recent studies have exposed this reality. Praveen Perumalla in his study reveals how Gospel workers in Andhra Pradesh such as evangelists, missionaries, pastors and believers in Jesus Christ are focusing more on doing Amway Network Business than on devotion to God. Sometimes Amway network marketing concept is equated with gospel too.[11]

Traditional distinction between the market and spirituality is gradually blurring. It is puzzling to see how certain churches which are very much concerned of otherworldliness are indirectly enjoying the fruits of modern market economy. We know that the conservatives are mostly neo-liberals. It is not surprising that such doctrines mix liberal freedoms and authoritarianism - even fundamentalism - in an uneasy and unstable fashion.[12] Pradeep Thomas feels that while the market orientation of religious fundamentalists varies, Christian fundamentalists in general are great believers in the market precisely because economic globalization has played an important role in the export of this tradition from the West to the rest of the world. Having said that, and given the reality of complexity in any social formation, there are bound to be those within the Christian fundamentalist fold who eschew the embrace of the market because it is perceived to be tainted by the hands of "fallen" human beings.[13] In a similar fashion Joseph Nathan Cruz speaks of a hybrid sub-culture of the mega churches where capitalism backed technology and Google backed

---

[11] *Ibid.*, pxvi-xvii.

[12] Anthony Giddens, *Beyond Left and Right: The Future of Radical Politics,* Cambridge: Blackwell Publishers, 1996, p40.

[13] Thomas, Pradeep, p157.

praise and worship and the use of high-tech technological gadgets define the 'techno-spiritual' mega churches and give them a transnational outlook.[14]

Power of Music in the Business

The language of sound originates from instinct and develops into the art of music as cultivated by different communities. Sign-language too originates from instinct and reason, and consists of signs and gestures in which the limbs of the body - the hands, the face, the lips, the tongue, the eye-brows and the cheeks - come into play.[15] Every human being is stirred up with religious emotions, and music intensifies it. Religion and music are in themselves capable of softening the beastly qualities of human and a combination of the two is sure to bring about wonderful results. But religion is the only agent which succeeds where music fails and which can really tame unmusical persons too.[16] Yet music has the potential power to surpass all the people cutting across creed and caste.

Music plays a cutting edge position among the modernization process uninformed of the difference between market and religion. Similarly people do not always know whether something belongs to religion or it belongs to market. Today to a large extent music is controlled by the market. Market commodifies everything including music for its own interest. Particularly people who indulge in rock concerts and other such concerts know that their music ultimately stimulates their fans to be one with the rhythm of the music and respond to it with movement of the body. In such situations many people make strange noises, break down or faint or become unconscious. With the kind of music now used in charismatic churches we can detect that similar kind of body movements and emotional ecstasy are unavoidable in the religious circles too. What is common in both cases is a sort of ecstasy accompanied by loud noises, fainting,

---

[14] Joseph Nathan Cruz, "A Spectacle of Worship: Technology, Modernity and the Rise of the Megachurch" in *Mediating Piety: Technology and Religion in Contemporary Asia*, edited by Francis Khek Gee Lim, Boston: Brill, 2009, p 125.

[15] H.P. Krishna Rao, *The Psychology of Music*, New Delhi: Asian Educational Services, 1984, p2.

[16] *Ibid.*, p 16.

and so on while there is an outburst of new spirit and energy. In these situations music has become an important means of hypnotizing and controlling people.

Much of the modern Christian music comes from mega-churches in the USA, the UK and Australia and effective marketing ensures that the music has international impact. Gertrud Tonsing, a hymnologist writes that the praise and worship movement has had a global impact thanks to the charismatic movements. She cites Robert Webber to maintain that this movement is characterized by a concern for the immediacy of the Spirit, a desire for intimacy and a persuasion that music and informality must connect with people of a post-Christian culture. English speaking American Lutheran Congregations celebrating services dominated by organ music and the hymnal are now celebrating services with worship teams, guitars, drums and visual presentations.[17] Tonsing thinks that this development is questionable in terms of theology and so urges that we must resist the cultural shift towards globalizing the American style of worship which in trun pushes aside local and indigenous singing traditions. [18]

Resonance with Rock Concerts

The New Year celebrations of 2011 began with midnight Christian worship along with noises from a chain of crackers, whistles, jubilation coming from Hindu neighborhoods. This was very unusual for the city of Madurai. Generally the New Year of the common calendar was celebrated by Christians. Now everybody joins in the celebration. In few places the New Year celebrations started with midnight dances in bars, pubs, restaurants, hotels, and theatres. This kind of jubilation is spreading every where in Indian cities and towns. Modern media today focuses its attention on advertisements about music concerts, pop music, mid night parties at star hotels to boost their business. Young couples and persons are attracted to that. Incidents of suicides by crazy fans over the death of their favorite heroes and heroines, celebrities like Michael Jackson are also growing. These kind of emotional

---

[17] Gertrud Tonsing,, "A Lutheran Critique of Popular 'Praise and Worship' Songs" in *Lutherans Respond to Pentecostalism*, edited by Karen L. Bloomquist, Minneapolis: Lutheran University Press, 2008, p99.

[18] *Ibid.*, p100.

outbursts are happening among Christians too. The Christian youth are attracted to the MTV style Gospel rock music. It is a watered-down version of Christianity. The lyrics may be modern but in essence those are the same as the triumphalistic hymns of yesterday that celebrated the primacy of the "Christian" God. Choirs in the programmes of televangelists follow the same looks and styple that sometimes it's difficult to differentiate it from the secular music programmes.[19] Nevertheless music, the organization of noise, is one such form. It reflects the manufacture of society; it constitutes the audible waveband of the vibrations and signs that make up society.[20] The game of music thus resembles the game of power; monopolize the right to violence; provoke anxiety and then provide a feeling of security; provoke disorder and then propose order; create a problem; create a problem in order to solve it.[21]

Use of Sophisticated Communication Technology

While the pre-colonial and colonial Christian eras were marked by oral communication and print communication respectively, the post-colonial Christian era is characterized by satellite and digital communication technology.[22] In similar way Jonathan D. James cites Escobar's analysis how the history and expansion of Christianity was linked to following aspects:

A. Sword in the seventeenth century;

B. Commerce in the nineteenth century;

C. Information technologies in the later part of the twentieth century.[23]

Somehow televangelism was introduced in India when satellite television made its entry into India during the 1990 Gulf War.[24] Most

---

[19] Prakash James, p10.

[20] Jacques Attali, *Noise: The Political Economy of Music*, Manchester: Manchester University Press, 1985, p4.

[21] *Ibid.*, p28.

[22] Jonathan D. James, *Ibid.*, p xxii.

[23] *Ibid.*, p26.

[24] *Ibid.*, p114.

of the analysts come to the conclusion that satellite technology is inevitable in any field in the modern age. The very fact that contemporary forms of terrorism make full use of new technologies-mobile phones, computing, websites and planes-indicates that religious fundamentalists are not averse to using the tools of the West to destroy its power or at least make a dent in its aura of power.[25] There is no doubt that the Christians, especially the right wing conservatives, are no exception to this trend.

Rupert Murdoch has been dominating the field of Media in the world for more than fifty years. Evangelists in USA have strong connections with Murdoch's networks. Christian fundamentalists in particular, rank among the world's foremost users of the media, because they consider every medium of communication as a gift from God and a potential ally in the dissemination of God's unchanging eternal truth. Instrumentation, professionalism and pragmatism are typical attitudes underlying the use of media by religious fundamentalists. High ranking evangelical crusaders like Pat Robertson others in the USA are backed by the technologies of marketing that has played a key role in their ascendance in popularity.[26] Pat Robertson himself controls vast media empires and, in addition, has substantive interests in wealth-creation activities such as banking and education. His Christian Broadcasting Network (CBN) is one of the largest cable providers in USA. Synergies and links with secular media moguls such as that which is done through the sale of the channel International Family Entertainment (IFE) to Rupert Murdoch illustrate the inroads made by fundamentalist media in the mainstream. Televangelism, however, is a lot more than an adaptation of television for religion to be experienced by a vast number of people.[27]

Following such western patterns there were plenty of advertisements by the modern Indian evangelists to get God's blessings via satellite. Dish antennas to receive Christian Satellite TV channels are available now twenty fours a day. New offers such as – "credit cards accepted," "one time investment," and "no monthly charges" -

---

[25] *Ibid.*, p20-21.

[26] Thomas, Pradeep, *Ibid.*, ppx,xi.

[27] *Ibid.*, pxii.

are few of the things advertised.[28] On the whole one could see clearly how market economy is in operation in the name of religion and blessing. Everything is done for financial benefits and profits and not simply to serve the people. Profits thus made are eventually invested on allied industries like private educational institutionss and engineering colleges in India.

New Evolution of Hindu Televangelism

Hindu televangelism has borrowed many production and commercial aspects from charismatic Christian televangelism and is flourishing in India. Hindu extremists are following the same methodology with channels like Aastha, Sanskar, Maharishi, Sadhna, Jagran and Om Shanti. Most of the Hindu channels are created in the name of rectifying the West's harmful influences.[29] Jonathan James describes this new phenomenon as 'Om Economics' for without its discourse orientation and strong element of orthodox beliefs, Hindu televangelism seems even more commercialized than charismatic Christian televangelism.[30] In fact, such forms of organized religion, at this level of sophistication, are hard to come by in India, although for sheer numbers. Hindu Godmen such as Satya Sai Baba and Sri Sri Ravishankar drew massive audiences.[31] According to sociologist Shiv Visvanathan these gurus would not tell the adherents to renounce everything and lead frugal lives, instead they offer "market-friendly" techniques to deal with their life's stress and problems.[32] However for Jonathan James the two pillars of religious globalized television in the charismatic Christian and Hindu context are technology and the market. While technology is the new medium for the teaching and discourse of the faith, the market encourages the recoding of the message legitimizing it for this world,

---

[28] English Channels include God TV, Day Star, TBN, EWTN (Catholic-Live Coverage: The Pope Benedict High Mass), 3ABN, Apostolic Oneness Network, Total Christian Television, The Church Channel, JCTV, Smile of a Child TV (Kids Christian Cartoon Channel). The Tamil channels include Aseervatham TV, Holy God TV, Angel TV, Satyam TV, Blessing TV Kids, JTV etc. Malayalam Channels include Power Vision, Shalom TV, Jeevan TV etc.

[29] Jonathan D. James, p119.

[30] *Ibid.*, p3.

[31] Thomas, Pradeep Ninan, *Ibid.*, p159.

[32] Jonathan D. James, p129.

rather than the world to come. Christian and Hindu televangelism both seem to have married their respective faiths to commercialization.[33]

Sale of Spirituality

The globalization of religion has led to a billion dollar new spirituality market, a market where every human problem has a modern solution that often comes packaged and includes a hefty fee.[34] Once people identify such potentiality, the sellers of the products are tempted to use religion for money making. New miracle healers and prophets, new messiahs are on the scene. For instance the accent on miracles and the miraculous is shared by millions of Christians around the world and Benny Hinn (an American televangelist) is considered first and foremost a miracle healer. The crusades conducted by people like Hinn are expressions of the globalization of a particular form of Christianity, neo-Pentecostalism, and its related theologies, such as Prosperity Theology. These crusades offer a stage in which faith, practice and belief can be corporately validated on a mass scale. This process of mass validation that is globally consumed via television and DVDs is taking over all the tired and bankrupt forms of traditional Christianity.[35]

Sale of Christian products is a part of this successful business. There is a case to be made that the media is a special commodity. It is a commodity with a difference because unlike ordinary commodities – soap, toothpaste, and biscuits – media products affect consciousness, what we think, and how we assign value to ideas, ways of behavior, and ways of conceptualizing the world and 'others'. CDs, DVDs, key chains, stickers, calendars, Bible covers, handy bibles and spiritual clocks were sold systematically.

India is yet to witness the full frontal marketing of Christianity as is the case in USA and elsewhere. The Hebron bookshop in Chennai seemed to be the closest expression of what Christian marketing could eventually become. The online marketing of Christian goods remains a fledgling enterprise. However, it is during crusades and conventions that there are large business opportunities for the merchandising of

---

[33] *Ibid.,* p132.

[34] Thomas, Pradeep, *Ibid.,* p165.

[35] *Ibid.,* p162.

Christian products. At Every Tribe and Tongue Convention that was held in Chennai in early January 2006, there were many stalls that sold all sorts of Christian products- from Bible to DVDs, CDs, stickers, crucifixes, book marks and the like. From a political-economy perspective, it was interesting to observe that the CDs and VCDs that were exhibited and that featured Gospel music, the sermons of popular televangelists, and coverage of Christian crusades, sold for Rs. 60-150.[36]

Crusades, a new market

The usage of the term crusade, although questionable in many ways, today takes us to another connotation within the Christian circles. Some Christians prefer to use this terminology for their own convenience at any time. It starts with crusade against Muslims and then crusade against terrorism and now crusade against people of other faiths. For Christians in India the crusades and revivals are certainly not a new phenomenon. It began with evangelistic crusades by Billy Graham in the 1950's. Yet the Benny Hinn crusade is different in the sense that Benny Hinn is a full-time global crusader, backed by a sophisticated global management and marketing machine, and is in the business of religion as spectacle. His religion is tailor-made for the era of wall-to-wall television and he himself is a representative of a resurgent, global and largely mediated form of Christianity.[37]

The modern crusades are projects involving millions of dollars. For instance, the Crusade in Bangaluru shows how much of infrastructure was used in the one square mile of 215 acres - 300,000 chairs, 60 large 45-feet video screens, 45 sets of large speakers and 100,000 watts of sound, 50 miles of cable, 15,000 ushers, and parking space for 60,000 cars and buses in addition to a Gulfstream III jet, helicopters, 20 security dogs, a 100-strong private security network, two floors of the exclusive Leela Penta Hotel, 10,000 state security personnel, billboards, television spots, and advertisements in the major newspapers, with many VIPs including an ex-Prime Minister of India (Deva Gowda) and the then Chief Minister of Karnataka state, Dharam Singh in attendance. There were at least a million people who attended the crusade. With a 2,000 voice backup choir and the support of 10,000

---

[36] *Ibid.,* p172.

[37] *Ibid.,* p157.

churches this crusade organized by the flamboyant US-based televangelist Benny Hinn took place at the Jakkur Airport Grounds, Bengaluru, 21-23 January 2005.[38]

Paradox of earth negation and free market affirmation

Although the messages of the Rightist conservative churches revolve around the biblical concepts of prophecy, second coming, judgment and punishment, their understanding and outlook of this earthly life is slowly changing. They are increasingly becoming more market friendly than earlier. A crusade is visual feast and in the case of spectaculars like the Festival of Blessing, once can see that meticulous choreography, impressive arrangement of seats, technology-based fit between the aural and the visual lead to a careful build-up of an eager expectation of miracles. Many were not converted by the experiences but were willing to suspend disbelief, even to believe that 'the cool, gentle breeze that blew across the airfield' was somehow related to the presence of God. The size of such extravaganzas and the presence of thousands of people all wanting a share of the miraculous make such gatherings unique.[39] North American Protestant fundamentalists are of course great supporters of the free market than they believe in a divinely- inspired system that will lead to the greatest good in society. Jannaconne in a paper entitled the "Christian Worldview of Economics" by an evangelical organization called 'the Coalition on the Revival' that states the following:

> "We affirm that the free market economy is the closest approximation that man has yet devised in this fallen world to the economy set forth in this Bible, and that, all of the economies known to man, it is the most conducive to producing a free, just and prosperous society for all people..."[40]

The recent tendencies in the western churches are to emphasise the social responsibility of corporations and to use their power as investors to influence the policies and behavior of corporations. American churches have often sought to influence the conduct of American corporations abroad. Universities and foundations exert pressure as

---

[38] *Ibid.*, p157.

[39] *Ibid.*, p159.

[40] *Ibid.*, pp20-21.

stockholders as well, but they are less aggressive than the churches.[41] But this approach is doubtful in India. In this connection Jonathan use the term 'McGospel' to the gospel originating from the USA, with all the cultural and technological additives of America including the capitalistic and corporate aspects of Christianity.[42]

Concluding Remarks

If we closely look at the use modern methods of communication by the conservative Christians, we can see a strong element of religious adaptation rather than a critical evaluation of such methods. For Bergunder, it is 'a process of religious adaptation, in which the traditional religiosity of people is tuned to the demands of modernity surviving in new forms'. Thus American Pentecostalism is nothing but a response to the pressure of secularization and modernization. This is how Pentecostal spirituality is the "the union of the very old and very modern." In the Indian Pentecostal movement too there is a connection between the old piety and new Western modernity. This results in tendencies to Westernizing worship and community life which we can observe especially in congregations dominated by English speaking and western-oriented elites.[43]

Hostility to technical things is quite alien to the south Indian Pentecostal movement and so the religious television industry and sophisticated communication technologies in India are gaining ground. Given the fact that the Christian television market is quite small and there is limited possibility for using it as a platform to sell religious goods and services, it would seem that for the foreseeable future, this industry will remain as it currently is, with perhaps a few enterprising Christian businesses using the internet for variety of online services including radio and video on demand.[44] Among this new business trends few of the people are genuinely worried about the gospel message too. And so in India, sooner than later, there will be attempts

---

[41] John C. Bennett, "Protestantism and Corporations" in *The Judeo-Christian Vision and the Modern Corporation*, edited by Oliver Williams and John Houck, Notre Dame: University of Notre Dame Press, 1982, pp83, 97.

[42] Jonathan D. James, *Ibid.*, p10.

[43] Michael Bergunder, pp128-129.

[44] Thomas, Pradeep Ninan, *Ibid.*, p187.

to start family oriented, Christian values-based channels, given the potential for a large multi-faith audience and the possibility, therefore, of spreading the message of the Gospel to 'non' Christians.[45]

Bergunder finally identifies how such a new spirituality has strong connection with the material reality, particularly economic rise of the congregation members, "..it should not be overlooked that ethical rigorism is affected by congregations' general economic rise in to the middle class....The connection between the holiness and unworldliness has long kept the south Indian Pentecostal movement from preaching a prosperity gospel. The appearance of the Faith Movement in the 1980s and the propagation of the 'financial aspects of the gospel' went parallel with an increasing turn away from the original separation. Indeed it was only then that the idea of a prosperity gospel struck a chord with many south Indian Pentecostal congregations".[46] For them the market economy is the closest approximation that human has yet devised in this fallen world to the economy set forth in this Bible. Nevertheless it is open secret that the history of western theological 'development' has been always closely linked with capitalist development. All the major corporations originate from the West closely associated with the Christian Churches in the West.[47] Therefore Indian Christians need discriminate the issues of modernization of religion from the emerging capitalist economic reality. The time has come to reexamine some of our theologies as to how much they serve corporate market interests rather than God. In this connection Dr.Israel Sevanayagam's excellent contribution both by writing and speaking in exposing the myths of false spirituality, modernism and market with the Biblical basis is commendable.

---

[45] *Ibid.*

[46] Michael Bergunder, *Ibid*, 2008, p189.

[47] J. M. Razu, "The Meaning of Christian Existence and the Mission of the Church in the Present Global Empire-Capital" in *Work, Worship, Witness*, edited by Brian Wintle, Jesudasan B. Jayaraj and others, Bangalore: Theological Book Trust, 2003, p303.

Inter–Faith Dialogue as Mission in the Israeli – Palestinian Context: Possibilities and Problems

Kanagu Nelson

I am delighted to contribute an essay to the Festschrift for Rev. Dr. Israel Selvanayagam who is my teacher, colleague, friend, well-wisher, and mentor. More than anyone else it was Israel *annan* (elder brother) who instilled in me a spirit of dialogue and guided me into deeper understandings of interreligious dialogue. His openness and simplicity, and his dialogical engagement coupled with a deep sense of commitment to Christian faith have influenced me greatly in my ministry of dialogue and on my life as a whole.

Background and Context

The world we live in is a world of religious diversity and of ideological variety. We have Hindus, Christians, Muslims, Sikhs, and others belonging to various religions; and we have non-religious people such as atheists, agnostics, and so on. To add to this diversity we also have fundamentalists, fanatics, secularists, humanists, activists, inclusivists, pluralists, pessimists, and optimists and each have a different vision about humanity and the world. This variety exists in every region and in every country as well. As far as the history of Israelis and Palestinians is concerned, their context is not exempt from the above said realities. In 1948 Israel was established as a Jewish State. Then Israeli military occupied the Palestine land in 1967.[1] It is observed by many people that this is the main cause for the structural violence in the life of the Palestinians that is political, economic, cultural, religious and environmental.[2] Consequently, it is said that the practice of Israeli occupation and control by Israeli Authorities have systematically hindered the development of Palestinians in their daily life. This view is shared by many Jews as well.

Today one feels a sense of urgency with regard to this issue. The complex relations between Jews, Christians and Muslims have become a critical situation for fear and anger and as well as hope.[3] Jews in both Israel and abroad may justify their engagement with Palestinian reality appealing to their peculiar history, the idea of a promised land, and the need for security and protection. Some may interpret all these in the light of religio – cultural and socio - political Zionism. Admittedly, both Jews and Palestinians have parallel historical experiences of suffering in the past and present. Since both Jews and Christians use the Hebrew Bible, it is a religious issue common to both Christians and Jews. From this point of view, one may understand that this cannot but be a religious issue too. In this connection, more importantly, Jean Zaru, a Palestinian woman and Dialogue activist argues: "It is a religious issue, with implications for the integrity of people who are Jews, Christians, and Muslims alike. All three traditions stress the dignity of each human being, the justice and the judgment of God, and the importance of peace making. The inability of people of these faiths to make serious progress in resolving this issue stands as an indictment of us all".[4] This is true in the life of many Jews, Christians and Muslims in a religiously plural country like Israel.

---

[1] Benny Morris, *One State, Two States, Resolving the Israel-Palestine Context*, London: Yale University Press, 2009, P. 4. See also Thomas Mandal, Ecumenical Accompanier in Yanoun, *Living with Settlers, Interviews with Yanoun Villagers*, Revised Edition, Jerusalem: Norwegian Church Aid and EAPPI, 2011, p30.

[2] Jane Sami Hilal, "Palestinian Environment and the Israeli Occupation" in *Corner Stone, A Publication by Sabeel Ecumenical Liberation Theology Center*, Jerusalem, Issue 61, Winter 2011, P. 14. See also Jean Zaru, *Occupied with Non Violence, A Palestinian Woman Speaks*, Minneapolis: Fortress press, 2008, pp55 – 56.

[3] Cf. Margaret O. Thomas, "The Neighbor" in *You Shall Love Your Neighbor, Church & Society*, Presbyterian Church (USA), ed. by Kathy Lancaster, Vol. LXXXIV, No.3, January – February, PP. 6 -7.

[4] Jean Zaru, *op. cit.*, P. 58.

Pluralists may argue that religious pluralism is a blessing in many respects, in terms of inter-faith relationship and working towards a harmonious and peaceful life that helps and supports each other in human life. Admittedly, in Israeli – Palestinian social milieu, this issue of pluralism, has at present become more complex. It is a well known fact that the issue inter-religious harmony is connected with nationalism, territory, racism, ethnicity, language, culture, and politics. It can be viewed in terms of intra religious and inter-religious, intra cultural and inter-cultural, intra national and inter-national, and so on because of the many layers in this composite and complex issue. Such pluralism in this context is a human existential problem which raises acute questions about how people of different faiths and nations are going to live their lives in the midst of territorial occupations, displacements, alienation, frustration, fear, conflict, tension, humiliation and suffering. Is it possible to address this issue in a friendly manner as people of different communities without launching into heated debates? Is there a Biblical vision and demand to create a feasible encounter to study, discuss and sharing in this regard? Since both Israelis and Palestinians are people of God, let us see how this concern could be addressed.

Biblical Vision and Demand

According to the Jewish, Christian and Muslim religious traditions, God has created all human beings in His own image and in His own likeness. There is no partiality in His act of creation. Hence He gives equal share of His love to all persons. This is affirmed by the statement of the Kairos Palestine by saying 'Love is seeing the face of God in a word of love for all human beings, which demands forgiving, reconciling, peace and justice'.[5] Love is basic in the life of every human being. One could provide many illustrations from the Biblical teachings. For example, Jesus Christ said: 'Just I have loved you, you also should love one another (Jn 13: 34). More significantly, he said with great authority, "love your enemies and pray for those who persecute you" (Matt 5: 44; Luke 6:27; Cf. Prov. 25:21 – 22; Rom 12: 20). Similar ideas about love are present in other epistles in the New Testament as well. For example, if we cannot love those whom we are

---

[5] "Introduction – A Word of Faith" in *Kairos Palestine, A Moment of Truth,* booklet, 8th print, Jerusalem, 2011, pp11–15.

able to see, the passage reminds us, it is impossible to love God whom we cannot see. In fact, the claim of fellowship with God can be no more than a lie if we do not love those about us (1 John 2: 9 – 10; 4: 20 – 21). With this insight, let us love one another, for love is of God, and every one who loves is born of God and knows God. Therefore, be kind to one another, tender hearted, for giving one another, just as God in Christ forgave you (Eph 4: 32). The impact of love says that evil should not overcome by evil but by good deeds. This is what we see in the letter to the Romans, " Do not repay any one evil for evil" (Rom 12: 17) and in Peter's epistle "Do not repay evil for evil or abuse for abuse"(1 Pet 3: 9).

Love is a criterion for the legitimacy of all relationships, both with fellow human beings and with God.[6] Thus loving and forgiving is not only Christian principles but also neighborly religious values. This is what we need to this social milieu, where genuine love is absent. As far as God is concerned, His love is for all people irrespective of all differences. His providence, goodness and plan of salvation is extended to all communities (Acts 14:17; 17:26; Rom2: 6-7; 1 Tim 2: 4). Thus God is the God of all and He is not limited to any particular community (Amos 9:7). This is applicable in this Israeli- Palestinian context. Then how do we go for discussion, sharing and engaging one another? And which is the platform to carry out this message of hope in the hopeless situation to the people of different faith communities? In this environment, dialogue is the platform to foster a spirit of toleration with mutual learning and right understanding.

Inter – Faith Dialogue

Jean Zaru rightly points out that

> Religion is the problem where its structures of dominance have oppressed us Palestinians, as women, or as any other people who have been on the down side of religious chauvinism. Religion is also a solution where its vision of liberation or equality has generated powerful social and political movements for change…So religion can be the bond of kinship that binds us together and binds us to God. Religion includes those deeply held traditions and values that shape our ways of thinking and our hopes for

---

[6] See Julia Neuberger, "Jews Christians, A shared Responsibility" in *Dialogue with a Difference, The Manor House Group Experience*, ed. by Tony Bay Field and Marcus Bray Brooke, London: SCM Press Ltd, 1992, pp119–124.

change. Religion should also be spiritual in order to breathe life in to a world weary of conflict.[7]

Such a view of the twofold nature of religion is underscored in the liberative message of God proclaimed by the Hebrew judges and prophets, Jesus and his disciples, and the early church missionaries. In it, God engaged in a dialogue with all communities. God invites us to engage in conversation with one another. As Thomas Thangaraj has argued,

> A dialogical engagement with one another is an open possibility…It has to take its public character seriously and engage in dialogical engagement with people of other religious persuasions. Issues of public concern are not matters pertaining to one religion alone. People of all religions are invited to engage in the discussion of public issues. For example, how could anyone deal with a concept such as "Justice" without taking into account the varying perspectives that one finds among Christians and people of other religious traditions?[8]

At this juncture, it is an urgent task that we work together to consolidate a culture of justice and peace. We believe that all those who are directly involved in the confrontation should adopt a bilateral cessation of hostilities, opening the possibility of dialogue. In this milieu, dialogue is the answer and a way out; and in due course this would become a message of hope and bringing reconciliation is possible for the people.[9] For this reason, the people of Judaism Christianity and Islam who live in and around Israeli – Palestinian milieu, need to engage in inter – faith dialogue. There are many groups and organizations that focus on dialogue, ecumenical efforts, and peace making in this context and these are important for community building. As S. Wesley Ariarajah writes, "dialogue is about building a community of conversation and community of heart and mind across racial, ethnic, and religio –

---

[7] Jean Zaru, *op. cit.*, pp127–128.

[8] M. Thomas Thangaraj, "The Challenge of Religious Plurality" in *Plurality, Power and Mission: Inter Contextual Theological Explorations on the Role of Religion in the New Millennium*, eds. by Philip L. Wickeri, Janice K. Wickeri and Damayanthi M.A. Niles, London: The Council for World Mission, 2000, pp200 – 201.

[9] Stewart Vriesinga, "Dialogue is the Answer", in *Christian Peace Maker Teams*, Chicago, Vol.XX1, No. 3, July – September 2011, pp10 – 11.

political barriers".[10] This orientation needs to be instilled in the heart and mind of the People of God and Peoples of God those who are not aware of the need for a spirit of dialogue for bring peace in a religiously plural world.

More significantly, religious pluralism and inter-faith dialogue encourages different communities' participation in terms of living together in friendship and fellowship, thereby sharing with one another and discussing socio -political and national issues together and working together for peace building and reconciliation.[11] Thus inter – faith dialogue is an indispensable condition in the establishment of a climate of trust, friendship and collaboration. Otherwise, there will be a kind of ridicule, cynicism or hatred in the knowledge of the other.[12] We need to have a clearer understanding and fuller knowledge of what dialogue is all about. "Inter – faith dialogue is not debate, where one attempts to convince an opponent. It is not negotiation, where one strives for the lowest common denominator. In this dialogue we meet as believers to learn about, and from, each other"[13]. This means that there is a need to have more initiatives where we can build common platforms and common concerns in which we can work together for human development, creating an environment of peace.[14] Since there are many glaring inequalities and injustice among different faith communities, this kind of motivation and engagement is needed to transform and change the society.

In this process of change, there would be positive, transformative, and liberative values, and new patterns of socio – political behavior

---

[10] S. Wesley Ariahrajah, *Not Without My Neighbor, Issues in Inter – Faith Relations*, Geneva: WCC Publications, 2000, p20.

[11] Quoted Wenona Giles and Jennifer Hyndman, "Gender and Conflict in a Global Context," in *Sites of Violence, Gender and Conflict Zones*, ed. by Wenona Giles and Jennifer Hyndman, London: University of California Press, 2004, p9.

[12] "Jerusalem One city Two Peoples and Three Religions in search of Peace," in *Al – Liqa'' Journal*, ed. by Geries S. Khoury, Jerusalem, Vol. 37, December 2011, p27.

[13] *Broacher*, The Centre for Inter Faith Dialogue, Diocese of Stockholm, Sweden, during the Lecture on 01.03.12.

[14] Helene Egnell, *Other Voices, A Study of Christian Feminist Approaches to Religious Plurality East and West*, Uppsala: Studia Missionalia Svecana C, 2006, p81.

will emerge bringing hope to a hopeless situation. Thus the wounds of the society inflicted by many decades of religio – political and national rivalries, social isolation and political antagonism may be healed. A realization of this possibility will foster mutual co – operation among the religious communities and encourage like-minded and politically involved people toward creative and constructive dialogue and ultimately that will reduce the fear and tension in this context.

Ron Kronish, Director of the Inter religious Coordinating Council of Israel (ICCI), and also the Center for Inter Religious Encounter with Israel, has described the dialogue of life in a helpful manner. He discovers four different aspects to the dialogue of life that will help the processes in peace making. These are: 1. Personal sharing of life and experience, 2. Inter – religious right understanding, 3. Listening and sharing of issues of political conflicts, and 4. Action.[15] This is indeed a good observation. However, these processes depend upon the mood, spirit, desire and potentiality of all persons concerned. This task is not only an individual one or an activity of a group of people; it is also the mission of church. Since God-in-Christ engages in dialogue with humanity in human history dialogue is the mandate of the church. Let us see how dialogue is as an integral part of the Church's mission.

Dialogue as an Integral part of Church Mission

Inter – faith dialogue is one of the major concerns of the church, and it is an integral part of mission in the light of the Biblical vision. This has been highlighted in the World Missionary Conferences (WMC) in 1910 at Edinburgh, 1928 at Jerusalem and 1938 at Tambaram, Chennai (South India). This position was maintained and promoted by the World Council of Churches (WCC) from its inception (1948). WCC has been taking a major role for dialogue as an integral part of mission, starting a sub - unit for Dialogue for inter-religious understanding and peace making between Jews and Christians, Muslims, Hindus, Buddhists and the alike. On the Roman Catholic side the Second

---

[15] Notes, from the lecture on Dialogue of Religions as Peace Building, at the Swedish Theological Institute, Jerusalem on 13.02.12. For story telling, See Prasanna Kumari, "Theology of a Crucified Reality: An Exploration of Feminist Experiences" in *Challenges and Responses, Church's Ministry in the Third Millennium: Implications for Theological Education,* ed. by Gnana Robinson, Bangalore: Asian Trading Corporation, 2000, pp237–241.

Vatican Council (1965) from its starting point has been encouraging the study, encounter and experience of neighboring faith traditions and cultures of the peoples for engaging in dialogue as a missional activity. Both WCC and Vatican have held a number of meetings, consultations, conferences and proposals for peace making and human development at global level. Their works in this area of concern are commendable and thus they stimulate the churches in the plural world. To fully understand dialogue as mission of the church, one needs to look in to the Bible.

"Love your neighbor" and "Do not bear false witness against your neighbor" give us the mandate for the mission of the church. If these two are taken seriously, witness cannot be shouting out our message at others or trying to win over people to our side; rather it becomes sharing - sharing what is most important in human life, and what in fact controls our lives. Such witness demands that we consider dialogue as mission.[16] This is a great challenge to our Christian faith and practice within the church as well as in the society.

Jesus was open to neighboring faith communities in his dialogue of life. For example, Jesus dialogued with the Roman Centurion, Canaanite woman, Samaritan woman and others. As he was a man of genuine dialogue, he respected, admired and appreciated the people of neighboring faiths. For example, Jesus appreciated the faith of the Centurion and said: "Assuredly, I say to you, I have not found such great faith, not even in Israel" (Matt 8:10). When we have mutual respect, openness, commitment and inner awakening, there is no need to renounce our religious identity. This is what we see in Jesus. Jesus was born as a Jew, lived as a Jew and died as a Jew. He never broke his traditional identity. But he was open to others.

This courageous and honest example of Jesus gives us hope to continue to dialogue. With this spirit, St. Peter says: "Always be ready to make your defense when any one challenges you to justify the hope which is in you. But do so with courtesy and respect" (1 Pet 3: 15). For such engagement in dialogue, she or he needs to be quick to listen, slow to speak and slow to be angry (James 1: 19). Taking this as a

---

[16] Quoted Israel Selvanayagam, *A Second Call, Ministry and Mission in a Multi - faith Milieu,* Chennai: CLS, 2000, p117.

norm, inter- faith dialogue is a fresh path for the church that is called to be a community of conversation. For this, it needs to become a participatory church, requiring creative and constructive dialogue of life in Jesus way. When God is seen as the parent God of all communities, it is possible to dialogue, discuss and negotiate for making peace and reconciliation in the life of Israeli –Palestinians. In this way, one could understand that God acts in the history of the human's suffering through dialogue, ecumenical and peace making groups.

More over, dialogue attempts to promote shared living and thereby understanding of the neighbors to rebuild confidence and strengthen the bridges between the communities with dignity and freedom.[17] This is what we observe in the values of the Kingdom of God (Mark 1:15). This Kingdom of God in Jesus Christ demands us to live as a public witness to the goodness of God and the dignity and self – respect of all communities. As inter-dependent communities, we can be sharing and struggling together in suffering, and thus experience joy and hope in hopeless situations. One may consider that the dialogue mission of the church is prophetic and authentic to share the word of God lovingly, courageously and honestly with kingdom values of equality, and justice. When we involve in this task in a pluralistic atmosphere, we need not give up our beliefs, convictions and traditional identity and there is no need of betraying one's commitment to Christian faith.

More important, in relation to this concern, is what Pope John Paul II ascribed: "It is my hope and my desire that commitment to dialogue...should be strengthened throughout the church"[18] In

---

[17] "Editorial – We need a Religious Discourse which Unites and does not divide", in *Al – Liqa News Letter*, The Center for Religious and Heritage Studies in the Holy Land, Jerusalem, No. 43, December 2011, P.16. See also for the activity of the Council of Religious Leaders at the Vatican in Israel and the Muslim – Catholic Forum in Amman, in Fouad Twal Latin Patriarch of Jerusalem, " The Christian Message from the Latin Patriarch Jerusalem", in *Bulletin, Associated Christian Press*, ed by Jerzy Kraj, ofm, Jerusalem, NO. 479, November – December, 2011, pp3–4.

[18] Joy Thomas, "Dialogue as Mission", in *Dimensions of Mission in India*, ed. by Joseph Mattam, Bombay: Saint Paul Society, 1995, P. 111. Cf. *Roman Catholic Documents, Statements by Vatican Authorities in Stepping Stones to further Jewish-Christian Relations, An unabridged Collection of Christian Documents*, compiled by Helga Croner, London: Stimulus Books, 1977, PP. 7 – 8. Cf. the followings are

addition to, Israel Selvanayagam says that the church is an apostolic body of God. It needs to recapture the vision of the God and activity under His guidance as a dialogical community. This means the congregations of the church are to be vulnerable to each other and to others in the world.[19] This is a challenge for the churches and Christian institutions of today. Many denominational churches have very little interest in activating and involving dialogue as a mission. By and large, they are particular about the spiritual activities, worship services, financial management and evangelization for bringing the people to Christian faith. For them, mission includes only these. But they need to be reminded of what Jesus said about religious conversion efforts in Matthew 23:15. While some Christians see efforts at conversion as important, people of neighboring faiths see those as an irritatingly intolerant approach to others and such a perception leads to many conflicts and tension in Asian context as well. Therefore, friendship, mutuality and inter dependence are necessary for a peaceful future. In today's world, we are bound together addressing common problems. The well being of one is intricately interrelated to the well -being of the other. If so, what are the steps we need to take to further the cause of interreligious dialogue of life and action and encourage individuals, groups and churches to offer their support?

Possibilities, Problems and Challenges

Possibilities are endless. For example, peace-making education may be made compulsory in the public and private schools, colleges, universities and other training centers so that students will grow with the sense of right understanding and involvement. This peace education may start in the family itself. Parents should accept their responsibility to teach their children the need for involving in peace and reconciliation processes. Moral and value education needs to be

---

from the *Flyers - Operation 1325 Women as Peace Builders, evolving further collaboration*, Stockholm, February 2010, P. 9., *SIDA Policy Promoting Peace and Security through Development Cooperation, for Environmental Peace*, Stockholm, Sweden, Swedish International Development Corporation Agency, 1st October 2005, *SIDA Policy Promoting Gender Equality in Development Corporation*, Stockholm, Sweden, Swedish International Development Cooperation Agency, 10th October 2005, pp7–8.

[19] Israel Selvanayagam, *A Dialogue on Dialogue, Reflections on Inter faith encounters*, Madras: CLS, 1995, p6.

intensified among the students for right attitude and commitment to do her or his socio- political duties. Religious ignorance and misinterpretation of religious scriptures is prevalent all over the world. This is one of the reasons for the conflict and tension. Therefore, dialogue, ecumenical and peace making groups need to encourage the people to study their religious scriptures with care and encourage involvement in inter-religious cooperation and dialogue.

From the Israeli – Palestinian contextual sources, we may provide some models for these possibilities. For example, as *Wahat al – Salam / Neve Shalom*[20] suggests, there is a need to maintain the following the educational principles to promote peace:

a)   Equal participation by Jews and Palestinians in the administration and teaching.

b)   Providing a natural on-going frame work that enables the day-today meeting between Israeli and Palestinian children.

c)   Use both Hebrew and Arabic in teaching all the children.

d)   Nurturing each child's identity by imparting knowledge of his or her culture and tradition while inculcating respectful familiarity with the culture and tradition of the neighboring people.

---

[20] *Hand out,* During the lecture on 29.02.12, *Wahat al- Salam / Neve Shalom* is a village in Israel of Jews and Palestinian Arabs of Israeli citizenship. Its programs focus on open inter – religious and inter – cultural dialogue and advancement of peace. Its educational system was the first Jewish – Palestinian bilingual Children's educational programme. This is also the Pluralistic Spiritual Center in memory of Bruno Hussar, the Founder of this Institution. But the *Arab Educational Institute(AEI) and the Sumud* program support education in values, culture and identity to build a cadre of Palestinian inter religious and cultural sources of inspiration able to develop a strong value - based message summarized in the Arabic concept of *Sumud*. One may identify that both AEI and Sumud are for the Palestinian community in the area of *Bethlehem*. Another wing is for the *Palestinian women's Research and Documentation Center* (PWRDC). It functions as a resource and documentation center and carries out net working, advocacy and policy oriented research for gender equality and the human rights of Palestinian women with commitment to the values of equality, justice, freedom, and human dignity for the better future. The above said are taken from the *Broacher* during the lecture on 14.02.12.

e)   Encounter workshops on the conflict for Jewish and Palestinian youth in Israel.

f)   Encounter workshops, in service training and seminars for adult groups, including teachers, journalists, lawyers, social workers and university students.

g)   Encounter work between citizens of Israel and Palestine NGOs.

h)   Courses for empowerment of Arab and Jewish women.

i)   Encounters for raising awareness towards inter group conflicts within Arab and Jewish society.

These principles and systems are apt and appropriate to this conflict context. What are the practical things one can do to promote peace?

Kathy Bergen[21] proposes that we can share our experiences in Palestine and Israel with people in our own peace making and dialogue groups, churches, synagogues, mosques, temples, Gurudwaras, schools, colleges and universities. We can join a group in our area that is working for peace and dialogue with justice for Palestinians and Israelis so we can find support for our work to neighbors working on these issues. Just like the way Ramallah Friends Meeting Quakers do in the dialogue of life, we may organize for lectures for students, NGO study tours, and fact finding visits in the affected areas. We may also organize educational and cultural events, lecture series on pertinent issues, workshops on women's role in peace making, and providing space for local NGOs and faith – based groups to meet.

We can conduct a signature campaign among the people of all faith communities to resolve the conflict. We may organize inter – religious prayer once a week and invite the people to read different religious scriptures with short reflection and pray for the issues by the participants. In this way, we may help people awaken to the present context.

---

[21] *Hand out,* Kathy Bergen, Program Coordinator, Friends International Center in Ramallah, (Israel), during the lecture on 22.02.12. See also for women empowerment, *Gender – based Violence in the Middle East Region: Research, Policy, and Action,* a Document booklet, oxfam, Norway, December 2010, p15.

The process of dialogue is for mutual – learning to understand and accept each other. This is further striving towards changing the mind set of Israelis and Palestinians from mere tolerance of one another to one total acceptance of plural society. Eventually people learn to be comfortable with the multiple identities, seeking equal opportunities and rights for all. This is the sign of integral development for everyone.

Being citizens of our country implies being committed to make justice prevail in our country. So we need to speak out against all forms of injustice. For this reason political involvement becomes a moral responsibility for Israelis and Palestinians. In this dialogue endeavor, there is a need to speak out, when there is an imbalance in the distribution of public services. It is our vital socio – political duty to raise our voices, maintaining a clear, honest and caring attitude in matters that concern all in our society. This is something we owe to one another. There is a growing need for mobilizing grass root level dialogues to get the support from people for our efforts at conflict transformation and our actions toward coexistence and harmonious life. Since both Israelis and Palestinians are living in fear and frustration in this political conflict, people who are involved in dialogue and peace making should engage in prayer to strengthen the Jews, Christians and Muslims in faith, hope, and love. This prayer may be offered by ndividuals, families, and of interfaith groups to humanize the neighbors and look forward to a future of peace, of living together.

There are some challenges and questions of how conflict transformation may be carried out in a dialogical and non-violent manner. What is needed here is dialogue both at the mirco and macro levels. Both in the Middle East and outside of the Middle East Israelis and Palestinians should be offered opportunities for dialogue, conversation, and peace making. Most often churches are not really motivated to evolve or devise dialogue as mission of the church. There is a fear of compromising one's Christian faith if one is engaged in the dialogue of life with the people of neighboring faiths. The leaders of the churches need to motivate and mobilize the congregations for recognizing dialogue as mission and take initiatives for furthering dialogue as mission in future.

In this connection, Roland De Corneille understands that the communication of God is by personal encounter; but the church has lost sight of it. It has tried to spread the Gospel but it has forgotten the personal relationship with the communities.[22] The good news is that there are many groups both women and men working for dialogue, ecumenism and peace making. They need to come together and act together. The question remains as to who will organize and integrate all the various groups for solidarity and collective action to raise voice against the socio – political conflict and tension. For many years there have been many consultations, meetings, resolutions and proposals, initiated and run by dialogue, ecumenical and peacemaking groups, NGOs, United Nations, and other International organizations to resolve the conflict. But the issue still remains unresolved. The burden rests on the people of God and the peoples of God. These are the challenges and questions that are placed before us for engaging in further study, research and joint action.

---

[22] Roland De Corneille, Christians and Jews, The Tragic Past and the Hopeful Future, Newyork: Harper & Row Publishers, 1966, pp81–83.

Mahatma Gandhi's Gospel of Truth Enabling Interreligious Dialogue

A. Pushparajan

I am delighted to make this contribution to honour Rev. Dr. Israel Selvanayagam, as a well-informed theologian, known for his original thinking and contextual interpretation of the Bible. It was always an enriching experience for me to enter into dialogue with him in Madurai. Those discussions mostly centered on theological matters to back up our dialogue-mission in which we were both involved, organizing many seminars together, and travelling together to participate in national seminars. It was always an exhilarating experience for me when he shared his views, views that were mostly complementary to my own.

Dr. Israel was a dynamic executive in all the innovative programmes he initiated in and through the 'Religious Friends Circle', which functioned for so many years in TTS, Madurai. These dialogue programmes even included Peace Marches and Common Prayer-Meetings, when he skillfully wooed the cooperation of likeminded organizations, such as the Commission for Dialogue of which I was the Secretary, the Gandhi Museum, the Islamic Study Circle etc, always showing his skill as both theologian and practitioner. Parallel to these two prominent features of Dr. Israel, my paper has both theological orientation and practical implication.

The paper primarily intends to elucidate the concept of Truth as evolved by M.K. Gandhi (1869-1948). This concept is highly theological, I contend, because it provides me with a tool to understand my Master better and fathom some of the dimensions of his personality that have not been disclosed during these two millennia. It unravels a trait of my Master which otherwise has been a puzzle to many all these years, thus proving itself a 'Gospel' to me, a Christian.

At the same time, this concept of Truth by Gandhi is of great practical relevance to our dialogue mission today. It gives believers as well as non-believers a common platform of action and collaboration and enables them all to involve themselves in common projects for betterment of society, despite the differences in their viewpoint or worldview. It enables them all to be engaged in common action, not simply out of good will, but by providing them with a sure and solid ground that is epistemologically and metaphysically valid.

To have a clear grasp of this Gospel, it is first necessary to be aware of Gandhi's personal search for Truth. For, it is in and through his life-long search for attainment of spiritual transcendence that he himself arrived at this concept of Truth. So, in the first section below an effort is made to outline his search for Truth. With this background, an effort is then made to elucidate this concept of Truth in order to see it as a Gospel, as a way of better understanding Christ. The final section will be devoted to drawing out the practical implications for interreligious action and cooperation.

1.   GANDHI'S SEARCH FOR TRUTH

Jesus the Nazarene is on trial, standing before the Roman governor as a convict. Pontius Pilate is not easily carried away by the accusations by the Jewish authorities, even being bewildered by them. Therefore he quietly calls Jesus inside and asks him: "Are you a king?" The retort of Jesus is mild: "You say that I am a king. However, I was born and came into the world for this one purpose: to witness to truth". Pilot is all the more confounded. Then he asks the crucial question: "What is truth?" At his point, however, Jesus keeps silent. Now, the question is: Why did Jesus not answer Pilot? He was not ignorant of the right answer. Was his silence perhaps the sort of contempt he had showed to King Herod? It cannot be, as he has answered other questions of Pilot.

This was a big puzzle to me for many years. However, it was resolved easily when I took pains to understand the notion of Truth as enunciated by Gandhi. Hence, for me describing Gandhi's teaching as 'Gospel of Truth' is entirely fitting. What is that gospel? We need to bear in mind that Gandhi was primarily a spiritual seeker and that his whole life was a journey in search of Truth:

> What I want to achieve - what I have been striving and pining to achieve these thirty years - is self-realization, to see God face to face, to attain Moksha. I live and move and have my being in pursuit of this goal. All that I do by way of speaking, writing and all my ventures in the political field are directed to this same end.[1]

It is also important to remember that his life-long effort was amply rewarded. That is why after narrating all the different experiments of his search, he could write at the end of his Autobiography: "My uniform experience has convinced me that there is no other God than Truth."[2]

1.1.   Earlier search

Gandhi was **a most ordinary man** in his early days. Intellectually not a brilliant student, he was a rather mediocre and slow learner. Emotionally he was a hot tempered husband, psychologically a weakling, fearful of darkness, ghosts and snakes. Morally, the boy succumbed to almost all the possible vices of a teenager: stealing, smoking, even visiting a brothel. Professionally he was utterly a failure in the beginning.

But there was **one thing that was extraordinary** in the boy: his commitment to truth-telling. He was so truthful to himself that he accepted every one of his defects, and thus was able to find an alternative way towards perfection. Acceptance of himself as he was, was itself an instance of his truth-searching. Especially seeing the street-play of Harichandra made such a lasting impression upon his youthful mind that he resolved always to play the role of Harichandra in life.[3] Even in the minutest details of life he became a truth-seeker. For instance, when the inspector of schools, on the occasion of his annual visit to his school, gave a dictation test, he miss-spelt a word. All other

---

[1] M.K.Gandhi, *An Autobiography Or The Story of My Experiments with Truth*, Ahmedabad: Navajivan Publishing House, 1927, Reprint 1976 "Introduction", p. x

[2] *An Autobiography*, p.382.

[3] *An Autobiography*, p.4

students of his class fared well in the test. Even the class-teacher was so concerned about him that he hinted he should correct it by copying from his neighbour. Even then he refused, being clear this was against truth. Looking at his puny body, a stout bodied friend persuaded him to eat non-vegetarian food. Only then would he become strong enough to fight against foreign rule. This motive seemed sufficient reason for him to decide in favour of meat eating, although it was against his family taboos. After the first experiment of meat-eating with his friend one evening on the banks of the river, he came home with a heavy stomach and refused his mother's prepared meal. When asked for reasons, the boy first escaped by saying he was not feeling hungry. Then he lied, saying it was probably indigestion. However, this pricked his conscience so painfully, that, in spite of what seemed good reasons, he decided to stop the whole experiment after a short time.

Gandhi also committed many petty faults common to boys of his age. He was even persuaded by his friend to pay a visit to a brothel, being saved only on account of his shyness. He was so perturbed by his various failings that he even decided to commit suicide. But there was an inner voice indicating a way out: 'Confess these pitfalls to your father and get forgiveness…start again a new life of truthfulness.' Not daring to speak directly, he wrote his sins and showed this to his father, expressing his readiness to receive punishment and pledging never to commit them again. Unexpectedly, his father shed tears, by which the boy felt that his sins were washed away. To young Gandhi this was "an object lesson for Truth and Ahimsa".

1.2. Gandhi's Deeper Study of Religions

Gandhi's deeper search for truth related to what he found in religions. Even during his childhood he became acquainted with numerous religions, both his parents being very religious minded. As Saivites, they would generally visit a Siva temple, but they were never averse to Vaishnavite temples. Jain monks too used to visit his house frequently, as well as Muslim and Parsi friends who often discussed religious matters with his father, especially when he was nursing his ailing father.[4] Further, during his student days in London he became friendly with Theosophists, whose teaching led to his reading the Gita

---

[4] *An Autobiography,* pp.22-23.

in Sanskrit. He also became acquainted with the Bible, reading the whole book, as well as classical essays on Islam and Buddhism.

Gandhi's contact with other religions, especially Christians and Muslims in South Africa, created a serious challenge to his native faith, and he was almost at the point of conversion. Unable to make a choice between Christianity and Islam, Gandhi took recourse to a certain Raychandbai, a living witness to the way of spiritual transcendence. With further guidance, reading in various religions, and a prayerful waiting upon God, he felt able to make a right choice. This was a transforming search, as he put into practice what was learnt by reading. While Christianity did not seem perfect, nor did Hinduism, especially when faced with the defects of Untouchability. His search led him to believe the following:[5]

- All religions are basically one in that all inculcate morality and self-purification. They all serve a fundamental need of society.

- "Religion" in a non-sectarian sense means basically "Truth": 'truth of living' involving a life of morality and self purification.

- Each particular religion has produced both 'peaks of morality', great attainments of spiritual transcendence, as well as utter degeneration, and manifestations of cruelty. So, there is no one religion which is all true, nor is any one religion all false.

- There is no question of superiority/inferiority between religions.

- Every religion is valid to its own followers and is capable of becoming more and more perfect by its followers' life. In fact the native factors might be even more congenial to the growth of spiritual fervor.

Therefore, in ordinary circumstances, conversion from one's native religion may not be advisable. On this basis he took a clear decision regarding his personal conversion.

---

[5] *An Autobiography*, pp.101-102.

1.3. A Search in Common Action

In South Africa, as he launched the campaign of the indentured labourers against unjust, colour-based discrimination, he drew in people of different religions to join in common action for non-violent resistance. Later, his nationwide freedom-struggle too involved people of different religions and even of no religion, thus widening the horizons of his understanding of Truth, and leading to startling conclusions **about God**.

Gandhi had started his search for truth by seeing the world's faith in terms of his own tradition: e.g. the different attributes of God and the one thousand names of God spoken of in the Hindu scriptures. Then, he came to know that Islam too had many names for God, leading him to see even then that there can never be an exhaustive list of the divine names.

Later still Gandhi came to be convinced that of all the numerous predicates of God, Truth is the best to describe God. All other attributes, he argued, could be vague and ambiguous. Even the most common description of God as 'love' can mean many things, including degrading passion. In contrast, about 'Truth' there is no ambiguity. "Nothing is (exists) in reality except Truth".[6] Combined with the suffix *ya*, the term *Sat* means 'endowed with Being', pointing to the most primary attribute, and so most appropriate to designate the ultimate Being, not subject to change. "Only God is; nothing else is". So Gandhi said that the most appropriate way of describing God is "God is Truth".[7]

In the course of his relentless search, he went a step further and said: "It is more correct to say 'Truth is God' than to say 'God is Truth'.[8] This change of the subject into predicate and the predicate into subject is what Aristotelian logic would call 'converse of proposition', and this converse forms the core of Gandhi's formation of the trans-religious concept of God.[9] For, in any statement, the subject is what we start

---

[6] M.K. Gandhi from *Yeravda Mandir, Ashram Observances*, Td. V.G. Desai, Ahmedabad: Navajivan Publishing House, Reprint 1980, p.1.

[7] *Ibid.*

[8] As quoted from Gandhi's *Autobiography* by R.K. Prabhu *op. cit.*, p.4.

[9] For a full treatment of the subject, please see A. Pushparajan, "Gandhi's Trans-religious Understanding of God" in *Romancing the Sacred*, Bangalore: Asian Trading Corporation, 2007, ACPI Publications 8, pp.373-406.

with. It is that which is taken for granted as known. It is the key term about which the predicate states something you do not know. Not all people claim to know about God. But none can deny knowing what is meant by the 'truth of life.'

Gandhi had such an attitude of openness to all sorts of thinking that he began to accept the genuineness of their claims as well as their life. Those who were avowed atheists had raised serious doubts about God. He agreed with their honest criticism that numerous atrocities and hypocrisies were committed in the name of God.[10] And he also realized that the life of genuine and sincere atheists was often far superior to the lives of some believers. In fact he found that God is denied more by the un-truthful theists than by the honest and sincere atheists. Hence Gandhi preferred its converse proposition as more appropriate. Human reason can reject everything, but not Truth, as being that which exists. With this starting point, the subject, Truth can be really God, rather than a blind religious notion.

2.   GANDHI'S MEANING OF TRUTH

Now, putting together the glimpses of a sincere spiritual seeker such as Gandhi, as well as the outcome of his search, we will be in a position to formulate what he means by 'Truth'. To realize the significant contribution of Gandhi's concept of truth, it may be good to contrast it with the well-accepted meanings of truth in the history of Western Philosophy.

2.1.   Truth as conceived in Western Philosophy

In Western Philosophy one finds three major strands of thought defining what truth is: ontologically, morally and epistemologically.

a.   Ontological meaning of Truth

Even 2500 years ago, Parmenides (and later Plato) is said to have first explored the properties co-extensive with 'being-as-such'. However, it was Aristotle who first spoke of the 'transcendental' properties of Being, so named because the properties of Being transcend categories like time and space, and are not contingent upon cultural diversity,

---

[10] GORA, *An Atheist with Gandhi*, Ahmedabad, Navajivan Publishing House,1951, Reprint 1971

religious doctrine, or personal ideologies. Being is said to be One, Good and True (*unum, bonum, verum*), later followed by St. Thomas Aquinas as he developed his doctrine of God.

b.   Truth in Morality

Granted the ontological Truth of God, and granted that human beings are created as the 'image and likeness of God', it followed that we are truly human only in so far as we strive after the 'transcendentals', for these are to be the ultimate desires of humans. Human perfection is found in the perfect attainment of these transcendentals. And moral truth was usually identified with veracity or the habit of speaking the truth. As social animals we cannot live together if we did not believe one another to be speaking the truth. "Hence the virtue of veracity comes to some extent under the head of justice (*rationem debiti*)."[11] Moreover, the gift of speech, of its very nature is intended for the communication of knowledge by one to another. It should be used, therefore, for the purpose for which it is naturally intended. If one fails to speak the truth, one not only misuses, but destroys the efficacy of the gift of speech, thus destroying our instinctive belief in the veracity of the neighbour.

c.   Epistemological Meaning of Truth

Epistemologically, truth in Western Philosophy has been explained in various ways. The Correspondence theory of truth defines truth in terms of correspondence between what one states and what is there in reality. In contrast, the Coherence theory of truth denies the one-to-one correspondence between statements and realities. What we call a 'fact' is itself a formulation of certain concepts in the form of a proposition. So, by 'truth' what one can validly accept is at the most a relationship of coherence of one statement with a set of statements. As a result of the incompatibility of these two theories, there emerged the Pragmatic theory of truth. It simply claims that what works is true. Obviously this kind of meaning of truth cannot be accepted as it will lead to utter relativism. Thus the whole treatment of truth in western philosophy by and large remains inconclusive.

---

[11] Thomas Aquinas, *Summa Theologiæ* II-II.109.3.

2.2. Gandhi's specific contribution

In contrast to these three Western formulations of truth, Gandhi arrives at a conception which would eliminate the defects of each one, while at the same time combining the merits of all three. First, Gandhi basically concedes, as we saw, the ontological sense of truth. Literally *sat-ya* means 'being endowed with the "Being" or the "Real" or the "Truth". In its primary meaning 'to be', it indicates '**What is, permanently'**, or the **fundamentally Real,** as against all transient beings; what Paul Tillich would call the **Ground of Being** or the Bible the **"I am who am".** Gandhi also understands the term *'sat'* as the **moral force** holding the universe together, or '**cosmic order and harmony',** what is traditionally called '*Rta*' or '*Dharma*'. It is indefinable, but surely if dimly perceived. While everything is ever changing and dying there is a living power that is changeless, binding and holding all things together.

'*Sat*' in both these senses is seen by Gandhi as **Absolute** Truth, though in relation to humanity it is **relative truth,** because each human differs in subjective conditions and so in conscious awareness of the 'Truth'. This is all the more reason for humans to aim conscientiously to live in consonance with that immutable one and eternal order.

'Truth', then, for Gandhi means not merely truth-telling (what the moralist would demand), nor merely correspondence between statement and reality (as an epistemologist would require). He goes one step further and says we human beings must strive after the One, Perfect and True Being. Accepting both usual meanings, Gandhi moved beyond this to aiming for truth even in thought and actions, implying thereby consistency between thought, word and deed. Truth then means that which affects the whole of one's being, all realms of life. Truth in thought, means that our ideas reflect reality as it is; we are not to allow our prejudice to influence us. So, truth according to Gandhi means "truth of living", where there is not only consistency of my thoughts and words with reality, but also there is a consistency between my actions and thoughts and between my actions and words.

Thus it is again an ontological conception of truth that Gandhi is hinting at, though it is not an abstract Aristotelian ontological truth. Striving after the Ideal, we are to integrate our life around that Idea, that absolute Truth. And the truth of human being lies precisely in striving after the eternal One.

2.3. Absolute Truth versus Relative Truth

Here, Gandhi is very realistic in understanding human nature as it is. A perfect harmony is perhaps impossible for us in this world for two reasons: (1) Imperfect as we are by nature, it is not possible for us to realize a perfect consistency here on earth. (2) Given the wide variety of people and their subjective conditions, individual perceptions of Truth are bound to be different and varied. Thus he introduces a distinction between Relative Truth and. Absolute Truth. **Absolute Truth** is the perfect consistency of thought, word and action. This is Truth in its fullness, the only ultimate reality, the immutable One, and the eternal Order, the pure ideal. And this is God. **Relative Truth** is that very same Truth perceived differently by different individuals, in relation to their different geographic, historical and cultural conditions.

As Truth is experienced by humankind, imprisoned in this mortal frame, by its very nature it is bound to be relative. Absolute Truth can only be visualized in imagination. Hence humans have to be content with **relative truth**. It is, though, 'relative' not in the sense of relativistic, but in the relational sense, that is in relation to our subjective conditions and variety of contexts. To put it in his own words: "Relative truth is the truth as we perceive it in relation to a particular set of circumstances. It is not the whole truth. What may be true under one set of circumstances may not be true in relation to a different set of circumstances." Even so, the different relative truths are in relationship with the Absolute Truth. Truth is manifested to everyone in relation to our own space, time and condition. Relative Truth is the truth of the Absolute manifested to you here and now.

2.4. Crucial Importance of the Distinction

Of its very nature, relative Truth is bound to be numerous and diverse. That means, for Gandhi, pluralism is an accepted norm of life. This does not mean ethical relativism in which there is no absolute Truth. Rather, all relative truths are to have participatory relationship with Absolute Truth, seeking correspondence with that Truth. What appears to be different truths are like the countless and apparently different leaves of the same tree. Hence Gandhi asks: "Does not God himself appear to different individuals in different aspects? Yet we know that He is one. Hence there is nothing wrong in every one following Truth according to his lights. Indeed it is his duty to do so. Even if there is a mistake on the part of any one so following Truth, it will be automatically set right because of the *tapas*, self-suffering even unto death".

The best way for the closest approximation of relative truth with Absolute Truth, according to Gandhi, is abiding by the indwelling spirit and listening to the dictates of conscience, whose voice should never be stifled. The biblical statement "Every sin will be forgiven, but not the sin against the Holy Spirit" (Mk.3:28) actually refers to the act of stifling of one's conscience. The more you stifle it, the farther and farther you will go from God's presence and a time will come when this soul cannot take a turn towards God at all, though by its very nature it was meant to be in the presence of God always. The expression 'Wrath of God' needs to be understood as a result of one's making rather than an attribute of God. What is within your control is the relative truth: accept it and abide by it. One's conscience is nothing but the voice of God, the mirroring of the Absolute Truth in the subjective conditions. It is the inner voice, the voice of purified reason, instinct. Its whispering is heard in every heart.

Can we be sure that the inner voice is definitely from God, rather than from the devil or from one's own selfish desires? To determine the nature of the voice, Gandhi appealed to the resulting fruits in life. Moreover, there is an inner compulsion to follow the voice of conscience without any external proof. The inner voice is itself its own proof. When the inner voice tells you, "you are on the right track", keep straight on. However, serious training is needed in order to listen to one's inner voice. Self-purification is a pre-requisite. And one who claims to follow the inner voice will be hesitant to be self-assertive, will be always humble, always ready to listen and ever willing and even anxious to admit mistakes.

Vindication of relative truth involves self-suffering (*tapas*) on the part of the seeker. What appears to be Truth to one person will appear as untruth to another person. This is bound to be the case since the human mind works through innumerable media and since the evolution of mind is not the same for all. Hence, tolerance is a necessity.

In fact, for Gandhi the golden rule of conduct is mutual tolerance. We will never all think alike and we see Truth in fragmentary forms and from different angles of vision. While conscience is a good guide for individual conduct, imposition of that conduct upon all will be an insufferable interference with everybody's freedom of conscience. If one wants to establish that the other is at fault, and vindicate one's own truth, this can only be through the path of suffering. Here lies the value of prayer, fasting, persuasion, negotiation, dialogue etc

2.5. The Gospel of Truth

The very fact that one speaks of 'relative Truth' means one ought to accept other truths contrary to one's own perception. Granted that the evolution of human mind is not the same for all and that we all work through different subjective conditions, Gandhi accepts that "what may be truth for one may be untruth for another". Everyone is to follow truth according to his or her lights. If there is a mistake on the part of anyone so following Truth, it will be automatically set right. For, according to Gandhi, the quest of Truth involves *tapas* - self-suffering, sometimes even unto death; there is to be no trace of self interest in an honest seeker. In such a selfless search for Truth nobody can lose his bearings for long. One who takes to the wrong path stumbles, and is thus redirected to the right path. This pursuit of Truth is true *Bhakti* (devotion). It is the path that leads to God. In this connection, Gandhi puts forward the lives and examples of Harichandra, Prahlada, Ramachandra from Hinduism, and great souls like Imam Hasan from Islam.[12] It is in this way that all the martyrs of early Christianity could be listed as saints who conformed their relative Truth closer to the Absolute Truth.

Another implication of Gandhi's distinction between relative and Absolute is that his Nonviolence or *ahimsa* gets an ontological basis. No perception of relative truth can be forced upon another as if the only revelation of Absolute Truth. Rather, tolerance and patience is needed, precisely because all perceptions of that Absolute are bound to be imperfect and varied. This implies Nonviolence.

---

[12] *From Yeravda Mandir,* p.3.

I can vindicate my perception of Truth only by suffering for what I hold to be true rather than imposing this on somebody else. This is how Gandhi developed the technique of self-suffering such as fasting, penance, and prayer as a valid technique of resolving conflict with the perceptions of others. Thus Gandhi's non-violent technique is not born out of expediency but a logical exigency from the ontologically valid plurality of relative truths parrticipating in the one Absolute Truth. That is why he called it *Satyagraha*, literally 'clinging to truth' (one's relative truth) unflinchingly, undergoing sufferings patiently, as a price for what one holds to be true, thereby enabling the other to realize his/her own truth. In other words, Gandhi's *ahimsa* is a logical concomitant of Truth. That is why Gandhi, at the end of his Autobiography has this to conclude:

> My uniform experience has convinced me that there is no other God than Truth. . . .The little fleeting glimpses, therefore, that I have been able to have of Truth can hardly convey an idea of the indescribable lustre of Truth, a million times more intense than that of the sun we daily see with our eyes. In fact what I have caught is only the faintest glimmer of that mighty effulgence. But this much I can say with assurance, as a result of all my experiments, that a *perfect vision of Truth can only follow a complete realization of Ahimsa.*[13]

2.6. Jesus the Supreme Satyagrahi

Now, in the light of the Gandhian implications of the Truth, it is easy to answer the question we raised earlier: "Why did not Jesus answer the question 'What is truth?'" Obviously the 'truth' that Jesus Christ came to witness to was not something to be told by words, or explained by theories. But it was a truth lived, to be established primarily in life. It was not an epistemological discussion, but an ontological confirmation that he needed to demonstrate. It pertained to his being, what he had to realize in his life, and what he would make of his being till his last breath.

It is true the Lord knew his identity and revealed it also to his Apostles in his last discourse with them: "I am the way, the truth and the life" (Jn. 14: 6). That way was to be the nonviolent way, willingly offering himself to be lifted up and voluntarily undergoing the most

---

[13] M.K. Gandhi, *An Autobiography, op. cit.,* "Farewell", p.382-83, emphasis is added

ignominious death on the cross. It is by dying that the grain of wheat was destined to give life. It is in taking up the nonviolent way, and giving life through dying that the real 'Truth' of his 'relative truth' lies. It is not propositional, not even a moral truth to be disclosed, or an ethical truth to be expounded. Rather it was on ongoing striving for that Absolute Truth within the relative, a pursuit of 'historical ontological' truth by the human Jesus seeking to approximate this to the eternal absolute Truth of the Father. It was only by the end of the journey that "everything was fulfilled". Prior to that, there was the deep agony in the garden of Gethsemane, when during agonizing prayer Jesus came to a clear conviction that he has to give up his life. The hardships of flagellation, crucifixion and ignominious death on the cross are the final tests of his claim to be that Truth.

That truth cannot be established orally by the power of rhetoric, nor theoretically by any amount of argumentation, but only through living it, and living through it.[14] It would have been irrelevant to talk to Pilot about a truth that cannot be talked about. It was only by living all the trials patiently, and dying his ignominious death voluntarily, that he could establish that he was really the Way, the Truth and the Life. And so he could utter the last word: "all is consummated"

That is why Resurrection proved to be not only the reward but also the vindication of the truth of the living he realized. That is why, again, it was after Resurrection that his Apostles, the timid and illiterate disciples became so courageous to speak about this living truth, and live it to the core, even by giving up their life voluntarily for it. It is in this connection that the most loved disciples wrote the following words:

> That which was from the beginning, which we have heard, which we have seen with our eyes, which we have looked at and our hands have touched - this we proclaim concerning the Word of life. The life appeared; we have seen it and testify to it, and we proclaim to you the eternal life, which was with the Father and has appeared to us. We proclaim to you what we have seen and heard, so that you also may have fellowship

---

[14] A.Pushparajan, "Professing the unique Lordship of Jesus in a Religiously Pluralist Context: A Lay Perspective" in W.S. Milton Jeganathan, *Mission and Religious Pluralism*, Chennai:The Department of Mission and Evangelism of the Church of South India, 2003 pp.177-191.

with us. And our fellowship is with the Father and with his Son, Jesus Christ. (1 Jn.1:1-4).

In fine, then, the Gospel of Truth challenges us to be fully perceptive of one's relative truth, and live it with all one's ability, so as to go thereby nearer and nearer the ideal Absolute Truth, allowing others also to go nearer, in their way, to that Truth. For Christians, the call is that they should not merely claim Jesus as their Lord, Life, Truth and the Way. They will rather make Him such with all its implications, follow the Way consistently, live the Life with all its costs, thereby realizing the Truth in and through their own being.

3.   IMPLICATIONS FOR INTERRELIGIOUS DIALOGUE

After theoretically solving the unsolved riddle regarding the silence of Christ with the help of Gandhi's conception of truth, it is appropriate now to examine the potentials of the same concept for undertaking interreligious dialogue.

3.1. Need for Interreligious Dialogue

If one applies the Gandhian distinction between relative truth and Absolute Truth to the field of religious plurality, it will be obvious that the various religions are relative truths, derived from the one source, namely God, the Absolute Truth. So, Gandhi theoretically establishes that all religions are true, since they all perceive and participate in the one Absolute Truth. That they all have the same God as the Source is established phenomenologically, according to Gandhi, by the fact of saints. This Gandhi emphasized as against the former missionaries' polar model and their accusation of other religions as being false.

Gandhi also held that all religions are imperfect by reason of the human instrumentality both in receiving the Absolute Truth (divine revelation) and later by commentators of that revelation. Exegetically, there have been varied interpretations and even interpolations and extrapolations in Scripture. These imperfections arise not because of any deficiency on the part of the Truth, but because of subjective conditions, the cultural and historical background.

If thus, all religions are both true and imperfect, then there is the need for every religion to grow from imperfection to Truth. It is to fulfill this need that interreligious dialogue is required. In this context evangelization has a meaning. Through such a process of interaction all the religions are bound to come closer to the Absolute Truth and establish the Kingdom of God. So God is not only the source but also the convergence of religions.

3.2. Pluralism is a must

Another implication of Gandhi's Gospel of Truth is that one will have to accept the diversity of relative truths. Just because I follow that Absolute Truth (AT) manifested to me according to my particular conditions and context (let us call it 'RT^1'), does not mean that someone living in a different context should follow my RT. The AT that is manifested to the other in a different context and received by a different person according to a different mould of subjective conditions, would be a different RT (say RT^2) and he/she is expected to follow RT^2 not RT.[1]

Human beings see the AT in fragmentary forms and from different angles of vision. Hence, no one can claim that what is true for one is necessarily true for all. Thus plurality of religions, understood as RTs of the one Absolute Truth is to be accepted as normal and necessary.

3.4. Not merely Tolerance but even Respect

Given the validity of diversity, it is necessary for us to be tolerant of other RTs. Just because I follow a particular RT in a particular way, I cannot impose my RT on anybody else or expect others to follow the Truth in the way I follow. Even among the most conscientious persons, Gandhi said, there must be room for honest differences of opinion. The only possible rule of conduct in any civilized society is mutual tolerance.

Yet, Gandhi was not satisfied with mere tolerance. Tolerance may imply a gratuitous assumption of the inferiority of other faiths to one's own. Or, one may develop toleration towards another, just because the other has proved to be invincible. This type of tolerance is born of convenience, whereas Gandhi's attitude results from the very understanding of RT. So, he goes one step beyond mere toleration. We should cultivate *respect* for other RTs and esteem for the followers of other RTs, and for their ways of life and thought, except where the difference is fundamental.

3.4. No oblivion of defects of RTs

Tolerance towards other RTs does not mean, according to Gandhi, being oblivious of the numerous defects or degradation that might have been accrued within the different religions in the course of their history. When a particular RT is seen to be evil or false, one must reject it. But before arriving at that conclusion, one must find out carefully whether the sum-total of that RT is bad for its followers. It also means being keenly alive to the defects of our own standpoint and making greater effort to overcome them as a result of encountering other RTs. Further, respectful tolerance purges us of harshness towards others, and their molehills are not made into mountains. This in turn provides for greater scope for learning from the acceptable features of other religions, purging us of an over-pampered attitude towards ourselves, and so enabling us to grow into greater and greater perfection. Thus the position of Gandhi is indeed a paraphrase of the biblical maxim: "Do not judge others so that God will not judge you. Why do you look at the speck in your brother's eye? First take the log out of your own eye" (Mt.7: 1-5).

3.5. Tapas

This process is only enabled through suffering for what I hold to be true rather than imposing my RT on somebody else. Gandhi developed the technique of inflicting suffering on self, especially through voluntary suffering, fasting and prayer, as a valid technique of resolving conflict with other RTs. His nonviolence is not born out of expediency, but is a logical exigency from the distinction between AT and RT. That is why he called his nonviolent resistance **Satyagraha,** 'clinging to truth', (one's RT) unflinchingly, undergoing (in the social realm) all sufferings patiently, as the price for what one holds to be true.

At the religious level, no one can dare think that one's own position is the sole revealed truth. Other religions also surely contain Truth. If they are imperfect, one's own religion is equally imperfect. Realizing this is the basis for entering into dialogue with one another. The purpose of their dialogue will be to learn from the riches of others and thereby enrich one's own religious pursuit. Equally, there will be sharing one's own riches with others and enabling others to go nearer to the Absolute Truth. Thus the whole world would be moving from imperfection to perfection, and so hastening the coming of God's reign on earth.

CONCLUSION

This paper has, hopefully, elucidated the Gandhian concept of Truth. Further, availing itself of the light derived from this this, the paper has unraveled an important, often unnoticed, dimension of Jesus Christ. In this respect, then Nonviolence or self-suffering is not an expedient technique but a logical concomitant of Truth, flowing from the ontological pursuit of the RT with the eternal *'ontos'* of the AT. That is today's 'Gospel' for us Christians.

This 'good news' that we have been able to draw out from Gandhian thought not merely satisfies my intellectual curiosity, giving a plausible explanation about our Satguru's silence regarding the meaning of truth; it also paves the way for making progress in interreligious dialogue, showing its great practical relevance too.

To understand both these aspects of this Gospel, it was found necessary to know the personal journey Gandhi was making in striving after the Truth in his life but also in conceptualizing it. I hope this recounting of Gandhi's search proves an inspiration to many of us to be more authentic in our pursuit of truth, as we profess to follow Jesus the Lord, who is the Way, Truth and Life.

In fine, then, the Gospel of Truth challenges us to perceive our RT candidly, and live it carefully so as to approximate the AT as closely as possible, at the same time allowing others also to go nearer to that Truth. We should never force our perception of the Truth on anybody. Neither should we simply keep quiet. In a dialogic spirit we witness to others and learn from others. Thus we would enhance other 'relative truths' while allowing our own to be enriched by those others. Thus all our 'relative truths' can move on towards a full effulgence of the Absolute Truth even here on earth, thus realizing the vision of the 'New Heaven and New Earth'.

Epilogue:
Weakness and Strength:
Living within the Gospel Paradox

Donald Eadie

When we honestly ask ourselves which person in our lives helps us most, we often find that it is those who, instead of giving much advice, solutions, or cures, have chosen rather to share our pain and touch our wounds with a gentle and tender hand. The friend who can be silent with us in a moment of despair or confusion, who can stay with us in an hour of grief or bereavement, who can tolerate not knowing, not curing, not healing and face with us the reality of our powerlessness, that is a friend who cares.[1]

I am writing for such a friend - the Revd. Dr. Israel Selvanayagam - one who is familiar, in his own words, with the years of 'darkness, oblivion and the abyss,' and who also knows what it is to be 'still alive' and to discern 'an implicit, imperceptible hand sustaining him underneath.' In the form of a meditation, I want to explore the Gospel paradox of weakness and strength through story, borrowed wisdom, reflections and wonderings. In seeking to relate to others, perhaps especially those whose story and life-reflections are very different from our own, rather than arguing our strengths, can the acceptance of our weakness become in the end the way to more effective engagement?

Mysteries are to be entered and explored not explained. 'When I am weak, then I am strong' writes Paul.[2] And, Christ crucified, the man tortured, flogged, abandoned by his friends and in the extremes of humiliation, 'is the power of God and the wisdom of God.'[3] A contemporary expression of the paradox comes in the writing of Barbara Glasson. '.........in Jesus we find the agonising process of transformation to be the very nature of God's engagement with humanity. To be followers of Jesus is to go to the depths of who we are, into the soup of metamorphosis, into the possibility that we might be consumed, destroyed, annihilated. To risk finding God, we must lose everything, and I mean everything, even God.'[4]

I first consciously began the search for an authentic vocabulary within this Gospel paradox following a visit to the Caribbean in 1984, not long after the invasion of Grenada by US forces. I met Alan Kirton in his office in Bridgetown, Barbados, a young Methodist Minister serving as General Secretary of the Caribbean Council of Churches. On behalf of the Churches Alan had spoken out deploring the invasion. His was a prophetic voice. Alan was called to Government Offices and threatened with deportation. There were those who labeled him 'communist'. He was forbidden to preach from some Methodist pulpits. Alan embodied the paradox, silenced yet powerful, gentle yet strong, wounded by a sense of betrayal by the Church which within the kairos moment, the critical hour, lost its nerve. He was sustained, he said, through the prayers of small communities of Catholic Sisters who prayed for him daily and phoned him regularly

Through the years my own attempts to explore with others our living within the Gospel paradox have generally met with a respectful yet unsettling silence. There are, however, notable exceptions and among them a couple who live in a village in the forest areas of central Sweden. Kjell was a social worker until in his early 40s he discovered he had Parkinson's disease. Great tiredness and angst belong to his reality, his hands shake, he props up his head and physical movement is limited. He expresses the deep things within him through poetry, painting and now through singing, 'nobody knows the trouble I've seen, nobody knows but Jesus.' Why is it that he only discovered such remarkable creativity when he became so ill? His wife, Ingela, is a physiotherapist in the local hospital and is strong; she also knows her weakness. In the summer she is both lost and found in her garden, in the winter she skis great distances through the silent forest. They live the paradox within themselves and also within the interplay of their relationship.

What are we learning within the paradox? There is a stripping away of so much within us which, through fear, seeks to control and manipulate. We are brought to the core, the heart of things. We learn a new openness, an inner freedom. We resist the culture of deceit, give things their proper names. We let go burdens which no longer need to be carried. The mystery of our becoming authentic human beings and human communities lies not in our weakness or strength but rather in their essential interplay. Here we learn 'the curious alchemy of risk, hope and struggle and the growing in love while remaining vulnerable and woundable.'[5]

In recent years I have encountered this paradox poignantly within my own life and in my relationship with my wife, Kerstin. In a variety of unanticipated, unwelcome circumstances I am learning about 'letting go' and 'handing over' and 'entrusting.' What has been new has been the rare yet real sense of having neither the energy nor the will to live through where the journey might lead. And yet it has been within this terrain that I have experienced what I can only describe as a cracking open of life, an eruption within the depths of my being, a welling up, an out-pouring.

Day and night for weeks, months I scribbled into note books random jottings, insights, phrases, images, resonances, echoes, bits of wisdom, stories, lines from poets and hymn writers. I had more time to listen to the radio, watch television and read newspapers and was almost overwhelmed by encounters with the weakness/ strength paradox, emerging like mysterious watermarks within the wonder and horror of the life of the world. Here are a few of the many cameos which for me embody those encounters.

- A woman arrives in a refugee camp in Kenya having walked for many weeks from Somalia with her six children. She is reported to have first walked a distance both carrying and also holding the hands of three of her children, and then she leaves them in order to bring the three who remain waiting for her. On arrival in the camp she is exhausted, the children hungry, thirsty and needing medication. *What, I wonder, of her inner strength, resolve, determination within physical weakness?*

- A crazed gunman first plants bombs in cars in the centre of Oslo, then travels to an island where young people are gathered in summer conference and mindlessly shoots so many, intelligent, socially committed young people. It is an attack, we are told, on 'aspiring multi-culturalism.' And within the grieving of the nation thousands gather in vigils carrying torches, lighting candles in the night, 'We want to remain open as a society, open to difference and this may mean that we leave ourselves vulnerable to extremists.' *What, I wonder, inspires such a corporate commitment to a way of openness and vulnerability?*

- A report on BBC's To-day program told that the Burmese opposition leader, Aung San Suu Kyi was making her first political appearance outside of Rangoon since her release after seven years of house arrest, a one day trip to meet supporters in two towns north of Rangoon despite Government warnings of riots.[6] A few weeks earlier she had delivered secretly the BBC Reith lectures. Of poetry and faith she said: 'Passion translates as suffering and I would contend that in the political context, as in the religious one, it implies suffering by choice: a deliberate decision to grasp the cup that we would rather let pass. It is not a decision made lightly - we do not enjoy suffering; we are not masochists. It is because of the value we put on the object of our passion that we are able, sometimes in spite of ourselves, to choose suffering.' *I wonder about solitude, confinement, silence and the birth of insight, wisdom and inner freedom?*

- A heartbroken father, Tariq Jahan, spoke publicly following the death of three young men including his son, knocked down and killed by a car in Winson Green, Birmingham. In front of a restless crowd he said that the deaths should not be treated as a race issue. 'To-day,' he continued, 'we stand here to plead with all the youth to remain calm, for our communities to stand united. I lost my son. Black, Asians, whites - we all live in the same community. Why do we have to kill one another? Why are we doing this? Step forward if you want to lose your sons. Otherwise, calm down and go home.' *From what deep spiritual well, I wonder, does this Muslim father draw within his profound shock and grief? And what has fashioned such a man?*

During the long period of my convalescence we received many cards, one was a candle card with the words, 'When the candle is lit angels gather.' Angels, I am learning, come in many forms. In my reading of the Gethsemane story I had failed to notice the angel who strengthens but who does not remove the cup of suffering. 'Then an angel from heaven appeared to him and gave him strength. In his anguish he prayed more earnestly, and his sweat became like great drops of blood falling down on the ground.'[7]

Sarum College in Salisbury has hosted four weekend conferences for those living with impairments. The theme of the most recent conference explored was 'Vulnerability as the heart of transformation.'[8] The Biblical texts for exploration were the first chapters of Paul's 2nd letter to Corinth. He writes of 'the afflictions experienced in Asia; for we were so utterly, unbearably crushed that we despaired of life itself. Indeed, we felt that we had received the sentence of death so that we would rely not on ourselves but on God who raises the dead.'[9] Paul's testimony is to 'the God of our Lord Jesus Christ, the Father of mercies and the God of all consolation, who consoles us in all our afflictions, so that we may be able to comfort those who are in any affliction with the consolation with which we ourselves are consoled by God.'[10] The word 'comfort' has the same verbal root as 'fortify' with resonances of encouragement, strengthening. The word 'courage' is derived from the French word coeur, heart. It means the ability to stand by one's heart or to stand by one's core.

More and more I wonder about the nature of transformation and tremble within this awesome crucible. I have read and re-read words by Barbara Glasson in which she points to mysteries we cannot grasp. She uses the language of the threshold/liminal place, '…I have spoken of the liminal place as a place of paradox, but I do not intend this to imply an either/or process, during which there is a natural progression from one state of being to another. On the contrary, the liminal threshold is messy and full of confusion and contradiction. It is this very messiness that is the medium for re-creation. It is a troubling place, a place where the waters are disturbed and the self becomes immersed into new dimensions of being.' And later '………crucially this process holds the potential to bring about transformation not just for the individuals concerned but also for communities who would take the risk of entering the liminal space and accompany the transitional person across the threshold into new life'.[11]

In Sweden the Baptist, Methodist and Missionkyrkan (the sister Church to URC) share a remarkable journey into the creation of one new Church. I addressed their winter conference in Stockholm on the theme, 'Vulnerability as the Heart of Transformation.' We were reminded of God's call to be drawn into the mystery of the Body of Christ, to share in his life, suffering, death and resurrection. I had the audacity to encourage others to be 'strong enough to be weak,' 'strong enough to be gentle.'[12] *I wonder how we keep the paschal mystery, the suffering, dying and resurrection of Jesus, as the heart of the creation of the Church? How to form congregations where we are strong enough to bring our weakness, open enough to bring our different experiences of pain, and hopeful enough to recognise that these could also be transforming gifts?*

Within our incompleteness, flawedness and fragility we are called into an inner yielding toward something more profound, a following within the breaking open and breaking through, a trusting into the unimaginable beyond. All this and so much more belong to the consent to be transformed. All this, too, cannot but be an essential part of any dialogue with others that springs from faithful discipleship. To engage with others whose life-experience and faith-journey may be very different from our own calls us to be open to weakness, and open to that inner transforming by which others too can become transformed.

These things are written for a companion who inhabits the Gospel paradox within weakness and strength and who is a friend indeed.

Endnotes

[1] Adapted from *Reaching Out* by Henri Nouwen (Collins Paperbacks 1976).

[2] 2 Corinthians 12:9-10.

[3] 1 Corinthians 1:24.

[4] Barbara Glasson, *The Exuberant Church - Listening to the Prophetic People of God* (DLT 2011). p44.

[5] Gillian Rose, *Love's Work* (Chatto and Windus 2011).

[6] BBC Radio 4, Sunday 14th July 2011.

[7] Luke 22: 42-44.

[8] See also D.Eadie, *The Faith Journey of Impaired Pilgrims*, a small book gathering papers, stories, poems and prayers (Sarum College Press 2007).

[9] 2 Corinthians 1:8.

[10] 2 Corinthians 1: 3-5.

[11] *Op. cit.*, p.44.

[12] Vinter Konferens, Stockholm January 2011. En Kyrka utan väggar (a Church without walls). 'Vulnerability as the heart of transformation' is available from Donald Eadie.

Israel Selvanayagam's Publications in English

1. "The Centrality of Cross in Dialogue", *International Review of Mission*, LXXIV/296, Oct. 1985.

2. "A Peoples Movement in the Making - The Scavengers Association in Madurai", *East Asia JL OF THEOLOGY*, Occasional papers, 1986.

3. Review of 2 books, "Orthodox Perspective".....and "Will the Future Work" in *Asia JL OF THEOLOGY*, I/1, 1987, 253-258.

4. "Effective Leadership and Evangelised Administration: Some Reflections", *AJT*, III/2, 1989, 639-642.

5. "Towards a Dialogical Approach to Reality and Religions", *AJTR* (Arasaradi Journal of Theological Reflection), I/2, 1985, 24-33.

6. "Towards a People-Centred Theology", *Ministerial Formation*, 27 (PTE, WCC, July 1984), 3-9.

7. Review of *Sharing Jesus in the Two Thirds World* in *BTF* (Bangalore, Theological Forum), XVIII/2-3, 1986, 141-143.

8. "The Role and Meaning of Saiva Symbols in Manikkavacakar's TVM" in *BTF*, XV/1, Jan-April 1983, pp.21-38.

9. "An Integral Approach to the Study of Religion: Insights from an Indian Christian Perspective", *BTF*, XIX/2, 1987, 104-120.

10. "Is Religious Conversion Possible in the Process of Inter-Faith Dialogue?", *Discernment*, III/2 Autumn, 1989, pp.2-11.

11. "The Tension between Mission and Dialogue: Some Observations", *MASIHI SEVAK*, Vol. XIV, 1989, pp.1-6.

12. "Learning in Mission and for Mission" (with M. Gnanavaram), *Venturing into Life*, TTS Story, 1990, pp.89-96.

13. "Learning with People of Other Faiths" (with S. Gangadharan), *Venturing into Life*, TTS Story 1990, pp.97-108.

14. "Hindu-Christian Dialogue in India: Some Recent Developments", *The Challenge of Dialogue*, Papers from the Meeting of the Dialogue Workshop, Casablanca/ Morocco, June 1989, WCC, pp.72-77.

15. "The Cross Bearers" (with Esther Retnaraj) in *Stories Make People*, compiled by Sam Amirtham, Geneva; WCC, 1989, pp.23-28.

16. "Communalism in Contemporary India: A Christian Response from Dialogical Perspective", *Arasaradi Journal of Theological Reflection*, Vol.III, No.2, July-Dec., 1990, pp.21-25.

17. "Floating Ark and Shipwreck: Contrary Biblical Models for Multi-Faith Context and Christian Living", *Asia Journal of Theology*, 5/2, Oct.1991, 338-345.

18. "Inter-Faith Dialogue: Some Programme Models", *Indian Missiological Review*, Vol. 13, No.2, July 1991, pp.48-54.

19. "Some Methodological Insights for Theological Writers in India", *The Theological Writer*, August 1992, pp.6-9; *The North India Churchman*, XXIII/5, May 1993, pp.6-9.

20. (With Dr. S. Gangadharan), "The Communion of Saints: Christian and Tamil Saiva Perspectives", *Hindu Christian Studies Bulletin*, Vol.5, 1992, 13-19; *Voices from the Margin*, ed. R. S. Sugirtharajah, Orbis/SPCK, 1995, pp.381-393.

21. "Asoka and Arjuna as Counterfigures Standing on the Field of Dharma: A Historical-Hermeneutical Perspective", *History of Religions*, 1992 Aug., pp.59-75.

22. "Inter-Faith Dialogue: A Clarification of Perspectives and Issues", *Current Dialogue*, WCC, No.23, Dec.1992, pp.20-25; *THE SATHRI JOURNAL*, 1/1993, 22-29.

23.   Edited and contributed an essay on "Non-Biblical Literary Resources for Theological Writing in India", *The Multi-Faith Context of India - Resources and Challenges for Christians*, Bangalore: BTTBPSA, 1992, pp.24-40.

24.   "Inter-religious Communication - The Primary Blockades on the Way", *Arasaradi Journal of Theological Reflection*, V/162, 1992, pp.183-194.

25.   (with Bishop Samuel Amirtham), "Ministry by God's People - The Significance of Lay Participation in Christian Ministry", (*ALL TO MINISTRY AND MISSION*, (Essays in Honour of Rt. Rev. Kenneth E Gill), ed. S. Vasanthakumar, SCM India, 1993 pp.48-59.

26.   "Who is this Jesus? - A Biblical Outline for Clearer Self-Understanding and Communication in a Multi-faith Context", *Asia Journal of Theology*, 7/2 Oct. 1993, pp. 231-243.

27.   Book Review - A. Pushparajan, "From Conversion to Fellowship", *Gandhi-marq*, 15/1, April-June 1993, pp.96-98.

28.   "Role of Religions in Secular India", *UNITE*, Madurai, 1/2, Dec. 1993, pp. 96-98.

29.   "Jewish-Christian Relationship from a Third World Perspective", *Current Dialogue*, No. 25, Dec. 1993, pp.20-31.

30.   *Towards a Humanist Theology of Religious Harmony - Insights from the Writings of Dayanandan Francis*, Madras: CLS, 1994.

31.   (With C.R.W. David), "Liturgy and Symbols: Reflections in view of Liturgical Renewal in the Church of South India", *AJTR*, VI/2, July-Dec., 1993, pp.19-28. *Greater Peace, Closer Fellowship, Fuller Life*, Ed. By Lily & Sam Amirtham, CSI Golden Jubilee Publication, Madras, 1997, pp. 310-322.

32.   "The Ayodhya Issue: A Review from a Dialogical Perspective", *National Council of Churches Review*, Vol.CXIV, No.2, Feb.1994, pp.123-134.

33.   "A Study of the Life of Abraham", *The Bulletin*, HMISS, Jan.-June1993, (12/1,2), pp.30-35.

34.   *Evangelism and Inter-Faith Dialogue - Are they Incompatible or Complementary?*, Occasional Paper No.13, Selly Oak Colleges, 1993. Indian Edition, Tiruvalla: CSS, 1996.

35.   "Challenges to Religious Pluralism in India: The Nature of Hindu Fundamentalism", *Challenges to Religious Pluralism*, ed. A. Pushparajan, Madurai Arch Diocese: The Commission for Dialogue, 1994, pp.28-38.

36.   Co-editor (with Dayanandan Francis), *many Voices in Christian Mission* (Essays in Honour of J.E. Lesslie Newbigin, Madras:CLS, 1994. Contributed an essay on "Towards a Humanist Theology of Religious Harmony", pp.172-209. (Reproduction of No. 31)

37.   "Twenty Five Years of Theological Reflection in Arasaradi", *Arasaradi Journal of Theological Reflection*, VII/1,Jan.-June 1994, pp.10-14.

38.   Ed. (Authored 20 articles), *Biblical Insights on Inter-faith Dialogue*, Bangalore: BTTBPSA-BTESSC, 1995.

39.   Five Bible Studies (A Great Name etc.), *Fundamentalism and Secularism - The Indian Predicament*, ed. Andreas Nehring, Madras: Gurukkul (Summer Institute), 1995, pp.364-383.

40.   "Children Laugh and Cry: Authentic Resources for Creative Christian Theology in Asia", *Asia Journal of Theology*, 9/2, 1995, pp. 352-366

a.   *A Dialogue on Dialogue - Reflections on Inter-faith Encounters*, Madras: CLS, 1995.

41.   "A Journey of Understanding Hinduism Through Study and Dialogue", in *CHRISTIAN CONTRIBUTION TO INDIAN PHILOSOPHY*, ed. Anand Amaladass, Madras: CLS, 1995, pp.201-212.

42.   Bible Studies (2,3,5-10) in *I Delight in Thy Law* (WCCI Bible Studies), ed. Moses P. Manohar, Nagpur: NCCI, 1995.

43.   "People of God and Peoples of God: Asian Christian Discussions" and "An Indian Christian View of Religious Pluralism" in *People of God, Peoples of God, A Jewish -Christian Conversation in Asia*, ed. Hans Ucko, Geneva: WCC, 1976, pp.67-83, 100-110.

44. Same Article, *People of God, Peoples of God* A WCC Consultation on The Church and Jewish People, Budapest - Oct. 15-21, 1994, ed. By Rabbi Leon Klenicki, Anti-Deformation League & CCJP, pp.37-48.

45. "Jacob and the Nature of Blessing", *The Bulletin* of the Henry Martin Institute of Islamic Studies, Vol.13, No.3&4, July-Dec. 1994 pp.94-98.

46. "Inter-Religious Lyrics by a Christian Poet", in *Doing Theology with the Poetic Tradition of India-Focus on Dalit and Tribal Poems*, ed. By Joseph Patmury, Bangalore: PTCA/SATHRI, 1996, pp.136-147.

47. (ed.) *Writing Theological Textbooks - Some Guidelines*, Bangalore: BTTBPSA & BTESSC, 1996; a revised version is published in *Theological Writings: Guidelines, Hints and Tips*, ed. By Samson Prabhakar, Bangalore: BTESSC/SATHRI, 2006, 2008, pp. 23-69

48. *Gospel and Culture in Tamilnadu*, Geneva: WCC, 1996.

49. "Pastoral Counselling for Creative Encounters with the People of Other Faiths", *AJTR*, VIII/1 & 2 (Jan.-Dec.), 1995, pp.40-60.

50. *The Dynamics of Hindu Religious Traditions - Teape Lectures on Sacrifice, Gita and Dialogue*, Bangalore: Asian Trading Corporation, 1996.

51. *Vedic Sacrifice: Challenge & Response*, New Delhi: Manohar, 1996.

52. "Originality in Theological Writing in India", *Theological Writer*, No. 7, June 1996, pp.2-4.

53. "Pointers and Particulars for an Historical Approach to Hindu Religious Texts: The Case of the Bhagavad Gita", in *Revisioning India's Religious Traditions*, (Essays in honour of Eric Lott), ed. By Israel Selvanayagam and David Scott, Published for UTC by ISPCK, New Delhi, 1996, 22-46.

54. "The Roots of Hindu Fundamentalism - A Historical Overview", Asian Journal of Theology, 10/2 Oct 96 pp. 440-450.

55. "Inter-religious dialogue and national integration : A Christian Viewpoint", *THE BULLETIN*(Henry Martin Institute of Islamic Studies), 16/3&4, July-Dec., 1996, pp. 106-111.

56.   Christian Theology and Mission in the Midst of Many Theologies and Missions", Lutheran World Federation *DOCUMENTATION* 41/1997 - Theological Perspectives on Other Faiths, Geneva, LWF, 1997, pp.181-201.

57.   "A Mission Spirituality for a United Church - Reflections from 50 years of experience of the Church of South India" (St. Thomas Unity Lecture delivered in Aberystwyth, Belfast, Edinburg and London during April - September, 1997 - hundreds of copies of the manuscript of 27 pages were sold and a summary published in *Pilgrim.*

58.   'Introducing the Church of South India', 'Strangers in a Foreign Land', 'Liberation and Confrontation of Culture' in *The Lotus and the Cross*, Newsletter & Swanwick Conferance Digest 1997, Issue no. 161, Methodists for World Mission, UK.

59.   "Mission in a Pluralist Society", in *Greater Peace, Closer Fellowship, and Fuller Life*, Ed. By Lily & Sam Amirtham, CSI Golden Jubilee Publications, Madras, 1997, pp.216-225.

60.   "With the Cross and the Lotus - The Church of South India in Fifty Years", *Epworth Review*, 25/1, Jan 1998, pp.107-114.

61.   "Indian Perceptions of Jesus" *Pilgrim*, no.12 April1998, pp.6-9.

62.   "Anglicans and Inter-faith Relations - a historical retrospect" in *Anglicanism - A Global Communion*, ed. By Andrew Wingate et. al. London: Mowbray, 1998, pp.341-346.

63.   "Components of a Tamil Saiva Bhakti experience as evident in Manikkavacakar's Tiruvacakam" in *Spitual Traditions- Essential Visions for Living*, edited by David Emmanuel Singh, Bangalore: UTC (ISPCK, Delhi), 1998, pp.418-439.

64.   "Mission Today: A World Church Perspective" in Harborne Papers No 39. May 1999.

65.   "Commitment and Openness in a Multifaith Context", *Thinking Mission*, USPG 'Sharing Faith in Today's World', December 1999.

66.   "Towards an Evangelical Theology for a Pluralist Age" in *Mission at the Dawn of the 21st Century – A Vision for the Church*, ed. Paul

Varo Martinson, Minneapolis: Kirk House Publishers, 1999, pp.201-218.

67. "Death by Dialogue: The End of Denominational Theology – A World Church Perspective", *Epworth Review*, 27/1, Jan 2000, pp.84 -93.

68. *A Second Call – Ministry and Mission in a Multifaith Mileu*, Madras (Chennai): The Christian Literature Society, 2000.

69. "Identity, Inspiration, Interpretation and Insights: The Significance of the Christian Scripture in the Midst of Scriptures", in *Bible Speaks Today* (Essays in honour of Gnana Robinson, ed. by Daniel Jones Muthunayagam, Delhi: ISPCK (for UTC Bangalore), 2000, pp.224-241

70. "The Interaction and the Integration between the Sanskritistic and Folk Traditions – Few Examples" in *Religions of the Marginalised – Towards a Phenomenology and the Methodology of Study*, ed. By Gnana Robinson, Delhi: ISPCK (for UTC Bangalore), 1998, pp.85-95.

71. "Crossing Over and Coming Back: Evangelical Openness and Dialogical Witness in a Multi-faith Context", in *A Great Commission – Christian Hope in Religious Diversity*, ed. By Martin Forward, Stephen Plant and Susan White, Bern: Peter Lang, 2000, pp.267-279.

72. "When Demons Speak the Truth! An Asian Reading of a New Testament Story of Exorcism", *Epworth Review*, 27/3 July 2000, pp.33-40.

73. "Sadhu Sunder Singh's Approach to the Scipture", *Arasaradi Journal of Theological Reflection*, XI,1-2, 1998, Jan-Dec, pp.54-68 (published in June 2000).

74. "INDIA – 2000 Years of Mission: Just 2.5%, Why or Why not?", *Pilgrim*, August 2000, Issue No. 17, pp.2-4.

75. "Discovering Christ in rural India" in *Discovering Christ-Advent and Christmas*, comp. by Maureen Edwards, Birmingham: International Bible Reading Association, 2000, pp.53-63.

76. "TRUTH and truths in Inter-faith Dialogue", *Religion and Society*, 46/1-2, March-June, 1999, pp.37-64.

77. "Foreword" A. Wingate, *Does Theological Education make a Difference?*, Geneva: WCC, 1999.

78. "A Study of the Life of Abraham" in *Approaches, Foundations, Issues and Models of Interfaith Relations*, ed. by David Emmanuel Sing and Robert Edwin Schick, Delhi: ISPCK&HMI, 2001, pp.372-378.

79. "From Orthodoxy to Modernity: The Transition of a Saiva Math in South India", *Humanitas: The Journal of George Bell Institute*, 3/1 October 2001, pp. 20-43; *Religion and Society*, 47/2 June 2000, pp.5-25.

80. "Learning from Each Other" Notes for *Words for Today 2002*, IBRA.

81. "The Bible and Non-Christian Scriptures", *Epworth Review*, 29/1 Jan, 2002, pp.49-58.

82. Edited and contributed an essay on 'What is Theology? Some Clues for Answers', *Moving Forms of Theology – Faith Talk's Changing Contexts*, Delhi: ISPCK, 2002.

83. Book Review: Hans Kung's *Tracing the Way-Spiritual Dimensions of the World Religions* in *Epworth Review*, Jan 2003, pp.90-91.

84. "Faces of Violence in the Ayodhya Conflict", *Religion and Society*, 47/4, Dec 2000, pp.27-46.

85. "Re-reading John 14:6 in the Context of Two Recent Events in the UK" *Current Dialogue*, No. 40, Dec. 2002, pp.44-51.

86. "Organic Learning in Mission Education", *Rethinking Mission*, 1/1, Spring, 2003, pp.18-25.

87. "In the face of a great majority: Contextual theology and mission in India", *The Anitepam Journal*, No. 40, Nov. 2003, pp.13-18.

88. "Theological Positions in Christian Approach to Religious Pluralism – The Fourth Way", *Arasaradi Journal of Theological Reflection*, XVII/1, Jan-June, 2004, pp.1-23.

89. "Interfaith Dialogue" (chapter 7) in *A History of the Ecumenical Movement*, Vol. 3 (1968 – 2000), Ed. by John Briggs, Mercy Amba Oduyoye and Georges Tsetsis, Geneva: WCC, 2004.

90. pp.149–174.

91. *Relating to People of Other Faiths: Insights from the Bible*, Thiruvilla: Christava Sahitya Samithi, BTTBPSA, 2004.

92. "The Good Samaritan Becoming a Human Rights Activist", Arasaradi Journal of Theological Reflection", Vol. XVIII, No. 1, Jan-June 2005, pp. 1-11; in Finnish: "Laupiaasta samarialaisesta ihmisooikeusaktivistiksi", in *Oikeus uskoon, toivoon ja rakkaauteen: Ihmisoikeudet ja kirkon missio*, ed. by Mari Pöntinen ja Mikko Helminen, Helsinki: Soumen Lähetysseura, 2005, pp.64-75

93. Book Review of *Asian Christian Theologies, A Research Guide to Authors, Movements, Sources, Vol. 1, Asian Region 7th-20th Centuries; south Asia; Austral Asia,* ed. by john England and others in *Studies in World Christianity*, 9/1, 2003, pp.145-146.

94. "Awake, Awake! The Call of the Tsunami – December 26 04", *Pilgrim*, No. 26, March/April 2005, pp.2-3.

95. "Learning about Civilisation", in *Mission Matters*, Issue:15, May 2005, p.5.

96. "Gal-ed versus Peniel: True Reconciliation in the Esau-Jacob/ Israel Story" in *Reconciling Mission: The Ministry of Healing and Reconciliation in the Church Worldwide*, ed. By Kirsteen Kim, Delhi: ISPCK/UCA, 2005, pp.1-22.

97. Book Review of *Unmasking Methodist Theology* in *Pigrim Post – Churches Together in England*, Issue 85, June 2005, p.12.

98. "The Significance of Studying South Indian Religions at Masters Level in a Theological Context", in *Shepherd of a Pilgrim People: Essays in Honour of Bishop J.W. Gladstone*, ed. by Gideon Sobhanam and Vinod Victor, Delhi: ISPCK for south Kerala Diocese, 2005, pp.32-39.

99. "Editorial: The Quest for Spirituality in the Secular Multi-faith Context of India", *Implicit Religion*, 8/2, July 2005, pp.101-117.

100. "Hebrew Laws and Indian Christians – A Contextual Reflection", *Indian Journal of Theology*, Vol. 45, No. 1&2, 2003 (published in 2006), pp.123-133.

101. "Encountering the Hindus: The Legacy of Ziegenbalg" in *Halle and the Beginning of Christianity in India*, Vol. II: *Christian Mission in the Context*, ed. By A. Gross, Y.V. Kumaradoss and H. Liebau, Halle: Franckeschen, 2006, pp.903-922.

102. "The Mission spirituality of the London Missionary society" in *Church of south India, Kanyakumari Diocese – Souvenir 2006*, pp.24-27.

103. "Foreword" to P. Collins, *Context, Culture and Worship: The quest for 'Indian-ness'*, Delhi: ISPCK, 2006.

104. " The Catholic Spirit in Action! – Methodists and the Formation of the Church of South India", *Indian Church History Review*, Vol.XLI No. 2, Dec, 06, pp.127-148.

105. "Syncretism or Symbiosis? An Investigation into the Impact if Hindu Piety and Vocabulary on the Tamil Christians as Evident in their Popular Lyrics", *Indian Journal of Theology*, Vol. 48, No. 1 & 2, 2006, pp.94-111.

106. "The Water of Life in Indian Cups: Protestant Attempts of Doing Theology in India" in Sebastian C.H. Kim (ed), *Christian Theology in Asia* (CUP, 2008).

107. Truth and Reconciliation: An Interfaith Perspective *International Journal of Public Theology* Volume 1 Issue 3/4, 2007.

108. Gandhi on Non-Violence – Does Merton's Appreciation have any Appeal today? *The Merton Journal*, EASTERTIDE, 14/1, 2007, pp. 2-14.

109. "Ready to Receive the Light: Devotions", *Words for Today 2008*, IBRA pp.361-370.

110. "Interfaith Dialogue in India and England: A Personal Reflection", *Pilgrim*, No. 31, August 2007, pp.7-13.

111. "Upon Our Lord's Sermon on the Mount: Discourse 12", in 44 *Sermons to Serve the Present Age*, ed. by Angela shier-Jones and Kimberly D. Reisman, Peterborough: Epworth, 2007, pp.168-173.

112. *Samuel Amirtham's Living Theology*, Banglaore: BTESSC/SATHRI, 2007.

113. *Tr & Ed. Christian Faith Step by Step: A Catechism for our Day*, Bangalore: BTESSC/SATHRI, 2007.

114. "From Congregationalism to Anglicanism with a Special Reference to Episcopacy", *Indian Church History Review*, XLI/1, June 2007, pp.50-79.

115. "Getting into Real Religious Commitment and Interfaith Dialogue", *Interreligious Insight*, 6/1, Jan 2008, pp.37-42.

116. Book Review *Robert Cardwell: A Scholar-Missionary in Colonial South India, Pilgrim*, No. 32, March/April, 2008, pp. 14-18' *Arasaradi Jornal of Theological Reflection*, XX, July-Dec 2007, pp. 80-84; *Bangalore Theological Forum*, XXXIX/2, Dec. 2007, pp.166-169.

117. "The Hindu Diaspora in the UK: Insights and Challenges for Christian Mission", in *Mission and Migration*, Hope Valley: Cliff College, 2008, pp.95-108.

118. "Apostle Judas! You have a Special appeal to Dialogue on Power and Authority", AJTR, XX, July-Dec 2007, pp.56-65.

119. "The Parable of the Prodigal son: A contextual Reflection" in *Light on our Dusty Path: Essays for a bible Lover*, ed. by I. Selvanayagam, Bangalore: SATHRI/BTESSC, 2008, pp.210-224.

120. "Christ's Body and Corporate Leadership" in *Masihi Sevak*, XXXIII/2, August 2008, pp.5-12.

121. "Interpreting a Riddle: Jesus' Subversion of the Davidic Legacy", *Black Theology – An International Journal*, 6/2, May 2008, pp.262-268.

122. "Truth and Reconciliation – An Interfaith Perspective from India" in *Peace and Reconciliation: in search of shared identity*, ed. by Sebastian Kim, Pauline Kollontai and Greg Hoyland, Farnham: Ashgayte, 2008.

123. "Theological Education and Participation in Global Mission", *Bangalore Theological Forum*, Vol. XL, No. 2, December 2008, pp.1-17.

124. "Easter Sunday" in *Mount of Olives*, Chennai: ICSA Books, 2009, pp.133-146.

125. "Rethinking Church in India", *Religion and Society*, 54/3, September 2009, pp.15-27.

126. "What is Religion? A Summary of an inconclusive Discussion" in *Harmony Flame Spreads Across India*, Edited by Gnana Robinson, Kanyakumari: Kanakumari Peace and Justice Publications, 2009, pp.120-133.

127. "Radical Difference! An Indian Review of a Defence of Henric Kraemer's Theology of Religions", *Pilgrim*, No. 36, March2010, pp.11-17.

128. "From Cosmetic Coverings to Heart Surgery: Power as Key for Creative Inculturation" in *The Church and Culture in India, Inculturation: Theory and Practice*, ed. by Paul Pulikkan and Paul M. Collins, Delhi: ISPCK, 2010, pp.185-201.

129. "'Fundamentalism Vs Fundamentals': Recent Attempts to Reread Scriptures with Special Reference to the Bible", *Indian Journal of Christian Studies*, I/1, Jan-June, 2011, pp.56-66.

130. "Revisiting *The Unknown Christ of Hinduism: A Tribute to Raymundo Panikkar*", *Gurukul Journal of Theological Studies*, XXI/2, June 2010, pp.61-70.

131. "Interfaith Dialogue: Perennial Questions, Yet Journeying with Provisional Answers", Editorial, and a Review of J.W. Bowker (ed.), *Conflict and Reconciliation: The Contribution of Religions*, *Gurukul Journal of Theological Studies*, XXII/1, January 2011, pp.2-8, 116-122.

132. "Christian Mission in the Midst of Many Missions" in *Participating in God's Mission Today*, ed. by Santhosh Kumar, Tiruvalla: Christava Sahitya Samithi & UTC Bangalore, 2011, pp.38-56.

133. "Paradigms of Religious Pluralism: A Clarification" *AREOPAGUS: Journal of the Association of Faculty for Religion, Philosophy and Culture*, 2011/1, pp.75-84.

134. *Being Evangelical and Dialogical: A Healthy Balance in a Multifaith Context*, Delhi: ISPCK, 2012.

135. "To Be a Sensibly Responsible Theologian in India – A Reflection", *Gurukul Journal of Theological Studies*, XXII/2 June 2011, pp.110-118.

136. (with S. Amirtham) *Glimpses in Life: 1. Human Lens and Divine Insights, 2. 'Satanic Verses' in the Bible, 3. Blessed to be a Blessing, 4. To Be like Children*, New Delhi: ISPCK, 2012.

137. "Guidelines for Christians on Interfaith Dialogue in India: Some Notes" in *Theology Beyond Neutrality: Essays to Honour Wesley Ariarajah*, Ed. by Marshal Fernando and Robert Crusz, Colombo: Ecumenical Institute, 2011, pp. 103-116; *NCC Review*, CXXX1/11, Dec. 2011, pp.38-56.

138. "Paradigms of Religious Pluralism: A Clarification", *Ariopagus: Journal of the Association of Faculty for Religion, Philosophy and Culture*, Vol. 1, 2011, pp.75-84.

139. "Majestic Elephant and Menacing Mouse: An Observation of Hindu-Christian Relationships in India" in *Among the People: Essays in Honour of Rev Dr P. G. Vargis*, Ed by V.D. John & Viju Wilson, Delhi: ISPCK & Hoshangabad: SALT, 2012, pp.95-100.

140. "Disability: An Interfaith Perspective" in *Sprouts of Disability Theology*, ed. by Christopher Rajkumar, Nagpur: NCCI, 2012, 2012, pp.21-30.

141. "Jewish-Christian Theological Rapprochement: Insights from the Book of Revelation", *Gurukul Journal of Theological Studies*, XXIII/ 1 Jan 2012, pp.50-64.

142. *65 Sermon Illustrations*, Chennai: Christian Literature Society, 2012.

Israel's Publications in Tamil (Selected)

1. *Uruvaakivarum Uraiyaadal* (Emerging Dialogue), Madurai: Arasaradi Publications, 1978.

2. *Aandavarin Adiyavarkal* (Servants of the Lord), Madurai: TTS Mission Institute, 1979.

3. *Iraivendal* (Prayer), with V.M. Gnanaraj, Madurai: Arasaradi Publications, 1980; Revised edition with the title *Unnadharudan Uraiyaadal* (Dialogue with God), 1985.

4. *Camayangal Urayaadukintana* (Religions in Dialogue, edited with CRW David), Madurai: Tamil Theological Book Club, 1987.

5. *Thirumaraikkuthirumpuvom* (Return to the Word of God), with Samuel Amirtham, Series of 20 booklets from 1980 to 2001 with several editions and finally revised and published in two volumes, Madurai: Arasaradi Publications, 2008, 2011.

6. *Soothira Sathiranka, Ithihasankal, Bhagavad Geethai, Puraanankal* (Sutras & Sasras, Itihasas, Bhagavad Gita and Puraanas), Madurai: TTBC, 1988.

7. *Narcheithiyai Nantruraippom* (Let us Proclaim the Gospel Properly, Ed. With CRW David, Madurai: Arasarasi Publications, 1989, 1992.

8. *Uraiyaadal Payanam* (Dialogue Pilgrimage), Madurai: Arasaradi Publications, 1984.

9. *Ciluvaiyin Caayalkal* (Images of the Cross, with CRW David), Madras: Christian Literature Society, 1984, 1993.

10. *Azhaikappattiruppathu Paniceiyave* (Called to Serve, Ed. With Gnana Robinson), Madurai: Arasaradi Publications, 1985.

11. *Inthiyachoozhalil Iraimakkal Pani* (The Ministry of the People of God in Indian Context, Ed. With Gnana Robinson), Madurai: Arasaradi Publications,, 1986.

12. *Visuvaasapporattom* (Struggle in Faith, with CRW David), Madras: CLS, 1989.

13. *Camayappattruthiyil En Ayalahatthaarum Naanum* (Tr. of *My Neighbours' Fath and Mine*, WCC Document), Madras: CLS, 1988.

14. *Inthiya Meyyiyal – Or Arimugam* (An Introduction to Indian Philosophy, with A.E. Inbanathan), Madurai: TTBC, 1994.

15. *Viviliya Iraiyiyal Cenchol Katturaikkovai* (Collection of Essays on Biblical and Theological Words, Ed. With 19 Essays of his own), Madurai: TTBC, 1993.

16. *Thiruviviliya Thunainool* (Companion to the Bible , Revised and Edited with two essays of his own), Madurai: TTBC, 1995.

17. *Mathamaattram – Oru Ulaviyal Nokku* (Conversion – A Psychological Approach, with D.W. Jesudoss), Maurai: TTS Mission Institute, 1984.

18. *Dhyaana Peedam* (Altar of Meditation; reflection on images and similes of the Psalms, after serializing in *Dhesopakaari*), Sivakasi: Cinie Printers for Programme on Lay Theological Education, 1996.

19. *Thiruviviliya Vilakkam: Ennikkai Nool* (Bible Commentary on the Book of Numbers), Thiruchi: Arulvaakku Mantram & Madurai: TTBC, 2001.

20. *Thiruviviliya Vilakkam: Viduthalaippayanam* (Bible Commentary on the Book of Exodus) –do-, 2012.

Plus several essays including over 25 published in *Iraiyiyal Malar* of TTS and text-books of TTBC; about 85 devotional songs of which 16 are published in CLS' *Hymns and Lyrics* and nearly 20 recorded in different albums.

Contributors

S. Wesley Ariarajah:

The Revd Dr S. Wesley Ariarajah, Methodist Minister from Sri Lanka, is currently Professor of Ecumenical Theology at Drew University School of Theology, Madison, New Jersey, USA. Before joining Drew in 1979 he served the World Council of Churches for 16 years, first as the Director of the Interfaith Dialogue Program for 12 years, and later as the Deputy General Secretary of the Council. His publications include: *The Bible and People of other Faiths* (WCC Publications), *Not without My Neighbour: Issues in Interfaith Relations* (WCC), *Axis of Peace – Christian Faith in times of Violence and War* (WCC), *Did I Betray the Gospel – Letters of Paul and Place of Women* (WCC), *Hindus and Christians – A Century of Protestant Ecumenical Thought* (Eerdmans), and *We Live by His Gifts – D. T. Niles: Preacher, Teacher and Ecumenist* (EISD, Colombo). His latest volume on the Theology of Religions, *Your God, My God, Our God – Rethinking Christian Theology for Religious Plurality* will be published in September 2012.

Dhyanchand Carr:

Dr. Dhyanchand Carr is an ordained pastor of the Church of South India, and he retired as Principal of the Tamilnadu Theological Seminary, Madurai in 2003, a seminary well known in ecumenical circles. After five years in pastoral ministry in his home diocese of Tiruchi, he studied for his M.Th in UTC, Bangalore, and after more years teaching at TTS, he went to King's College, London, where he completed his Doctorate in 1981, in New Testament studies. Returning again to TTS, he became immersed in social action for which the Seminary was renowned, and continued to teach New Testament. This combined role is reflected in his book *The Sword of the Spirit* (WCC, Risk Series 1991). From 1993-98 he worked as Secretary for Mission and Evangelism of the Christian conference of Asia, based in Hong Kong, and conducted workshops on Reading the Bible with New Eyes in 16 Asian Countries, published since. He returned to be Principal at TTS, Madurai, in 1998.

Kenneth Cracknell:

Revd Prof. Kenneth Cracknell is President Emeritus of the Cambridge Theological Federation where he held the Michael Gutteridge chair in Systematic and Pastoral Theology at Wesley House. He also taught Comparative Religion in the University of Cambridge. He most recently served in the USA as Distinguished Professor in Residence at the Brite Divinity School, Fort Worth, Texas. For ten years he was director of interfaith concerns for the British Council of Churches in London and was a long-term consultant for the World Council of Churches. His writings include *Towards a New Relationship: Christians and People of Other Faith* (Epworth 1986); *Justice, Courtesy and Love: Theologians and Missionaries Encountering World Religions (1846-1914)* (Epworth 1995); *In Good and Generous Faith: Christian Responses to Religious Pluralism* (Epworth, 2006); and with Susan J. White, *An Introduction to World Methodism* (Cambridge, 2006). He is married to Susan White and now lives in Vermont, USA.

Donald Eadie:

Prior to theological training the Revd. Donald Eadie chose to learn about life through working in a large warehouse in a Yorkshire mill. He studied at Didsbury College (1960-63) and then at the William Temple College (1963-64). He attended the European Ecumenical Youth Conference in Lausanne where he met Kerstin who later become his wife. Through marriage Sweden has become a second home. After ordination Donald worked at the Luton Industrial Mission and in 1972 joined the Notting Hill Ecumenical Team ministry. In 1982 he became tutor in Pastoral Theology at Wesley College, Bristol and in 1987 was inducted as the Chairman of the Birmingham District of the Methodist Church. He had to retire early due to a degenerative disc disease. Since 1996 much of his life is lived from a special chair in his beloved room. There has been contraction, limitation but also life has opened up, deepening and expanding. 'Go to your cell and your cell will teach.'

Donald listens to people from a wide range of backgrounds, churches, communities and places in life. He leads retreats and quiet days and writes. He is the author of *Grain in Winter - Reflections for Saturday People* published by Epworth Press in 1999. Donald lives in Moseley, Birmingham.

Christy Femila:

Prof. Christy Femila has served as a Lecturer at the Henry Martyn Institute in Hyderabad since 2008. After completing her Bachelor of Divinity from Tamilnadu Theological Seminary, Madurai, she has completed Master of Islamic Studies from Luther Seminary, Minnesota, U.S.A., through HMI. She has published articles and book reviews in the Arasaradi Journal of Theological Reflection, the Gurukul Journal of Theological Studies, the Journal of Henry Martyn Institute and the Journal of Deccan Studies. Her research interests include, but are not limited to, Interfaith Dialogue/Relations, Sufism, the Israel-Palestine issue, Conflict Transformation, and Religion & Gender.

Elizabeth Harris:

Dr Elizabeth Harris is a Senior Lecturer in Religious Studies within the Department of Theology, Philosophy and Religious Studies at Liverpool Hope University, specializing in Buddhist Studies. From 1996-2007, she was the Executive Secretary for Inter Faith Relations for the Methodist Church in Britain, whilst also teaching within the Graduate Institute of Theology and Religion at Birmingham University as an Honorary Lecturer. Prior to this, she was a Research Fellow at Westminster College, Oxford, a post that she took up after completing a doctorate in Buddhist Studies in Sri Lanka, where she lived from 1986-1993. She is currently President of the European Network of Buddhist-Christian Studies. Her publications include: *What Buddhists Believe* (One World 1998); *Theravada Buddhism and the British Encounter: religious, missionary and colonial experience in nineteenth century Sri Lanka* (Routledge 2006); *Buddhism for a Violent World: A Christian Reflection* (Epworth 2010, subsequently re-published by SCM).

Kirsteen Kim:

Dr Kirsteen Kim, a native of Britain, is Professor of Theology and World Christianity at Leeds Trinity University College, Leeds, UK. She has taught at a number of institutions in different countries, including from

1993 to 1997 at Union Biblical Seminary, Pune, India. Her PhD at the University of Birmingham (2002), now published as *Mission in Spirit* (ISPCK, 2003), was on Indian Christian theologies of the Holy Spirit. She later worked with Dr Selvanayagam as tutor and programme coordinator at the United College of the Ascension in Selly Oak (2001-2006). Prof. Kim has also lived in Korea and is currently researching Korean Christianity and theology. Recent publications include, *Joining in with the Spirit: Connecting World Church and Local Mission* (SCM, 2012), *Christianity as a World Religion* (with her husband Sebastian C.H. Kim; Continuum, 2008) and *The Holy Spirit in the World: A Global Conversation* (Orbis Books, 2007). She is Vice Moderator of the Commission for World Mission and Evangelism of the World Council of Churches.

P. Pratap Kumar:

Dr Pratap Kumar is Professor of Hinduism and Comparative Religions in the School of Religion, Philosophy and Classics, University of KwaZulu Natal, South Africa. In addition to several scholarly essays and articles his publications include *The Goddess Lakshmi in South Indian Vaishnavism*, Scholars Press, Atlanta, GA USA, 1997; *Hindus in South Africa: Their Traditions and Beliefs*, Durban: University of Durban-Westville, 2000; *Methods and Theories in the Study of Religions: Perspectives from the Study of Hinduism and other Indian Religions*, Delhi: Sundeep Prakashan Publications, 2004; *Religious Pluralism and the Diaspora*, edited by P. Pratap Kumar, Leiden: E.J, Brill, 2006. He was also one of the editors of the *Numen* Book Series of the International Association for the History of Religions, published by Brill between 2004-2007.

Suresh Kumar:

The Revd Suresh Kumar was ordained in the Trichy-Tanjore diocese of the Church of South India, having studied Theology at Serampore College, and later a Master's in Communication studies at Leicester University. He served on the teaching staff in Tamilnadu Theological Seminary from 1986 to 1999. During this time he helped the prison ministry and was among the pioneers to start the M.Sc in the Communication course for secular students. He served the Senate in the board of education for communication studies. He became Treasurer in the Trichy diocese and served the CSI in various capacities for 9 years. He wrote several articles about Tamil films, his research subject. He is also interested in ecological issues and concentrates on smaller community communications. He was editor of the Trichy diocesan magazine and is now editing the joint parish magazine in UK. Since 2008 he has been serving in the Church of England, Leicester Diocese. At present he is the priest in charge of St. Philips Church, Leicester.

Julius Lipner:

Professor Julius Lipner is Professor of Hinduism and the Comparative Study of Religion and Fellow of Clare Hall, in the University of Cambridge. He is of Indo-Czech origin, and was born and brought up in West Bengal. He obtained his Doctorate from the University of Birmingham, and after one year teaching there (1974-5), he moved to Cambridge where he has remained ever since. He has authored or edited 12 books, and has published over 80 articles or translations; his most well-known book is his comprehensive study *Hindus: their religious beliefs and practices* (1994, second much revised edition 2010). His book *Brahmabandhab Upadhyay* won an award in the USA as the best book in Hindu-Christian Studies 1997-99. He has lectured in many contexts around the world, and is a member of the editorial board of several academic journals. His specialist fields are Vedantic thought, 19th century Bengal, and truth in interreligious dialogue. In 2008 he became a Fellow of the British Academy. He was tutor to Israel Selvanayagam when he studied part of his Doctorate in Cambridge.

Eric J. Lott:

The Revd Dr Eric Lott came in 1959 as a Methodist mission-partner to the Dornakal Diocese of the Church of South India. After ordination in Dornakal Cathedral and rural pastoral work, 1963-88 he taught Worship and Indian Religions first in Andhra Christian Theological College, then in United Theological College, Bangalore, where he also edited *Bangalore Theological Forum*, was Dean of Doctoral Research, and Convenor of the Intercultural Worship programme. 1988-94 he was engaged in Inner City community and pastoral work in Leicester, UK. His publications (10 books and over 100 articles: topics include methodology in religious studies, art, liturgy, eco-theology, and issues of faith and culture, with occasional writing on bird-life), with two books in Telugu (on Indian Religions and on Christian Worship), as well as *Vedantic Approaches to God* (Macmillan 1980); *Vision, Tradition, Interpretation: Theology, Religion & Religious Studies* (De Gruyter 1988);

Religious Faith, Human Identity (the Cambridge Teape Lectures 2001, pub.2004); *Faces of Vision: Jyoti Sahi's Images of Life & Faith* (Christians Aware 2008). Retired in an English village, with his wife he is a keen bird-photographer.

V. Kanagu Nelson:

Dr Kanagu Nelson is the Head of and Professor in the Religions' Department, Dean of the External Studies Department, and Administrative Staff Officer in Tamilnadu Theological Seminary, Arasaradi, Madurai, S. India. He is an ordained Presbyter of the Church of South India, Madurai-Ramnad Diocese. His publications include, *Inter-Faith Dialogue for Relationship*, Tamil edition, Madurai, TTBC 2009; *Pali Manual, Part 1*, (Co- author), Madurai:TTBC, 2009; *Indian Religious Revolt Movements*, Tamil edition, Madurai, TTBC 2011; *Living Religions in India*, (soon to be released), Madurai: TTBC, 2012, and a number of articles on Mission, Dialogue, Theology, Ecumenism and Religions both in English and Tamil. He has contributed 42 Devotions in English for the Gurukul Devotions' book, published by the Gurukul Lutheran Theological College & Research Institute, Kilpauk, Chennai.

A. Pushparajan:

Dr A. Pushparajan, who retired in 2004 as Professor and Head, Dept. of Interreligious Relations, Madurai Kamaraj University (MKU), began his career in J T College at Gadag as Lecturer of Philosophy in 1971. He moved to teach Philosophy and Psychology at Arul Anandar College, Karumathur from 1972 to 1985, before joining as Reader in Gandhian Studies at MKU. He has authored 20 books, contributed over 300 articles in research journals, and presented over 350 papers in national and international seminars, symposia and conferences. He has been a Consultant to the Pontifical Council for Faith and Culture, Awardee of Charles Wallace Fellow in Dept. of Religions and Theology, University of Bristol, UK, paper presenter in the UN Peace Summit of the Religious and Spiritual Leaders, Founding member of the World Council of Religious Leaders, Secretary of the Commission for Dialogue, Archdiocese of Madurai, Consultant to several Commissions of the Catholic Bishops' Conference of India. Presently residing in Bengaluru, he gives guest lectures in his fields of specializations: Interreligious Dialogue, Gandhi and Ecosophy.

Neil Richardson:

The Revd Dr Neil Richardson is a retired Methodist minister living with his wife Rhiannon in a village near the English/Welsh border. He taught New Testament studies for many years at Wesley College, Bristol where, as Principal, he welcomed Israel as a colleague and Israel's family as members of the college community. His books include *Paul's Language About God*, (his doctoral dissertation); *God in the New Testament*; and, most recently, *Paul For Today, John For Today* and, (with the Revd Dr George Lovell) *Sustaining Preachers and Preaching*. He served as President of the British Methodist Conference in 2003-4, and is currently the Methodist co-chair of the British Catholic- Methodist Committee.

Gnana Robinson:

Rev. Dr. Gnana Robinson has been a minister of the Church of South India since 1960. After one year parish ministry in the Kanyakumari Diocese he has been teaching in three leading theological colleges in India, namely, the Tamilnadu Theological College in Thirumaraiyur (1962-1969), the Tamilnadu Theological Seminary (TTS) in Arasaradi, Madurai as Professor of Old Testament and as Principal for nine years (1969-1987) and the United Theological College (UTC), Bangalore as Principal (1993-2000). From 1987-1993 he taught at the Predigerseminar in Soest in Germany as the Ecumenical Guest Professor. During the periods when he was Principal in TTS and UTC, he was twice elected as the President of the Senate of Serampore College (University). Dr. Robinson has served as visiting professor in Trinidad, USA and U.K. He has authored a number of books, booklets and articles in English, Tamil and German. He is committed to the poor and the marginalized and as such most of his writings are around the theme of justice, peace and sharing. As such, *Good News to the Poor*, T.T.S., 1984; *Let Justice Roll Down Like Waters*, T.T.S., 1984; *Struggle is Life*, CLS, Madras, 1988; *Siding with the Poor*, CLS, 1989, are among his early publications. His latest publication is *Hindutva at Crossroads*, KJPP, 2010. Dr. Robinson is the founder president of the Peace Trust at Kanyakumari, the Movement for the Eradication of Corruption, and the Prophetic Forum for the Life and Witness of Churches, which is fighting against corruption in churches.

David C. Scott:

The Revd Dr David Scott began his professional career with the Methodist Church in India in 1962 as Director of Religious Studies and Chaplain at Lucknow Christian College. In 1969 Scott was appointed Director of the WCC-related Christian Retreat and Study Centre. Here, in the midst of a number of Hindu and Buddhist monasteries, he became deeply involved in inter-religious relations, which remains a significant vocation. Scott began a career in theological education at Leonard Theological College, Jabalpur (1974-1986) where he taught Comparative Religion and directed the Department of Research. Subsequently he was appointed Professor of Religion and Culture at the United Theological College, Bangalore (1987-1999). Here he also served as Dean of Doctoral Studies and Senior Tutor. Visiting professorships in the USA and S. Korea, as well as appointments to the Board of Studies and Examiners of Guru Gobind Singh Department of Religious Studies, Punjabi University, the Editorial Board of the Hindu-Christian Studies Bulletin, Centre for Studies in Religion and Society, University of Victoria, BC Canada have added an ecumenical dimension to Scott's engagement in theological education. In 1999, Scott was recognized by the Indian Council of Philosophical Research for "Significant Contribution to the Study of Indian Religions". His publications comprise several books, including *Kabir Mythology* and *Keshub Chunder Sen*, and numerous professional articles. Now retired, Scott lives in Washington, DC with his wife.

Ruth Tetlow:

The Revd Ruth Tetlow taught Geography in Kenya (1968-70) and then became Education Secretary of the British Council of Churches' Community and Race Relations Unit. She has taught English as a second language in Lancaster, Birmingham and Bulgaria, and Geography at St Philip's RC Sixth Form College in Birmingham (1990-1998). She was Tutor for External Programmes (many of which were interfaith) at the United College of the Ascension, Selly Oak, Birmingham 1999 – 2006. Since then she has worked with the Faith Encounter Programme to develop Faith Guiding courses in the West Midlands. She continues to be actively engaged in inter faith encounter in Birmingham, and is a Senior Adviser to Birmingham Council of Faiths. She is a founder member of the Jubilee Debt Campaign Multi

Faith Project. She contributed a chapter on 'Inter-Religious Reconciliation' to *Reconciling Mission* ed. K.Kim ISPCK 2005; and an article on 'Interpreting Faith to Visitors – reflections on a pioneering Faith Guiding course' to *Inter Religious Insight* July 2009.

M. Thomas Thangaraj

The Revd Dr M. Thomas Thangaraj retired in 2008 as Professor Emeritus of World Christianity at the Candler School of Theology, Emory University, Atlanta, GA, U. S. A. After serving as a Minister in the Church of South India in the Tirunelveli area, Professor Thangaraj moved to teach at the Tamilnadu Theological Seminary, Madurai, India from 1971 to 1988, before joining Emory. His publications include: *The Crucified Guru: An Experiment in Cross-Cultural Christology* (Abingdon Press, 1994); *Relating to People of Other Religions: What Every Christian Needs to Know* (Abingdon Press, 1997; *The Common Task: A Theology of Christian Mission* (Abingdon Press, 1999); "Indian Christian Tradition," in *Religions of South Asia: An Introduction,* (ed) Sushil Mittal and Gene Thursby (Routledge, 2006); and *Hermeneutical Explorations in Dialogue: Essays in Honor of Hans Ucko,* co-edited with Anantanand Rambachan and Rashied Omar (Delhi, ISPCK, 2007). Thangaraj's hymns both in Tamil and in English have also been published. Currently he serves as the Visiting Professor of Global Christianity at Boston University School of Theology.

Solomon Victus:

The Revd Dr Victus has been teaching Social Analysis for the last 22 years at the Dept. of Social Analysis of Tamilnadu Theological Seminary. He is an ordained minister of the Church of South India. He has published widely in India and abroad including, *Religion and Eco-economics of J.C.Kumarappa: Gandhism Redefined* (Delhi: ISPCK, 2003); *Jesus and Mother Economy:An Introduction to the Theology of J.C.Kumarappa* (ISPCK, 2007); *Christian Response to Fundamentalism* (Madurai: TTS, 2003); *Rainbow: Eco-Theology,* (ISPCK, 2007); *Sacrifice for the Dawn,* (ISPCK, 2007); *Bubbles: Convulsion of Pain and Suffering,* (TTS, 2010). He is a former Visiting Fellow of Birmingham University (UK),a regular resource person for the Society for International Pastoral Care and Counseling (SIPCC), and a pioneer in exploring Indian Christian theology of J.C.Kumarappa and Eco-theology in Tamilnadu.

Andrew Wingate:

Canon Dr Andrew Wingate is a Canon Theologian of Leicester Cathedral, and a Chaplain to The Queen. He was awarded an OBE in 2011, for services to Inter Faith Relations. He was a theological teacher at the Tamilnadu Theological Seminary, Madurai, and then as Principal of the West Midlands Course at Queen's College, Birmingham, and as Principal of the College of the Ascension, Selly Oak, Birmingham. He moved to Leicester in 2000, and was the Founding Director of the St Philip's Centre for Study and Engagement in a Multi Faith Society. He was Co-Chair of the Hindu-Christian Forum UK, and a founder of the Network for Inter Faith Concerns of the Anglican Communion. His publications include *Encounter in the Spirit, Muslim-Christian Dialogue in Practice* (WCC, 1989,91); *The Church and Conversion* (ISPCK, 1999); *Does Theological Education make a Difference* (WCC, 2001); *Free to Be* (DLT, 2002); *Celebrating Difference, Staying Faithful- How to live in a Multi Faith World* (DLT, 2005, 7, 9). He gave the Teape Lectures (Cambridge/St Stephen's Delhi Partnership) on Bhakti Movements in Britain, and has a contract for a book on Hindu-Christian Encounter in the West.